The Polish Diaspora

Volume II: Selected Essays from the
Fiftieth Anniversary International Congress of the
Polish Institute of Arts and Sciences of America

Edited by
James S. Pula & M. B. Biskupski

With an Introduction by
James S. Pula

EAST EUROPEAN MONOGRAPHS
DISTRIBUTED BY COLUMBIA UNIVERSITY PRESS

1993

EAST EUROPEAN MONOGRAPHS, NO. CCCXC

For Those Who Left

Contents

Preface

In June, 1992, Yale University was the site of the International Congress of scholars commemorating the fiftieth anniversary of the Polish Institute of Arts and Sciences in America. Several hundred participants met in more than forty sessions over three days to discuss many aspects of the history and culture of Poland and the Polish diaspora worldwide. This book, and its two companion volumes, reflect the variety and quality of these discussions. The three volumes comprise a selection of the papers presented at the International Congress grouped into three broad categories: the evolution of Poland's relationship to its European and world context; the history of the Polish community outside the historic borders of Poland, and the artistic and literary contributions of Poland to world culture. The essays are all revised and edited versions of papers originally presented at the Yale conference.

A few words are required concerning the conventions adopted by the editors in preparing the volumes. Regarding nomenclature, the Polish versions of place and personal names have been uniformly adopted with two exceptions: when a well-known English variant has become established it has been substituted (e.g., Warsaw, not Warszawa); or, in those essays dealing with contemporaneous events, the current spelling of names has been substituted for the established Polish practice (hence, Mensk and Vilnius, rather than Minsk and Wilno). Whereas this has resulted in certain inconsistencies, it attempts to retain a proper respect for the Polish tradition while acknowledging present realities. In those instances where confusion may result due to the existence of multiple designations for the same (occasionally obscure) place, the editors have provided alternative versions in parentheses at the first usage in the text.

The editors are honored to acknowledge the cooperation of their colleagues in the preparation of this volume, and the conference it reflects. Thaddeus V. Gromada, Vice President of the Polish Institute of Arts and Sciences, served as Conference Chair and coordinated innumerable matters throughout. Piotr S.

Wandycz, Professor of History at Yale University, was part of the conference planning committee and was the principle scholarly liaison to Yale. Joseph E. Gore, President of the Kościuszko Foundation, arranged the support of the Foundation in many ways, including vital financial support. Jane Gromada Kedron served as a valuable asset in planning and logistical arrangements. In addition, there is a long list of scholars who provided advice regarding the essays herein published. Their contributions, while anonymous, are nonetheless very considerable.

Whereas the editors have had the aid of many, the responsibility for any shortcomings in these volumes is theirs alone.

Unfortunately, limitations of space, as well as the need to retain thematic coherence, required the editors to omit many fine contributions. Consequently, in order that the reader may access additional information from authors of papers that do not appear in these three volumes, we have included the complete academic program from the Fiftieth Anniversary International Congress in the Appendix to this volume.

The Polish Diaspora

Recent Perspectives on the Polish Diaspora

by

James S. Pula[1]

Throughout the past two centuries, since the partitioning of Poland in the late eighteenth century, one of the recurring themes in Polish history has been the political and economic emigration of Poles to locations around the world. Most often, these emigrants established ethnic communities in their new adoptive nations and continued, to the extent possible, to be interested in and involved in providing aid to their homeland. While their individual circumstances and experiences varied, their collective experience was remarkably similar regardless of the countries where they settled.

The following essays, selected from among those delivered at the Fiftieth Anniversary International Congress of the Polish Institute of Arts and Sciences of America, are designed to provide readers with new insights into specific topics which may help to further an understanding of the collective experience of Polish political emigrés and economic immigrants. The essays are arranged into two general topic areas highlighting those dealing with immigrant assimilation in general, and those specifically relating to the influence of the host government policies on the assimilation of Polish immigrants.

---

[1]James S. Pula is a member of the Boards of Directors of the Polish Institute of Arts and Sciences of America and the Polish American Historical Association. He is also the Editor of *Polish American Studies*.

Part I

Essays on Immigrant Adjustment

Part I of this collection of essays deals with issues associated with the assimilation of immigrants into their host cultures and issues related to their contacts with the homeland. In the first article, Danuta Mostwin suggests a new theoretical model for understanding the relationship of ethnic identity and individual introspection. After outlining the development and inter-relationship of the psychological concepts of "self," "identity," and "ego," Mostwin reviews the need to understand the process of identity in contemporary society, the dynamics of the identity process, and the nature of the holistic approach which incorporates both psychological and physiological attributes into a unified "holistic" unit. The context for her model thus established, Mostwin begins her discussion of "ethnic identity" by referring to Erik Erikson's pioneering concepts which enjoyed great popularity during the 1960s. By applying Erikson's theories to her own work with Polish immigrant family adjustment, she develops her own working definition of "ethnic identity" as "an 'ethnic bond' influencing a person's self-evaluation."

After establishing her working definition of "ethnic identity," Mostwin postulates a paradigm for understanding what "ethnic identity" means in the context of group and individual relations. First established during the family socialization process, the elements of "ethnic identity" provide models of social roles and values that inform individual decision-making and serve as a point of reference when these values come in conflict with others in the assimilation process. "Ethnic identity," she contends, encompasses the individual's need for belonging and a sense of community, but the concept of the "Third Value" that she develops provides a means for understanding "ethnic identity" as it relates to the individual as a unique human being rather than merely a member of a group.

From this analysis of ethnic identity, we move to an essay by George M. Kapalka and Juliana Rasic Lachenmeyer that provides us with a unique analysis of the effect of acculturation on sex-role orientation. Beginning with a general review of literature on the separate nature of masculine and feminine dimensions, they explain that sex-typed individuals are those that strongly exhibit characteristics associated with their sex, while androgynous individuals reflect characteristics of both dimensions. To test the sex-role orientation of Poles living in the United States, the authors administered a Polish language translation of the Bem Sex-Role Inventory to fifty-three men and women whom they divided into two groups based upon their length of residence in the United States. Using ANOVA and correlational statistical analysis, they conclude that the more acculturated immigrants were significantly more androgynous than either the recent immigrants or American normative samples.

Because of their findings, Kapalka and Lachenmeyer suggest the need for additional studies on cross-cultural differences in gender development, the influence of stressors, comparative studies on other ethnic groups, and additional sex-type studies of American populations. They also assert that their findings should be considered when developing strategies for counseling activities.

The group effects of assimilation are also studies by Dennis Kolinski in his essay on "The Evolution of Polish American Wedding Customs in Central Wisconsin" which addresses the question, common in the literature on assimilation, of the influence of Americanization on the customs of immigrant groups. Unlike many who seek to trace what he characterizes as "a simple, linear, and one-directional process" that "implies that changes are the result of nothing more than the loss of Polish elements and acquisition of American" culture, Kolinski asks: "From where would isolated, rural immigrants and their children learn Anglo-American cultural patterns on a scale broad enough to assimilate them is the majority of the population in the region was not of Anglo-Saxon origin?"

Through his study of the evolution of Polish American wedding customs over a seventy-year period, Kolinski identifies "a process of change which wove together several different threads to create a new form of cultural fabric." Noting the ethnic diversity of rural Wisconsin, and the relative insularity of the ethnic communities until the post-World War II era, he rejects the view of dominant and minority cultures as "two extreme and mutually exclusive manifestations" and focuses on the process of ethnic change leading to a culture that integrates elements from many cultures and communities. His analysis suggests that to the extent that Polish American wedding customs changed, they did so as a result not only of Anglo-Saxon influences, but the introduction of French-Canadian customs, typically rural midwestern habits, and the normal process of cultural change over time. In rural Poland, he notes, culture has not remained static, but has evolved over the past seventy years. Similarly, some of the cultural change among Polish Americans in rural Wisconsin is simply the result of normal change over time; generational differences and the evolution of cultural forms to fit changing circumstances. The process is complex and interactive; it is not a simple elimination of one culture's characteristics for those of another as is frequently assumed.

Kenneth Lewalski also explores the effects of immigration by chronicling the experiences of Polish refugees in France following the November Insurrection in 1830-31. Under the terms of the amnesty that ended that conflict, leaders in the revolutionary government were required to emigrate. Thus, Lewalski notes, the "political, artistic and intellectual elite" were forced to leave the country. Although, they settled in many European countries, and nations as distant as the United States and Chile, more than 6,000 sought refuge in France becoming in exile an emigration of "highly articulate and influential character." There, those fortunate enough to have independent means or the sponsorship of an influential patron were free to locate in Paris or other communities, while the majority of refugees were barred from Paris, kept under close surveillance in special barracks in the provinces, and were "completely dependent upon the French government for subsistence."

Eschewing the traditional approach of focusing on the prominent exiles, Lewalski provides a fresh and illuminating account of the experiences of the average refugee in the provincial depots between 1831 and 1848. Emphasizing "the material, psychological and moral" aspects of their exile, he details in a very human way through the use of diaries, memoirs and letters, the food, drink, clothing and health of the average exile, their leisure time activities, the psychological and moral stress they endured, their methods and extent of adjustment, their relations with the local citizenry, and the degree to which they assimilated and became self-sufficient. In the end, Lewalski concludes, despite the obstacles and mistrust they faced, the Poles "more than compensated for the material assistance provided by the July Monarchy."

Anna D. Jaroszyńska-Kirchmann's contribution to the literature on ethnic assimilation analyzes the development of social relationships between the post-World War II "displaced persons" and the existing American Polonia. Characterizing the post-war immigration as political refugees rather than voluntary immigrants, somewhat more middle class and more highly educated than the previous migration to America, she notes that those who entered America by benefit of the Displaced Persons Acts harbored an "intense feeling of alienation and distinctiveness" resulting from the "psychological and emotional burden of the war, displacement, concentration camps, forced labor, and prolonged stay in the displaced persons camps while waiting for emigration." This unique experience led to specific psychological support needs which were not fully recognized or provided for upon their arrival in the United States.

Focusing on the process of resettlement and the development of social relationships between the displaced persons and the established Polonia, Jaroszyńska-Kirchmann emphasizes, through the use of specific examples, the mutual misconceptions that inhibited early formation of positive relationships. Polonia, she notes, expected the new immigrants to be socio-economic replicas of themselves, while the new arrivals, lacking any substantive knowledge of American Polonia, considered it a "fourth province" of Poland with all of the social and political consequences they ascribed to that view. With this as a basis for understanding the context of the situation, Jaroszyńska-Kirchmann proceeds to discuss Polonia's efforts to assist the displaced persons, the role of voluntary associations in the process, sources of conflict between the two groups, and the resulting positive and negative experiences. She concludes that the resettlement program was imperfect and sometimes chaotic, with the result that "The formation of social relations between the old Polonia and Polish displaced persons was probably the most difficult and emotional process" that the displaced persons faced.

Changing the focus from the effects of immigration on the immigrants, Donald E. Pienkos explores the institutional response of American Polonia beginning with Agaton Giller's famous essay in 1879 which called for the organization of Poles abroad to assist the Fatherland. Giller argued that American Polonia's organizational agenda must include *both* advancement of the Polish American community within the United States *and* organization of that community to assist the Fatherland. Pienkos argues that over six generations Polonia has fulfilled this dual mission, and he sees the continued existence and "dynamism" of Polonia reflected in its three continuing goals which he articulates as "the advancement of their own well-being in America, their concern for the Polish homeland and its people, and their consequent interest in preserving a general sense of respect in the United States for the Polish cultural heritage."

Pienkos sees two distinct phases in the development of Polish American organizational life, the first period taking place prior to the end of World War I and the second beginning with the end of that war and the creation of the Second Republic. Pienkos sees the first period as one of construction, the Polish American community just beginning and its organizations being new and not growing until people decided to stay in America. Preoccupation with growth, development of insurance benefits, and assistance for the homeland. Organizations reached peak of influence and cooperation in the effort to assist Poland just before and during the First World War.

With the end of the First World War and the re-creation of an independent Polish state, the unifying factor of "patriotism" for the homeland diminished causing a decrease in the cooperation between Polonia organizations. The most significant event dealing with the organization of Polonia during this period was the creation of the Polish American Congress as an umbrella organization during the Second World War. Pienkos devotes the latter portion of his essay to an analysis of the priorities and achievements of the PAC. Among its many accomplishments, he maintains, is the creation "among countless Polish Americans [of] a positive sense of identification in their own heritage based upon pride in their material achievements in America and a concern for the fate of their ancestral homeland." With Poland at last free, it is now time, he concludes, to use Polonia's resources "to enable more Polish Americans to better understand who they are."

John J. Bukowczyk's contribution to this volume also focuses on the institutional response of American Polonia, outlining the early history of the Polish American Historical Association from its beginning as the "Commission for Research on Polish Immigration" within the Polish Institute of Arts and Sciences to the beginning of publication of *Polish American Studies* in 1944 and its establishment as a separate organization shortly thereafter. Bukowczyk summarizes both the historical achievements and current aspects of PAHA, as well as existing problems such as its difficulty in maintaining membership. As a result of his reflections, he calls for a reassessment of how PAHA and other ethnic organizations, beset by the same difficulties, relate to membership, to their mission, to prospective clientele, and to other organizations.

The relationship between Poles and their homeland is also the subject of Jan Lencznarowicz's essay which examines the role of the Polish press in Australia in maintaining ties with Poland. Through the use of statistical content analysis, presented within the framework of historical context, he traces the changing content of newspapers as a function of the social and political currents of the time. One important conclusion that he reaches is that the Polish press in Australia remained almost exclusively an emigrant press rather than developing into a medium reflecting the perspectives of the more assimilated "Australians of Polish descent." Perhaps because of this, the majority of the press not only attempted to informed public but to actively shape public opinion.

Although there were some differences in tone and coverage among papers, Lencznarowicz demonstrated similar attitudes and interests among the major newspapers through the prominence given the various types of stories, with items related to internal Polish issues and religious affairs being the most prominent. In large part, these stories tended to be oriented toward stories emphasizing internal resistance and reminding Poles in Australia of their duty to support resistance to Communism in the homeland. The picture of Poland that they presented to their readers focused on the government repression and the hostility of the population hostile to the regime. Special emphasis was given to themes of deteriorating conditions in Poland, the exploitation of workers by the Communists, and the difference in living conditions between the prosperity enjoyed by Poles in the Australia and the relative economic deprivation of the homeland. Further, Lencznarowicz noted that the great distance between Australia and the homeland, which created a sense of isolation, led the press to establish contacts with large Polish communities in Great Britain and the United States.

Thomas Gladsky addresses another problem associated with ethnic identity, the difficulty of identifying and defining Polish American ethnic literature. According to Gladsky, "Current thinking about ethnic literature continues to be influenced by theoretical models that do not apply evenly to all ethnic groups and historical periods." A good example of this is Daniel Aaron's recent model which divides ethnic literature into three phases, assuming that all such work progresses through the same evolutionary stages. Such a model, Gladsky contends, does not adequately fit ethnic groups whose literary history does not span several generations and includes a large component of immigrant literature.

Through an analysis of the work of Stuart Dybek, Gladsky illustrates both "the limitations of traditional paradigms of ethnic literature" such as that espoused by Aaron, and "the special circumstance of the contemporary Euro-ethnic writer." Dybek, for example, is variously classified as a "regional" or "class" author, thereby ignoring the ethnic content and messages continued in his works. To complicate this, Dybek, himself of Polish American heritage, while placing many of his protagonists in Chicago's ethnic communities and including ethnicity as "a distinct and recognizable presence," quite often portrays a generic "form of urban trans-ethnicity" rather than a recognizable Polish American community. In Dybek's case, this results from his attempt to confront the modern realities of urban life where generations and cultures collide and redefine life in contemporary ethnic or trans-ethnic neighborhoods, rather than the traditional stereotypical immigrant communities of the early twentieth century. As a result, Gladsky concludes, Dybek actually "encompasses all three of Aaron's stages, functioning as a spokesperson for all generations of Americans of Polish descent and producing a multi-layered and multi-dimensional ethnic self."

In the final essay in Part I, Dirk Anthony Ballendorf examines the work of the little-known ethnographer Johann Stanislaus Kubary, a modestly educated man who spent twenty-six years in the Pacific studying the native cultures of Micronesia. Arriving in the Pacific in the late nineteenth century, Kubary focused his initial efforts on developing an understanding of the origin and usage of the traditional monetary system on the island of Palau, later expanding his efforts to the island of Yap and other areas within the Caroline Islands chain. Through his study of traditional monetary systems, Kubary attempted connect the legends of the Palauans and Yapese with other Pacific and East Asian cultural traditions, thereby shedding light on the origins of those peoples and their traditional cultural and economic connections.

According to Ballendorf, Kubary has not been remembered "commensurate with his contributions" to the fields of ethnography and Micronesian studies. Through his studies of the Palauan monetary system, and his related work tracing the cultural heritage of the Caroline Islands, the ethnographer contributed significantly to a greater understanding of the origins and culture of Micronesia. Further, his work brought some organization and understanding, in the Western tradition of scholarly study, to the ambiguities of Palauan money and culture. Yet, despite Kubary's long association with his subject area, Ballendorf maintains that contemporary scholars can learn much from the Pole's thorough and unobtrusive way of gathering information and his thoughtful interpretations. "He provided," Ballendorf concludes, "great insight into the Palauan society and culture of his time and as he saw it."

Part II

Essays on the Effects of Government Policy on Polish Immigrants in the United States

One of the factors that led to some differences in the experiences of Poles abroad was the attitude of the host government to the new residents. Kenneth Lewalski's essay on the Polish political exiles in Part I of this volume illustrates the importance of government attitudes in the lives and opportunities afforded Poles in nineteenth century France. As a major destination for a the mass migration of the period between 1880 and 1920, government attitudes and policies in the United States are of particular importance in the study of the Polish diaspora. In Part II we explore this question from various perspectives covering the period from 1920 to the present.

James S. Pula's essay examines the effect of United States government policies on Polish Americans between 1900 and 1925. Noting that prior to the American Civil War Poles generally enjoyed a positive image in American society and literature, he argues that increasing immigration and a change in the source of immigration from the countries of Northern and Western Europe to those of Southern and Eastern Europe in the 1880s brought about a revitalization of the nativist movement and corresponding attacks on members of the "New Immigration." One result was the creation of the United States Immigration Commission, an investigative body sanctioned by the U. S. Congress, which concluded that Southern and Eastern Europeans were generally undesirable people whose entry into the country should be restricted.

Pula examines the workings and conclusions of the Commission, arguing that its findings were based upon faulty methodology, evidence, and interpretation, as well as the preconceived biases of Committee members, which led to inaccurate conclusions. These negative and inaccurate stereotypes were, he argues, used by nativist writers as a basis for the publication of derogatory portraits of Southern and Eastern Europeans, and also led directly to the development of both an atmosphere conducive to immigration restriction and public acceptance of a new, negative image of Poles and Polish Americans. The First Quota Act in 1921 and the National Origins Act in 1924, which resulted from the activities of the Commission, reduced the influx of Poles to a mer trickle, thereby depriving the Polish American community of ongoing cultural contact with the homeland. Pula concludes that the resulting isolation of American Polonia from contacts with its homeland that would otherwise have fostered cultural renewal gradually created an ethnic community that became frozen in time and heightening feelings rootlessness, anomie, and marginality. Pula concludes that the policies of the United States government that resulted from the Immigration Commission's inaccurate portrayals contributed directly to the isolation of American Polonia from both its European heritage and its American environment.

Focusing on more contemporary times, Shelly Lescott-Leszczynski's article traces the evolution of Civil Rights legislation and its effect on Americans descended from the nations of the European continent. Beginning with an overview, definition and rational for the creation of federally designation "protected" categories of people, she discusses how the intent and application of affirmative action changed over a period of time from the initial conceptualization as steps to be taken to provided expanded job and educational opportunities, to contemporary goals, timetables, quotas and preferential treatment mandated by law.

Using education as an example, Lescott-Leszczynski contends that while "many of the same non-academic factors that have handicapped the designated minorities may well have impeded upward mobility of European ethnics," the promotion of race-based scholarships, admissions set-asides, and other such policies provides advantages to members of officially designated groups, regardless of personal circumstances, while denying those same advantages to many disadvantaged people based solely upon their race or ethnicity. Citing examples from business and employment, she notes that the development of requirements for "proportional representation" and "deadlines" for accomplishment developed by the Equal Employment Opportunity Commission have in many instances altered the traditional merit system to a "representationalist approach." Such policies, she argues, re-define affirmative action as both "remedial" and "compensatory" resulting in "social engineering" and a system where "the concept of group harms and group remedies, including proportionate representation in every sector and activity of society, often takes precedence over individual rights, individual merit, and individual responsibility for one's situation and destiny."

Despite legal challenges to federal policies such as the famous Bakke case regarding differential admissions criteria to college programs, these policies have continued to expand in scope. By promoting these policies, Lescott-Leszczynski argues, the federal government has created an atmosphere in which European ethnics have become "hidden factors" in the White data collection category. This has "blurred their ethnic distinctiveness in the eyes of the law. It has attached an aura of 'guilt by association' to the European ethnic." As an alternative, she suggests a reassessment of the basic principles underlying affirmative action and other government policies and the exploration of other alternatives that could provide assistance for those in need regardless of the group to which they belong.

Raymond Dziedzic, a practicing attorney, explains the development of the legal definition of "minority" used by the federal court system in cases involving racial discrimination. Beginning with *United States v. Carolene Products* in which Justice Stone opined the need for special inquiry in cases involving "prejudice against discrete and insular minorities," he explains how and why the courts have increasingly expanded constitutional protections to groups judged to have been previously excluded from equal protection. Key to an understanding of this movement is the Court's application of the definition of "discrete and insular" minorities to groups within American society to determine which deserve "special" protection based upon historical inequities generally referred to as "invidious forms of discrimination."

Continuing with his analysis, Dziedzic illustrates how the application of the legal definitions adopted by the Court act to promote racial stereotyping, inequitable protection, and favoritism toward selected "minorities" at the expense of European ethnic minorities who have also suffered historical discrimination but who are generalized because of their skin color to be members of the "dominant group." Further, despite specific requirements in Title VII of the Civil Rights Act of 1964 that specifically prohibit discrimination based upon "national origins," the Court has consistently refused to recognize or prosecute discrimination based upon that criteria. Despite this, Dziedzic explains how rulings in the *Al-Khazraji* and *Shaare Tefila* cases, which recognized the right to sue based on ethnic ancestry, may open the legal door that has thusfar been closed to Polish Americans seeking redress for discrimination.

The effects of the differential treatment documented by Pula, Lescott-Leszczynski and Dziedzic can be seen in Anthony Bukoski's unique combination of academic research and personal experience which explores the effects of government policies and the new "political correctness" on individual Polish Americans. Bukoski tells, with a very human sense of loss, of growing to maturity unaware of his heritage because of the dearth of materials and information available to him as a young man. His interest in his heritage finally aroused through his reading of Nelson Algren's depiction of Polish American characters in a university course, Bukowski details how this new-found heritage was again thwarted in his professional life when he was prevented from participating in the exploring of the diversity of Polish American culture because it did not "fall within the purview" of his university's diversity initiatives.

Bukoski illustrates in a very straightforward manner how, in the politically correct university culture of the 1990s, all Whites have become generic, lacking in cultural individuality, while "diversity" has become the sole domain of women, African-Americans, and to a lesser extent Hispanics, Asians, and Native Americans. Bereft for decades of any mention in secondary school and university courses and textbooks, it is cruelly ironic that they continue to be pushed aside as the emphasis on "diversity" focuses elsewhere. Bukoski laments that Polish Americans have failed to develop a strong cultural and political voice with which to battle this restricted perspective, and poses the crucial question: Who will bring the history and culture of Polonia before America in a positive light?

The editors hope that the essays in this volume stimulate scholars to pursue further topics of research on the Polish diaspora, seeking answers to the question Bukoski poses.

Part I

Essays on Immigrant Adjustment

In Search of Oneself:
From the Concept of Ethnic Identity
to the Idea of "The Third Value"

by

Danuta Mostwin[1]

In the words of the early Christian philosopher Clement of Alexandria, "to know oneself is the greatest of all disciplines, for when man knows himself, he knows God."[2]

While interest in oneself is as old as the human race, the art of introspection and the discipline of knowing oneself have remained until recently the privilege of a select group. The discovery of the unconscious in medical psychology cast a new light upon the under-explored territory of self. It is true that for ages thinkers and philosophers believed in the potential of the unconscious contents of the self[3] but it was Joseph Breuer who, at the end of the nineteenth century, first introduced the term "unconscious" to mean ideas which because of intense emotions were unable to enter consciousness.[4] Sigmund Freud, friend and co-worker of Breuer, gave widespread recognition to the unconscious, while his stu-

---

[1]Danuta Mostwin teaches at Loyola College in Baltimore, Maryland.

[2]As quoted in G.G. Jung, *AION, Researches Into the Phenomenology of the Self* (Princeton, NJ: 1973), p. 222, vol 9, pt. 2.

[3]*Ibid.*, p. 66.

[4]Ernest Jones, *The Life and Work of Sigmund Freud* (New York: 1961), Volume 1, p. 274.

dent and later opponent Carl Jung went even further from the personal unconscious to develop a concept of the collective unconscious.[5]

In further developments in medical and social psychology in this century,
the concept of *self* interchanged with that of *identity* and *ego-identity*. Related to
these concepts, the notion of *ethnic identity* became popular in the early 1960s
after the publications of the work of Erik Erikson.[6]

Erikson was a scholar of psychoanalysis and the theory of personality, a
student of Sigmund and Anna Freud, an immigrant to the United States from
Germany, and an excellent speaker and prolific writer. He captured attention and
quickly won the admiration of young people in colleges. Disoriented and dissatisfied with the political situation in America and the unpopular war in Vietnam,
young people were searching for meaning in life. Erikson's ideas appealed to
them.

At the same time, Martin Luther King was leading African-Americans into a
peaceful struggle for human rights, awakening their need for roots. Inflamed by
this movement, ethnicity burst from hiding and American ethnic groups began
to proclaim their differences, their shared heritage, their binding ties with the
past and emphasizing their cultural ethos.

It was at this time as a student at the Columbia School of Social Welfare
that I became especially interested in the concepts of *self* and *identity*, trying
without success to find clear and separated definitions which would make them
stand apart from each other.

It was not until 1970, while working on my research on Polish immigrant
family adjustment in the United States, that the theoretical concepts acquired a
different meaning. Concepts which had so far been distinct—i.e. self, identity,
self-identity, ethnic-identity and self-concept—began to overlap.[7]

---

[5]G. G. Jung, *The Archetypes and the Collective Unconscious*, p. 42: "The
collective unconscious is a part of the psyche which can be negatively
distinguished from a personal unconscious by the fact that it does not, like the
latter, owe its existence to personal experience and consequently is not a personal
acquisition, while the personal unconscious is made up essentially of contents
which have at one time been conscious but which have disappeared from
consciousness through having been forgotten or repressed, the contents of the
collective unconscious have never been in consciousness, and therefore have never
been individually acquired, but owe their existence to heredity, whereas the
personal unconscious consists for the most part of complexes, the content of the
collective unconscious is made up essentially of *archetypes*."

[6]Erik Erikson, *Identity, Youth, and Crisis* (New York, 1968); *Childhood and
Society* (New York, 1950); *Insight and Responsibility* (New York, 1964).

[7]Leland and Hinsi, *Psychiatric Dictionary* (Cambridge and New York, 1970),
define "Identity" as "the unconscious directional pattern of sensing apparatus
whereby the individual orients himself to others and to his environment. In part
it consists of identification and representations with primary love objects." They
defint "Self" as "The psychological total of the person at any given moment,
including both conscious and unconscious attitudes." Benjamin B. Wolanin,

I realized that for the purposes of my research I would need to construct my own working definition of identity which would embrace both *"identity"* and *"self"* and the concepts derived from them, but in such a way that the theoretical aspects of the definition could be translated into practice. I learned while conducting interviews with my respondents and examining their responses that *identity* possesses a special meaning for an immigrant, and that the knowledge of its structure and the processes of its transformation could be helpful to a person in his or her healthy adjustment to a new environment. My focus was on ethnic identity which is but a part of the total identity system, and my first article devoted to this subject bore the title "In Search of Ethnic Identity."[8]

In the following twenty years of research on processes related to immigration, clinical practice, observations, and creative writings, I moved my focus from the rather narrow notion of ethnic identity to a more elaborate structure of identity system. It was during that time the idea of the *Third Value* emerged. The purpose of this paper is to recount my experiences in the process which brought me to this new idea, which I feel is still in need of further development and refinement.

I would like to develop the following three related topics:

1. The need to understand the process of identity in contemporary society,

2. The dynamics of the identity process, and

3. The creative aspects of the *Third Value*.

1. The need to understand the process of identity in contemporary society.

Loneliness and confusion are the hallmarks of our time. An average person today is much better informed about many things than was his grandfather, but he is more dependent on the environment than the previous generations were, and

---

Dictionary of Behavioral Science (New York, 1973), defines "Ego-Identity" as "A person's experience of himself as persisting essentially unchanged on as a continuous entity through time as a result of the function of the ego which synthesis one's ideals, behavior, and societal role." Wolanin defines the "Self Concept" as "The individual's appraisal or evaluation of himself." The above definitions of the terms are but a few selected from the multitudes of definitions in dictionaries and professional books. Each one is somewhat different depending on the orientation (psychological, psychoanalytical, social or anthropo-logical) of the authors.

[8]Danuta Mostwin, "In Search of Ethnic Identity," *Social Casework*, May, 1972, pp. 307-316.

he searches desperately for his own place in the universe. He is a person liberated from the bonds of authority and community opinion, and in this sense, he has won his freedom, yet he is craving for a sense of belonging to a group which will accept him as a unique, special individual.

In this hunger for recognition and for belonging "to people who are like me" the needs of an individual's identity are expressed. Identity, therefore is not only an answer to the question: *"Who Am I?"* It is much more. I turn again to Eric Erikson, the messenger of identity, identity crisis, identity confusion, and related terms so popular on college campuses in the 1960s, yet not always understood on a higher level of abstraction. Erikson defines *Identity* "...as a process 'located' in the core of an individual and his communal culture ... the process taking place on all levels of mental functioning ... for the most part unconscious ... always changing and developing ... never established ... [an] internal sense of sameness and continuity."[9]

The sociologist George Herbert Mead has connected the concept of identity to the learning of social roles and to the mechanism of value transmission.[10] Existential psychology has explained the notion of identity as a result of man's attempt to find meaning in life.[11] Sociologists of religion have emphasized the role of religion in consolidating identity after disturbing experiences of change.[12] Other scholars have described identity as the result of a decision making processes, the motivation on which the decisions are made constituting a core around which the structure of identity crystallizes itself.[13] These references are but the tip of the iceberg of volumes of writings on the subject. In spite of this, or maybe because of it, I needed to construct a working definition which would integrate the available, selected knowledge from psychology, psychiatry, sociology, anthropology and related fields.

I planned that the frame of my working definition would be large enough to include both concepts: that of self and that of identity. I wanted this definition to have a dual purpose: to serve as an analytical device for a student of behavior and also as a diagnostic tool for a clinician. My purpose was to implement theoretical concepts into practice.

It was in practice, correspondence and clinical observation that I encountered the problems of behavior of young Polish immigrants (often children of immigrants) related to or resulting from identity confusion or identity crisis.

I recall two characteristic situations. In both, the client was a college student in his early twenties. Here are their brief histories:

---

[9]Erikson, *Identity, Youth and Crisis*, pp. 22-23.

[10]G. H. Mead, *Mind, Self and Society* (Chicago, 1967).

[11]S. Dixon and R. Sands, "Identity and the Experience of Crisis," *Social Casework*, Vol. 64, No. 4 (1983), pp. 223-230.

[12]"Identity and Religion," in Hans Mol, ed., *Saga Studies in International Sociology*, Vol. 16 (1978).

[13]E. James Marcia, "Identity and Adolescence" in Joseph Adelson, ed., *Handbook of Adolescence Psychology* (New York, 1980).

Jan was artistically inclined but insecure, tormented by anxiety and critical of America. He blamed immigration for all his miseries. But since he was recruited by a Cult, Jan changed. He now follows them with enthusiasm and works for them in all kinds of jobs. His decisions are made for him. The world outside, including his family, have become "they." He does not need them anymore, nor does he need or value his heritage. Jan experiences identity confusion. He has become a person he is not.

Tom immigrated with great expectations for a wonderful life in America. Soon he became disenchanted and critical, complaining that he feels different. He thinks he is ugly, not athletic. Being ambitious, he works hard in school and tries to overcome his depression, but he feels painfully lonely. He experiences crying spells, cannot sleep, thinks about suicide. Since he relates well to his mother, he can share some of his feelings with her. Tom's situation is acute. He is experiencing an identity crises.

Identity problems are not limited to young persons. I have met older immigrants with symptoms of identity confusion or identity crisis. In my experience, there were more men than women. The tragedies of mental breakdown or even suicide among Polish immigrants in the United States do happen, but we seldom relate those incidents to identity crisis.

2. The Dynamics of the Identity Process.

Over the years of teaching, practice, and research, I have developed a definition of identity which was helpful to me and my students in the analysis of identity-related problems. Gradually this formulation expanded into a larger, more detailed system which I refer to as the *Paradigm for the Systematic Analysis of Identity*. I present it here, fully aware that it is a construction in need of refinement and not a final product.

PARADIGM FOR THE SYSTEMIC ANALYSIS OF IDENTITY

Introduction

Identity, which provides a person with a feeling of sameness and continuity, is a dynamic process, a bio-psycho-social system enclosing and involving all the aspects of a person's functioning on both conscious and unconscious levels.

This hypothetical structure of *Identity* possesses a holistic[14] quality in the sense that all the structural and functional parts are organized around and subordinated to the main principle: the question *Who Am I?*

Structural Parts

1. Genetically inherited attributes.
2. Attributes and values acquired through family and community socialization.
3. Attributes and values adopted in re-socialization.

Functional Parts

1. Self-evaluations regarding:

   a. one's own status
   b. role (social and familial)
   c. potential
   d. priorities of values
   e. obligations
   f. abilities
   g. group solidarity
   h. religion
   i. nationality
   j. ethnic bond

2. Adaptive mechanisms—a source of energy which provides for dynamics in the identity process:

   a. synthesis
   b. transformation
   c. substitution
   d. destruction

In the analysis of identity we ask which structural parts contributed to, and which functions and mechanisms were put into action to produce the behavior observable after stressful events of change or loss. By examining the dynamics of functional parts (self evaluations and mechanisms), we can possibly learn how a person creatively operates in the process of adjustment. One of the results of this creative process of adjustment is the unfolding of *The third Value*.

---

[14]A. Angyal, *Foundation for a Science of Personality* (New York, 1969).

Discussion: The Holistic Approach

"The holistic point of view bridges ... the gap between mind and body....
The person is neither physiological nor psychological, but a holistic unit."[15] He
is also social, being a product of interaction with his social environment.
Genetically inherited attributes of physical characteristics are under constant
scrutiny of our self-evaluation. Compared and confronted with our "looking
glass self" (that is with the opinion of important others about us), these self-
evaluations contribute to the answer of the leading question of our identity process: *"Who Am I?"*
Early family socialization forges in us models of familial and social roles.
It writes our code of values and imprints it in our mind in a hierarchical order.
All our life, whether at the time of crisis or everyday decision making, we will
return to this rudiment of our identity. Rejection of this code might be followed
by a feeling of guilt.
In 1988 I conducted a study entitled "The Unknown Polish Immigrant."[16]
Among the twelve inherited values named by the respondents, the values named
with the greatest frequency were: *patriotism, hard work, family, religion,* and
tradition. Among the values adopted in America, those which were named with
the greatest frequency were *independence, work ethic, achievement, tolerance,* and
pragmatism.
In the process of decision making, when self-evaluations are called into action by adaptive mechanisms, the immigrant may be confronted with opposing
values, for example, ethnic bonds and loyalty to one's national heritage in confrontation with the social role in the new country.
Another example related to the socialization of the immigrant's children is
this dilemma: should the parents contribute to the survival of ethnic identity in
the next generation by teaching the language, customs, and values of the country
of origin, or should they rather help the children to separate from parental background and become like the majority? In this situation, the value of *patriotism*
(inherited from the parents) is confronted with the adopted values of *pragmatism*
and *achievement.* The final decision of the parents will be greatly influenced by
their self-evaluation process regarding their parental role, their obligations, and
their own ethnic bond.

Ethnic Identity

Ethnic Identity, included in the Paradigm as an "ethnic bond" influencing a
person's self-evaluation, is but one of many aspects of an immigrant's identity

---

[15]*Ibid.*
[16]Danuta Mostwin, "The Unknown Polish Immigrant," *Migration World*, No.
2 (1989), pp. 24-30.

system. Definitions of ethnic identity are numerous but not always precise. Ethnicity has been defined as the nationality group, a part of a larger community, as cultural ethos meaning values and symbols, as "people speaking the same language," or as a cultural bond historically derived.

In 1981 I was appointed by the President to serve on the National Advisory Committee of the White House Conference on Aging. While at the conference, I approached a group of ethnic leaders asking if I could join their debate. I was accepted with some reservation, and told politely but definitely that I did not belong to ethnic groups because the color of my skin was white and therefore I was not different from the majority. The irony of this situation is that at the Conference I was representing "American White Ethnics." Ethnicity emphasizes group, folks, "peoplehood," and togetherness. It does not stress the concept of the individual, personal development or uniqueness. It is the concept of the *Third Value* which is concerned with the individual as a unique human being.

I came to believe that ethnicity is a need for a bond with people sharing the same heritage. This need does not exist before emigration. It is first experienced after detachment from a familiar environment. It is felt when the immigrant realizes that he is a member of a minority. It begins with nostalgic sentiments and the yearning to be with people who are felt to be "like me." It may lead either to the rejection of everything new and a tendency toward isolation, or to a denial of one's own heritage and a determination to become like the majority. In this either/or conflict, the example of the first one is the isolation within one's own group of the old "bread emigration" of Polish peasants. They formed ethnic enclaves recreating old *"okolica"* (neighborhoods) and thus walled themselves off from the new environment. This isolation proved successful in safeguarding the emotional health of the group and solidifying its endurance since isolation without the support of the group threatened the emotional health of the immigrant and might precipitate depression. Nevertheless, it prevented many of the early Polish immigrants (and for a long time) from entering the mainstream of American life.

The determination to leave everything behind and become like the majority conceals danger. The immigrant, whether he realizes it or not, experiences the impossibility of completely cutting off the umbilical cord with his mother country. This invisible fabric of loyalty[17] presses the immigrant to repay his obligations to the parents who symbolize for him his cultural heritage. If disregarded or rejected, this trans-generational accounting of merits and obligations may surface in guilt feelings or the acting out of an unexpected nature. When I think about this, two examples come to my mind. First is the story of John.

John, a post-World War II immigrant, successfully joined the American mainstream. He became a professor in a leading university, married an American, and had several children with her. John came from an intellectual, patriotic Polish family, but he did not feel the need to be involved in any action for

---

[17]Boszormenyi Nagy and G. Spark, *Invisible Loyalties* (Baltimore, 1973).

Poland. He was interested, but too busy with his own life. He never wanted to go to Poland for a visit or to encourage his children to go there. Our meetings with John were not frequent. It seemed that he was avoiding his Polish friends. And then, one day he called unexpectedly asking if he could come see us. When he did, we talked for a long time. John recounted his war experiences and tearfully revealed the depth of his feelings for his Polish heritage. At that time he was already terminally ill and knew about it.

A few months after John's death his wife came suddenly to our home. She was excited and presented me with a newly published book. "You are the first person I wanted to offer this to," she said. "It is my testimony to John. This is what he wanted to leave to his children. He dictated it to me and I took it word by word and did not change anything."

Fascinated, I turned the pages of the book searching for a chapter describing John's American experience. There was his family history, reminiscences of his Polish boyhood, his experiences as an officer during the war, an emotional account of his despair after the defeat of Poland, and some photographs of John in a Polish Army uniform. The book ended with a description of John's liberation from a German Prisoner of War camp.

"Didn't he write anything about his experience in America?" I asked.

"You see," his wife explained, "when we approached this time of his life, he was already very weak. He was dying. So he had to end it right there."

The second example is the story of Frank.

After September 1939 Frank found himself with the Polish Army in the West. In 1945, while liberating one of the German prisoner camps, he met his future wife. Frank's childhood was not an easy one. He and his father were not on good terms. He was relieved and happy to have an opportunity to start anew in England.

He began using his mother's maiden name which sounded Scottish. He even discovered an old seventeenth century family link with the Scottish clan. In his speech, mannerisms, and choice of friends he made himself Scottish. His wife, from a prominent Polish family and with her own heroic past in the Underground Army, did not approve of Frank's choices in life. They had one son, brilliant and attractive. He completed successfully his higher education and then one day, after selling everything he had (or rather received from his parents), he left for India to join a Cult. From his letters they learned he was working as a helper in a bakery.

Communication between father and son remained distant. The mother, after years of desperate attempts to understand and repair a broken relationship, gave up. Only cold indifference remained. She knew he would never change and never return.

John and Frank tried to adjust to a new situation. In both cases the adaptive mechanisms put into action were that of substitution and destruction. There was no evolution into the synthetic mechanism which opens the gate to the *Third Value*. John could not reconcile his Polish past with his American present. He died not leaving the account of his American struggles to his children. Frank repressed his feeling and moved forcefully from his past to the new present. The son acted out Frank's feelings. It was as if he was saying to his father: "I understood what you wanted me to do but I did it even better."

The two cases presented are not exclusively limited to John and Frank since "In analyzing the experiences and attitudes of an individual we always reach data and elementary facts which are not exclusively limited to this individual's personality but can be treated as mere instances of more or less general classes of data, and can thus be used for the determination of laws and social becoming."[18]

John and Frank exemplify situations of immigrants who, disregarding the values of trans-generational accounting of merits and obligations, were not able to develop their own, unique value, the *Third Value*.

3. Creative Aspects of the Third Value.

The concept of the *Third Value* was borrowed from Jan Lukasiewicz, one of the most brilliant logicians of the twentieth century. Prof. Lukasiewicz, founder of the Lwów and Warsaw School of Philosophy, created a system of multilevel logic and introduced symbolic mathematical logic. His three values logic system is based on a non-Aristotalian way of thinking.[19]

In Aristotelian philosophy, events and objects are grouped into paired opposites such as cold and warm, dry and moist, and are independent of the situation. In non-Aristotelian logic transitional stages are possible (not necessarily black or white, but gray is also acceptable).[20] The dynamics of the process are always to be derived from the relationship of the concrete individual to the concrete situation...."[21] According to Lukasiewicz, there exists in addition to two propositions, true and false, a third one, which represents neither the first nor the second, does not reproduce the facts, but is an independent *Third Value* influenced by creative human energy.

The *Third Value* is thus the result of a creative process. It may be described as having the following characteristics:

1. The *Third Value* represents the creative choice of a person who has found himself between two opposite or different systems.

---

[18]William I. Thomas and Florian Znaniecki, *The Polish Peasant in Europe and America* (New York, 1958).

[19]J. Łukasiewicz, *Selected Works*, L. Borkowski, ed. (Amsterdam and London, 1970).

[20]Kurt Lewin, "The Conflict Between Aristotelian and Galileian Modes of Thought in Cont. Psychology," in *A Dynamic Theory of Personality* (New York, 1935).

[21]Lewin, p. 41.

2. The *Third Value* does not need to be limited to the situation of the immigrant. It can also develop in those cultures where a society is under constant pressure of change.

3. The *Third Value* provides a person with a greater ability to adjust to a changing ecology and in discovering one's own place in the world.

4. The *Third Value* eliminates absolute either/or decisions. It introduces a new creative choice which does not destroy the past nor negate the present.

5. From a holistic and pragmatic point of view, the *Third Value* introduces an element of time and therefore better understanding of the evolution of our identity.

6. The *Third Value* expands the inner life of a person and liberates him from complexes: an inferiority complex of being different from the majority and a guilt complex of not being able to ever repay the everlasting obligations to one's own cultural heritage. These complexes, usually repressed to the unconscious, are barriers to individual development. Weakened or eliminated they will release creative energy for inner development.

One of the examples of the *Third Value* is the blossoming of Polish American identity, a trend which I observed in my own research of the last twenty-five years. The individuals who responded to my questionnaire adopted selective American values, but by retaining their Polish heritage they enriched the American culture. Thus they converted the old one-way adjustment process to a two-way creative interaction.[22]

To complete the recounting of my experiences which brought me to the idea of the *Third Value* I return to the title of this paper, "In Search of Oneself: From the Concept of Ethnic Identity to the Idea of the 'Third Value'."

Ethnic Identity or "ethnic bond" is that part of our identity system which expresses itself in feelings of loyalty to a group of people with whom we share our historical and cultural heritage.

The *Third Value* is a broader concept which does not negate or eliminate that of the "ethnic bond." This "ethnic bond," however, is but one of many aspects of the *Third Value* which reaches beyond "ethnic ties" and is a higher form of in-

---

[22]For a discussion of the Third Value as a creative process in the immigrant identity, see Danuta Mostwin, *Trzecia Wartość* (Lublin, 1985), pp. 20-21, and her "Family Mental Health in a Pluralistic Society," in *Social Thought*, Vol. IV, No. 2 (Spring 1978), pp. 26-28.

dividual human development.

The *"Paradigm from the Analysis of Identity System"* presented in this paper is a suggested method for the analysis of our own identity system, how to perceive ourselves in relation to structural parts, self-evaluation, and adaptive mechanisms.

I hope that this ontological exercise will bring us closer to the question *"Who Am I?"* and further understanding of the choice making process and the unfolding of the *Third Value*.

Sex-Role Orientation
Change and Acculturation

George M. Kapalka & Juliana Rasic Lachenmeyer[1]

Since the pioneering work of D. Bakan, A. Constantinople, J.H. Block, and S.L. Bem,[2] masculinity and femininity have been viewed as separate dimensions, present, in various degrees, in both men and women. Additionally, the masculine dimension traditionally is viewed as embodying a cluster of instrumental abilities (including assertiveness, dominance, independence, competitiveness, and the like), while the feminine dimension includes characteristics related to expressiveness (including affection, compassion, tenderness, warmth, etc).

[1]George M. Kapalka is a member of the Department of Graduate Education, Rider College, Lawrenceville, New Jersey. Juliana Rasic Lachenmeyer is a member of the North Shore University Hospital, Cornell University Medical College, Ithaca, New York. An early version of this paper was presented at the annual meeting of the American Psychological Association in 1988.
[2]D. Bakan, *The Duality of Human Existence* (Chicago: Rand McNally, 1966); A. Constantinople, "Masculinity-Femininity: An Exception to a Famous Dictum?" *Psychological Bulletin*, Vol. 80 (1973), pp. 389-407; J. H. Block, "Conceptions of Sex-Role: Some Cross-Cultural and Longitudinal Perspectives," *American Psychologist*, Vol. 28 (1973), pp. 512-526; S. L. Bem, "The Measurement of Psychological Androgyny," *Journal of Consulting and Clinical Psychology*, Vol. 42 (1974), pp. 155-162.

The sex-typed individuals are those who endorse a high degree of characteristics from the cluster corresponding to their own sex, while endorsing a low degree of characteristics belonging to the other cluster. Androgynous individuals synthesize a high level of both feminine and masculine desirable traits, while undifferentiated individuals endorse a low degree of characteristics from both clusters. Finally, sex-reversed people endorse a high degree of characteristics from the opposite-sex cluster, while endorsing a low degree of characteristics from the cluster corresponding to their own sex.

Developmental studies of gender propose that sex-roles emerge out of the influences of family and the society at large.[3] Indeed, cross-cultural investigations have shown much variability in sex-role orientation of both men and women across various cultures. Orientals tend to be more gender-typed,[4] while western Europeans and Scandinavians appear to be close in gender-orientation to North Americans.[5] Australians and New Zealanders tend to be more undifferentiated.[6] Argentinian males tend to be more sex-typed than American males, while Argentinian females appear less sex-typed than their American counterparts.[7] Israeli subjects were found to be more sex-typed than Americans,[8] while

---

[3]See E. E. Maccoby and C. G. Jacklin, *The Psychology of Sex Differences* (Stanford, CA: Stanford University Press, 1974), pp. 275-374, for a comprehensive review.

[4]See T. Inagaki, "A Cross-Cultural Study of the Feminine Role Concept Between Japanese and American College Women," *Psychologia*, Vol. 10 (1967), pp. 144-154 and D. Tzuriel, "Sex Role Typing and Ego Identity in Israeli, Oriental, and Western Adolescents," *Journal of Personality and Social Psychology*, Vol. 46 (1984), pp. 440-457.

[5]See L. Rainwater, "Social Status Differences in the Family Relationships of German Men," *Marriage and Family Living*, Vol. 24 (1962), pp. 12-17; G. H. Seward and W. R. Larson, "Adolescent Concepts of Social Sex Roles in the United States and the Two Germanies," *Human Development*, Vol. 11 (1968), pp. 217-248; Block, *op cit.*; J. J. Cohen, A. D'Heurle and V. Widmark-Petersson, "Cross-Sex Friendship in Children: Gender Patterns and Cultural Perspectives," *Psychology in the Schools*, Vol. 17 (1980), pp. 523-529; J. E. Williams, H. Giles, J. R. Edwards, D. L. Best and J. T. Daws, "Sex-Trait Stereotypes in England, Ireland and the United States, *British Journal of Social and Clinical Psychology*, Vol. 16 (1977), pp. 303-309.

[6]See R. N. Hughes, "Bem Sex-Role Inventory Performance in Students: Comparisons Between New Zealand, Australian and American Samples," *New Zealand Psychologist*, Vol. 8 (1979), pp. 61-66; J. Gackenbach, "Sex-Role Identity Across Two Cultures," *Psychological Reports*, Vol. 49 (1981), pp. 677-678; J. D. G. Goldman and R. J. Goldman, "Children's Perceptions of Parents and Their Roles: A Cross-National Study in Australia, England, North America, and Sweden," *Sex Roles*, Vol. 9 (1983), pp. 791-812.

[7]See R. J. Havighurst, M. E. Dubois, M. Csiksentmihalyi and R. Doll, "A Cross-National Study of Buenos Aires and Chicago Adolescents," *Human Development*, Vol. 3 (1965), pp. 80.

[8]See P. Maloney, J. Wilkof and F. Dambrot, "Androgyny Across Two

investigations of several African cultures revealed similar gender-role orientation to that found in Western European and American samples.[9]

The Polish and American cultures differ substantially in historical, political, and economic perspectives. Poles, along with individuals from many other ethnic backgrounds, can be characterized as field-dependent, with a cluster of traits characterized by strictness of child rearing, emphasis on respect for authority and social convention in general, close ties to the mother, and a more formal relationship with the father.[10] The abolishment of traditional Victorian stereotypes of male and female roles has been retarded by Poland's political system. For example, psychology, as a science, has not gained as wide an acceptance within the Polish population as it has in the United States, and the women's liberation movement has not gained much recognition and found little support in the censored media. These factors may have implications for differential sex-role development in comparison to American society. Although some research investigations have suggested that the socialist political system fosters the development of flexible gender orientation,[11] methodological problems and use of methods of assessment incompatible with instruments used in most Western societies make interpretation of these results difficult. When using instruments developed and standardized in the Western cultures, it is more likely that Polish individuals can be expected to appear more sex-typed than their American counterparts.

Following migration to a divergent culture, individuals in situations of culture-contact are exposed to values and influences of the host society. The process of acculturation includes behavioral change in the direction of the dominant culture and internalization of the host society's norms and values.[12] Since gender orientation emerges from intra-cultural standards, exposure to different social expectations may result in gender-oriented change in acculturating individuals.

The Problem

This study set out to test the sex-role orientation of Polish individuals living in the United States. The hypotheses of this research were as follows:

Cultures: United States and Israel," *Journal of Cross-Cultural Psychology*, Vol. 12 (1981), pp. 95-102.

[9]See S. A. Basow, "Cultural Variations in Sex-Typing," *Sex Roles*, Vol. 10 (1984), pp. 577-585; R. L. Munroe, "Gender Understanding and Sex Role Preference in Four Cultures," *Developmental Psychology*, Vol. 20 (1984), pp. 673-682.

[10]See J. W. Berry, "Temne and Eskimo perceptual skills," *International Journal of Psychology*, Vol. 1 (1966), pp. 207-229.

[11]See M. Vorwerg, "Untersuchungen über Einstellungsstereotype," *Probl. Ergeb. Psychol.*, Vol. 16 (1966), pp. 47-86.

[12]See J. Goldlust and A. H. Richmond, "A Multivariate Model of Immigrant Adaptation," *International Migration Review*, Vol. 8 (1974), pp. 193-216.

1. Recent Polish immigrants would score highly in the direction of sex-typing, significantly exceeding the United States normative data.

2. Acculturated Polish immigrants would show significant change in scores in the direction of androgyny in respect to the group of recent immigrants.

Methodology

A sample of 24 male and 29 female Polish immigrants were administered the Bem Sex Role Inventory[13] translated into Polish by the present author. Subjects were divided into two groups; recent immigrants (residing in the United States for less than ten years), and acculturated immigrants (residing in the United States for ten years or more). Sample medians were derived by sex for each group. To test the first hypothesis, sample medians of recent immigrants were compared to American normative data reported by previous research. To test the second hypothesis, ANOVA was used to compare sex-typing between groups. For the whole sample, Pearson Product-Moment Coefficients were calculated to measure correlations of androgyny score with age of subjects and androgyny score with number of years spent in the United States.

Results

The first hypothesis was confirmed; both men and women in the group of recent immigrants were found to be significantly more sex-typed than American normative samples. The second hypothesis was also confirmed: significantly more androgynous men and women were present in the acculturated group than in the group of recent immigrants. Some 74% of the control group was classified as sex-typed, while only 19% of the acculturation group fit that classification. Moreover, medians of the acculturated group significantly exceeded those of American normative samples. The distribution of gender orientation for the whole sample is summarized in Table 1 and ANOVA results are provided in Table 2.

---

[13]See Bem (1974).

TABLE 1
Distribution of Subjects with Regard to Sex-Type

Sex Type	Whole Sample	Acc. Group	Contr. Group	Acc. F	Acc. M	Contr. F	Contr. M	All F	All M
Andr.	28	21	7	11	10	3	3	14	13
Sex-Typed	25	5	20	3	2	12	9	15	11
Total N	53	26	27	14	12	15	12	29	24

Percentages

Andr.	53	81	26	79	83	20	25	48	54
Sex-Typed	47	19	74	21	17	80	75	52	46

TABLE 2
ANOVA Results

Source	df	SS	MS	F	p
Between gr.	1	11.13	11.13	14.70	.001
Error	51	38.63	.76		
Total	52	49.76			

Polish immigrants (both groups combined) were more clearly balanced with respect to definite orientation towards either androgyny or sex-typing than American subjects used in previous normative research: no undifferentiated or sex-reversed subjects were identified in the present study. However, looking at the acculturation group separately, 81% of the subjects met the androgyny criterion. This figure is well above the percentages reported in American normative data. Furthermore, only 19% of acculturation group subjects were considered sex-typed. This figure is lower than reported by studies examining American samples. Conversely, 74% of recent Polish émigrés scored as sex-typed. That figure greatly exceeds American norms. Comparison data regarding distribution of percentages obtained in previous studies with American samples is summarized in Table 3.

TABLE 3
Comparison of Percentages

Sex Type	Present Study	Bem (1977)	Spence and Helmreich (1978)	Hyde and Phillis (1979)
Andr.	53	24	31	19
Sex-Typed	47	37	29	52
Undiff.	0	23	25	20
Sex-Rev.	0	16	15	9

No significant correlation was found between androgyny and age (r(51)=.03, p>.05), but a significant correlation was obtained between androgyny and years spent in the United States (5(51)=.46, p<.005).

Discussion

The findings of the present study seem to suggest that individuals migrating from cultures characterized by formal and conservative societal and familiar conventions exhibit a rigid gender orientation as measured by American standards and compared to American normative data. A society where women's issues have gained little recognition and support may indeed foster rigid and conservative gender attitudes. This seems to contradict findings reported by Vorwerg.[14]

The Polish woman, thus, may be at a disadvantage in comparison with women in Western Europe, Japan, Australia, and the Americas, lacking instrumental characteristics seemingly crucial in the Western cultures. As suggested by prior research, it is very likely that this can result in lower self-esteem, assertiveness, stress handling capability, and achievement motivation.[15] Fur-

---

[14]See Vorwerg (1966).

[15]See S. L. Bem, "Sex-Role Adaptability: One Consequence of Psychological Androgyny," *Journal of Personality and Social Psychology*, Vol. 31 (1975), pp. 634-643; S. L. Bem, "Beyond Androgyny: Some Presumptuous Prescriptions for a Liberated Sexual Identity," in J. Sherman and F. Denmark, eds., *Psychology of Women: Future Directions of Research* (New York: Psychological Dimensions, 1976); J. S. Wiggins and A. Holzmuller, "Further Evidence on Androgyny and Interpersonal Flexibility," *Journal of Research in Personality*, Vol. 15 (1981), pp. 67-80; L. C. Bernard, "Multivariate Analysis of Aew Aex Aole Formulations and Personality," *Journal of Personality and Social Psychology*, Vol. 38 (1980), pp. 323-336; J. T. Spence and R. L. Heimreich, *Masculinity and Femininity: Their Psychological Dimension, Correlates, and Antecedents* (Austin, TX: University of Texas Press, 1978); W. F. Gayton, G. Havu, J. G. Baird and K. Ozman,

thermore, she may be subjected to many negative stereotypical attitudes, such as being less competent, independent, and logical. This has further negative implications in terms of family relations, and personal and occupational satisfaction.[16]

Likewise, Polish men can feel the impact of sex-typing. Being stereotyped as instrumental rather than expressive, Polish men may be experiencing problems expressing their feelings and frustrations. Since high masculine sex-typing has been correlated with high anxiety, high neuroticism, and low self-acceptance,[17] such individuals typically display more Type A behavior and less stress tolerance.[18] Since coping with cross-cultural adaptation is most difficult and stressful, these individuals are at a clear disadvantage in comparison with androgynous males. Indeed, this may be a factor contributing to the high rate of suicide and alcoholism found in Polish males.[19]

As illustrated in the present study, however, gender orientation may be altered by exposure to socio-cultural atmosphere conducive to developing flexible gender orientation. This has significant implications for counseling of gender-typed women. Since socialization appears to be responsible for the individual's gender orientation,[20] it may be possible to alter the net effect by creating an environment that fosters androgyny[21] and counseling.[22] Exposure to non-

---

"Psychological Androgyny and Assertiveness in Females," *Psychological Reports*, Vol. 52 (1983), pp. 283-285.

[16]See W. J. Ickes and R. D. Barnes, "The Role of Sex and Self-Monitoring in Unstructured Dyadic Interaction," *Journal of Personality and Social Psychology*, Vol. 35 (1977), pp. 315-330; W. J. Ickes and R. D. Barnes, "Boys and Girls Together—and Alienated: On Enacting Stereotyped Sex Roles in Mixed-Sex Dyads," *Journal of Personality and Social Psychology*, 36 (1978), pp. 669-683; W. J. Ickes, "Sex-Role Influences in Dyadic Interaction: A Theoretical Model," in C. Mayo and N. Henley, eds., *Gender and Non-Verbal Behavior* (New York: Springer-Verlag, 1981); H. M. Klein and L. Willerman, "Psychological Masculinity and Femininity and Typical and Maximal Dominance Expression in Women," *Journal of Personality and Social Psychology*, Vol. 37 (1979), pp. 2059-2070; M. Campbell, J. J. Steffen and D. Langmeyer, "Psychological Androgyny and Social Competence," *Psychological Reports*, 48 (1981), pp. 611-614.

[17]See T. C. Harford, C. H. Willis and H. L. Deabler, "Personality Correlates of Masculinity-Femininity," *Psychological Reports*, Vol. 21 (1967), pp. 881-884; P. H. Mussen, "Some Antecedents and Consequents of Masculine Sex-Typing in Adolescent Boys," *Psychological Monographs*, Vol. 75 (1961), pp. 506; P. H. Mussen, "Long-Term Consequents of Masculinity of Interest in Adolescence," *Journal of Consulting Psychology*, Vol. 26 (1962), pp. 435-440.

[18]See N. Batlis and A. Small, "Sex Roles and Type A Behavior," *Journal of Clinical Psychology*, Vol. 38 (1962), pp. 315-316.

[19]See J. Staniszkis, "On Some Contradictions of the Socialist Society: The Case of Poland," *Soviet Studies*, Vol. 31, No. 2 (1979), pp. 167-187.

[20]See Maccoby and Jacklin (1974).

[21]See P. Remer and E. Ross, "The Counselor's Role in Creating a School Environment that Fosters Androgyny," *School Counselor*, Vol. 30 (1982), pp. 4-

stereotyped models, for example, has been found effective in producing lasting behavioral changes in women.[23] Because gender-role counseling is rather recent, more research is necessary to investigate other effective techniques for increasing sex-role flexibility of both men and women.

Many other questions also remain to be investigated. All the subjects participating in the present study are inhabitants of the greater New York/New Jersey/Penn-sylvania/Connecticut area, which is heavily urbanized and industrialized. It is possible that different findings might have been obtained with a group that became acculturated in a more rural setting.

The acculturation process involves many stressors, such as a language barrier, change of peer group, separation from family, and a change of profession, which many immigrants experience. More research is needed to determine the effect of these on acculturation, sex-role orientation, family and social satisfaction, etc.

Acculturation studies involving populations other than Polish may also provide insight into other cultures' adaptability to social change. By examining how various cultures adapt to acculturation within an environment, meaningful and enlightening comparisons can be drawn.

Finally, more recent norms of sex-typing among the United States population are also needed. The availability of norms representing the current state of sex-typing in the American population would increase the validity of comparative research.

14.

[22]See B. A. Kerr, "Smart Girls, Gifted Women: Special Guidance Concerns," *Roeper Review*, Vol. 8 (1985), pp. 30-33.

[23]See J. J. Walstedt, F. L. Geis and V. Brown, "Influence of Television Commercials on Women's Self-Confidence and Independent Judgment," *Journal of Personality and Social Psychology*, Vol. 38 (1980), pp. 203-210.

The Evolution of Polish American
Wedding Customs in Central Wisconsin

by

Dennis Kolinski[1]

When dealing with the ethnic question, many view America as having a relatively homogeneous, monolithic culture, when in reality there exist quite diverse regional and ethnic variations. In addition to larger regions such as New England, the Midwest, and the Southwest, culturally diverse enclaves resulting from an ethnic pattern of settlement have managed to create unique pockets of localized culture. The patterns that have developed in these areas are different than urban ethnic manifestations and are ethnically-based regional hybrids that have grown out of and which are cohesively tied to a given terrain.

One of these subcultures can be found in rural central Wisconsin, home to a large Polish American community. The Polish Americans living there even today are characterized by a certain attachment to tradition and resistance to rapid change, not unlike their ancestors who came from rural Polish villages over one hundred years ago. These traits can be seen particularly in special family celebrations. As in other parts of the state, "Polish Weddings" there have through time attained a degree of notoriety because of their lavishness and exuberance. It was this uniqueness that prompted me to embark upon a project ten years ago to document the evolution of wedding customs among the population.[2]

---

[1]Dennis Kolinski is a program administrator at the Illinois Humanities Council.
[2]The research for this paper was originally undertaken for Kolinski's M.A.

The research for this project focused on a period of some seventy years beginning in 1912 and ending in 1983. Wedding customs during that period underwent a steady evolution, while at the same time retaining a certain "Polish" character. Some elements of the wedding changed completely, others disappeared, and new elements were adopted. But it would be a gross oversimplification to regard this transformation merely as another case of assimilation, so frequently used to account for ethnic cultural changes among immigrants in the United States. Seen as a simple, linear, and one-directional process, it implies that changes are the result of nothing more than the loss of Polish elements and the acquisition of American culture.

The characteristic culture of rural Wisconsin contains, to be sure, many American elements, yet varies greatly from other regions in the country. Particularly, when confronting Polish central Wisconsin from an assimilationist point of view, one is forced to ask: From where would isolated, rural immigrants and their children learn Anglo-American cultural patterns on a scale broad enough to assimilate them if the majority of the population in the region was not of Anglo-Saxon origin? It would seem improbable that this numerically large ethnic group did not itself play a role in the development and evolution of its own culture.

In the case of Portage County in central Wisconsin, general settlement of the region began in the 1830s and was meager through the 1840s. The first Poles arrived in 1857 and soon became the dominant ethnic group in the country. Anglo-Saxons, concentrated almost exclusively in the county seat of Stevens' Point, constituted a minority in the region. In such a situation, it is very difficult to believe that a tiny Anglo-Saxon population, isolated from the rural settlements of Poles, had such an enormous influence on that population that the Poles (as well as other ethnic groups in the area) became "Americanized" with little trace of their native culture. What we see, rather, is a process of change which wove together several different threads to create a new form of cultural fabric.

In her study of primitive cultures, anthropologist Ruth Benedict comments on the process of cultural change by writing: "Every culture, every era, exploits some few out of a great number of possibilities. ... Change, we must remember, with all its difficulties, is inescapable. ... The diversity of culture results not only from the ease with which societies elaborate or reject possible aspects of existence. It is due even more to a complex interweaving of cultural traits."[3] Because all cultures, including American regional and ethnic cultures, are based on these same principles, so too is the culture of Polish American central Wis-

---

thesis "Obred weselny w spoleczenstwie polonijnym powiatu Portage, Wisconsin, USA.," at the Jagiellonian University, 1984. A partial treatment of some of the results from the research is found in Kolinski, "Przemiany obrzedu weselnego w polonijnej zbiorowosci powiatu Portage, Wisconsin, USA," *Przegląd Polonijny*, Vol. 8, No. 2 (1989).

[3]Ruth Benedict, *Patterns of Culture* (New York: 1934), pp. 33-34.

consin a "complex interweaving of cultural traits."

However, investigations of internal mechanisms of change in American ethnic societies are usually hampered by the manner in which those transformations are characterized. Buzz-words, such as "melting pot" or "salad bowl" are very fashionable and in the academic community we hear everything from "acculturation" to "accommodation" and "Americanization" without even possessing a consensus of exactly what each of those concepts truly means or how they work. All of these ideas in some way or another fall into two broad categories: assimilation and pluralism. "In both, however, there are variations that make it all the more difficult to describe the reality."[4]

A great degree of our inability to come to an understanding of the processes of ethnic change stems from the fact that instead of looking at a given culture as an integrated whole, we see it as having only two extreme and mutually exclusive manifestations. The most basic way this is done is through the names we use to describe the culture—in this case, Polish and American. Certain elements can be labeled with certainty as clearly "Polish," others as "American," but many in justice cannot be so labeled because they are really neither. Limitations imposed by the use of these two terms can lead to misunderstandings. Even the term "Polish American" implies a certain Americanizing gloss.

The other way of portraying two mutually exclusive extremes is through overuse of the term assimilation, which still does not evoke a consensus among scholars. Theories of full assimilation have long figured strongly in American thought, forming the foundation for most theories concerning ethnic groups in the United States. Many of them have been more of a cultural ideology than empirically proven theories, which easily justified the pressure on ethnic groups to conform to a certain "superior" American culture. In the United States, the oldest manifestation of this was a form of absolute assimilation—Anglo-conformism, in which all incoming immigrants were compelled to conform to the indigenous culture.[5]

Almost all theories of assimilation view it as a one-directional, one-sided process that is based on the principles of loss-gain. The basic premise behind this concept is the absorption of one group by another. It is a negative, denationalizing process that is both absolute and static, which has only two opposing poles, excluding the possibility of development in any other direction. Cultural change, however, develops in many directions. Assimilation constitutes only one out of many mechanisms at play, but need not even be the dominant force.

Noted Polish American scholar, Helena Znaniecka Lopata, however, writes: "Much of the literature on immigrants to American, ethnic communities, assim-

---

[4]Harold Abramson, "Assimilation and Pluralism," *Harvard Encyclopedia of American Ethnic Groups*, edited by Stephan Thernstrom (Cambridge, MA: 1980), p. 150.

[5]Jan Piekoszewski, *Problemy Polonii amerykańskiej* (Warsaw: 1981), p. 150.

ilation, the hyphenated-Americans, and so forth, has been simplistic and biased."[6] In the early years of the twentieth century, observers of immigrant communities such as William I. Thomas and Florian Znaniecki were not looking for a social structure but for disorganization. The sociologists following this were more concerned with ethnic life and assimilation than with the overall social systems the groups created. Many studies saw assimilation as a mechanism in which certain elements of a past ethnic culture are preserved, not taking into consideration new cultural elements which continually appear.[7] "Seeing change as nothing more than a loss of prior items oversimplifies the ethnic scene."[8] These views of Znaniecka Lopata are not unique and are shared by many scholars.

The majority of theoretical assimilationist concepts were born in the Chicago School of urban sociology, which concentrated its focus on the transformations of urban ethnic ghettos, as well as the physical, professional, and class mobility of successive immigrant generations.[9]

Sociologists, whose theoretical foundations were laid during this narrow treatment of early twentieth century analysis, treated entire ethnic groups and all groups together as a whole, not taking into consideration the fact that each group, and certain internal parts of a given group, do not behave identically and are not homogeneous entities. Above all, one has to remember that matters concerning minority or ethnic groups are exceptionally complex.[10]

Wedding customs provide unusually rich and fascinating material for the study of cultural change and the complex mechanisms governing it. Marriage forms a pivotal point not only for two individuals but for the entire community as well. In many cultures, customs surrounding it tend to preserve, to a larger extent than in other facets of everyday life, traditions of sometimes considerable antiquity. It presents, therefore, a measure of what elements from its past a culture has deemed worthy of preserving and which values from its past are most strongly rooted in its psyche. To chart changes within these traditions provides one measure of the extent to which that culture has distanced itself from its past.

To most people today, weddings are happy and important occasions in the lives of those around them, but few view them as subjects of serious study, as evidenced by the dearth of scholarly attention given to this topic in the United States. This is unfortunate because it deprives us of an analytical look at this moment which has always comprised one of the major thresholds through which individuals pass during the course of life's journey.

---

[6]Helena Znaniecka Lopata, *Polish Americans: Status Competition in an Ethnic Community* (Englewood Cliffs, NJ: 1976), p. xi.

[7]Lopata, p. xiii.

[8]Lopata, p. xiii.

[9]Andrzej Kapiszewski, "Ideologie i teorie procesów asymilacji w USA. Szkic problemu, Część I," *Przegląd Polonijny*, Vol. 7, No. 1 (1981), p. 11.

[10]Grzegorz Babiński, *Lokalna społeczność polonijna w Stanach Zjednoczonych Ameryki w procesie przemian* (Wrocław: 1977), p. 50.

In his brilliant and influential work *The Rites of Passage*,[11] Belgian anthropologist Arnold van Gennep analyzed the manner in which all societies treat critical phases of life such as birth, death, and marriage through the ceremonies associated with them. He wrote in the conclusion of his work that "an individual is placed in various sections of society in order to pass from one category to another and to join individuals in other sections, he must submit, from the day of his birth to that of his death, to ceremonies whose forms often vary but whose function is similar. ... Beneath a multiplicity of forms, ... a typical pattern always recurs: the pattern of the rites of passage.[12]

It is precisely because of the fact that marriage is probably the greatest threshold in life that, consciously or unconsciously, societies have always chosen to mark this passage with great ceremony and ensure its importance through a myriad of practices. In such moments people turned to tradition to give them not only a continuity with the past but also to give them ceremonies that created a sense of the significance they attributed to it. Many customs practiced during rites of passage have had archaic roots because it was the "ancient" that gave an aura of the sacred and therefore both blessed and eased the transition. The marriage bond was of exceptional importance because only through its success was the preservation of society guaranteed.

Weddings of the last several decades in America, on the other hand, have to an increasing degree come strongly under the influence of fashion in opposition to socially dictated custom. The popularized version of marriage stressing the American ideal of individualism runs counter to the emphasis upon the family and community which one often sees in most ethnic traditions.[13]

Yet, despite this individualistic mentality which tends to view tradition as old fashioned, we continue to see wedding customs which persist. Brides still follow the formula: "Something old, something new, something borrowed, something blue, and a penny in your shoe." Grooms still carry brides over the threshold. Rings are still worn on the left hand. Brides like to wear their mother's old wedding dress. And all this, despite the fact that most people could not tell you where or when the customs originated, or even why they are done. Most would say that the customs give greater meaning to the event. However, the reason they give meaning is that it links them to the past; to others who have made this passage before them; to numerous weddings stored in one's consciousness.

In retracting the evolutionary steps of the marital rite of passage among the Polish Americans of central Wisconsin, I hoped to discover what relationship this particular community held to its past—i.e., to tradition—during the course of several decades. In an attempt to establish a control group which would min-

---

[11]Arnold van Gennep, *The Rites of Passage* (Chicago: 1960).
[12]Gennep, pp. 189-194.
[13]Pamela B. Nelson, "Ethnic weddings American Style: Old Traditions in a New Culture," in *Something Old, Something New: Ethnic Weddings in America* (Philadelphia: 1987), p. 17.

imize outside influences of change to the greatest degree, I selected a single extended Polish American family consisting of over one hundred members, originating in the rural environs east of Stevens' Point, and which still contained living members of the immigrant generation. Through interviews with family members I obtained a fairly detailed picture of Polish-American wedding customs from that terrain spanning a period of seventy years. Although an attempt was made to take into consideration the greatest number of family weddings, in order to create as near an unbroken chain of samples as possible covering this period of time, not all weddings of family members were used as samples. In order to eliminate possible deviations which would provide a false representation of internal change, research was limited only to those family weddings which took place in central Wisconsin and within the context of the Polish American community.

The point of departure for this analysis was the wedding cycle of the nineteenth century Polish Village—a long, complex order of ritualistic practices characterized by their strong traditional context and belief in strict adherence to both form and content.

The first members of the control family arrived in central Wisconsin in the year 1891, but the area had already been occupied by large numbers of Poles for about thirty years. Many of them originated from the Kaszubian region of northern Poland, but Poles from numerous regions could be found living there. This fact of regional mixing, plus the immediate loss of certain cultural elements inherent in the immigrant process through which one is wrenched out of one's own socio-cultural context, led inevitably to a certain homogenization of Polish regional customs in that area. Nevertheless, the routines, structure, and atmosphere of village life were re-created to such a degree in this rural setting that we can easily talk of the first researched wedding customs prior to the end of World War I as fundamentally Polish.

If we look back to that time and view the wedding cycle from beginning to end, we see a progression of stages that reflect the traditional approach to marriage, in all its complexity, that had been both preserved and transformed in the Polish village for centuries. In a typical scenario from that period, the entire wedding cycle spanned several weeks or months, beginning with *"Zaloty."* The first concrete but delicate steps taken toward marriage were *"Swaty"* (the matchmaking negotiations) which had traditionally taken place between the girl's father and the young man or his representative. *"Zareczyny"* (the engagement celebration) soon followed and constituted a formal confirmation for the village that a match had been made.

Because every step of the passage to the marital state was decisive, even the dressing of the bride was ritualistically dictated. Many of the elements of what she and the groom wore were determined more by custom than by fashion.

The groom was obliged to appear at the bride's home prior to the wedding for the parents' blessing. Following this, the church ceremony was probably the only element of the wedding in which folk tradition did not play a large role. On the other hand, the manner in which the individual members of the wedding party travelled to and from the church, as well as in which order, was very important.

The wedding celebration, lasting until the following morning, was held at the bride's home. Meals were served in the house, with music and dancing in the barn. During the course of the evening, one of the highlights was the Bride's Dance, which not only provided moments of amusement, but also constituted the primary means by which guests bestowed gifts upon the couple. One custom, however, which had always been an integral part of traditional weddings in Poland, *"Oczepiny"* (the capping) was conspicuously absent from all weddings researched in this study.

The first day ended for the couple with the wedding night and was followed by one or more days of continued celebration called *"Poprawiny."* This process has been greatly simplified for the purposes of this article, but should provide a picture of the major segments which were integral to these weddings.

As years passed, elements of the wedding cycle underwent, as they always had, a slow and continual evolution. Although it may not appear to us presently as fast-paced change, it was taking place probably at a more rapid rate than at any time in the past. But, despite the fact that this was taking place on American soil, many of the initial changes were not a direct result of the influence of Anglo-American culture, but rather of internal mechanisms of cultural change and creativity.

By the time of the Second World War, we begin to see a number of new elements appearing in the wedding cycle, while its primary structure remained relatively unaltered. Wedding showers preceded the wedding, but were not the gatherings women see today. They were a celebration almost like a small wedding, with abundant food, drink, and music. The wedding rehearsal appeared as an integral part of the cycle. Brides began to carry flowers to the Blessed Virgin's altar as part of the wedding ceremony. Following the service, instead of departing immediately to the reception, the newlyweds accepted greetings as the guests filed out of the church. After breakfast at the home, a trip into town was required for pictures. And an interesting element of folk innovation was the "decoration" of wedding guests during the dance—bridesmaids pinned flowers from their bouquets onto lapels and dresses of family and guests. During the evening, alongside the Bride's Dance, the Grand March—a sort of *"chodzony"*—became part of the evening scenario. Once in a while, even a Mock Wedding was held.

The most radical and rapid changes in wedding customs did not take place until the 1950s and 1960s—a time when much of American and all of Western culture was reeling under the influence of new technologies and the mass media.

The essence of some of the weddings elements gradually changed, such as the engagement. Previously unknown, bachelor and bachelorette parties sometimes were held, and a reception was added to the rehearsal. Several new theatric elements became a part of the evening celebration: a Grand March in a form different from that seen previously, coupled with the dance of the wedding party, throwing of the bouquet, removal and throwing of the garter, cutting of the wedding cake, and the *Tatusiu Waltz.* Although expressions of appreciation for gifts were always conveyed in the past, the sending of "Thank You" cards now became customary.

All essential aspects of the wedding cycle can be categorized in two essential manners. In the first, specific elements can be grouped by type or function, giving major categories within which all wedding customs can be found. They are:

1. the order of specific persons in the wedding party (i.e., who followed whom) during certain staged components, such as the line-up for the procession to the church or the Grand March;

2. logistic elements (persons organizing various aspects of the wedding, those paying for specific parts of the wedding, etc.);

3. customary gifts and ways of presenting them;

4. wedding customs of a staged or theatric character;

5. types of food and drinks served;

6. participants of specific parts of the wedding cycle;

7. those persons filling a special customary (or ritualistic) function;

8. customary clothing and their elements;

9. objects of a ritualistic character.

The second manner of categorization groups specific elements by time and gives us the major sequential segments found within the progression of the customs. They are:

1. customs which take place up until the day preceding the wedding;

2. customs which take place the day before the wedding;

3. customs which take place during the wedding day, among which, five important parts can clearly be seen:

    a. before the church ceremony,
    b. during the church ceremony,
    c. after the church ceremony until the beginning of the wedding dance,
    d. the wedding dance,
    e. the wedding night;

4.   customs which take place the day after the wedding.

A chronological analysis of changes within the wedding scenario as a whole reveals to us some of the major parts of this tradition's metamorphosis. Two important elements eventually lost from the original wedding scenario of the early twentieth century were customs brought over by the first immigrants from Poland: the blessing by the parents and the moving of the bride to her new home, and the Bride's Dance (although this last custom has exhibited a revival in recent years). The blessing, given in Polish by the bride's father, passed out of use with the disappearance of Polish as a first language. The abandonment of the Bride's Dance, as attested to by respondents themselves, is connected with the fact that guests eventually began giving the newlyweds gifts, thereby replacing the money presented to the bride in exchange for a dance with her. However, even after its initial disappearance, the custom seems to have lived on in a slightly different form. Although no money was involved, guests frequently felt an obligation to engage the bride in at least one dance during the course of the evening.

Several newer elements beginning in the 1950s enriched wedding observances and diversified their theatrical character, something for which Poles always showed a strong affinity in their customs. This is most clearly seen during the wedding dance with the introduction of customs such as the throwing of the bouquet and garter. These customs, probably originating in England, became part of Anglo-American tradition, and in time made their way into the wedding scenarios of most ethnic groups in the country. However, each group adopted them in their own manner.

That the Polish American community of central Wisconsin was not driven to blindly imitate standard Anglo-American practices is attested to by the fact that certain wedding customs widely recognized throughout the U.S., such as the custom of carrying the bride over the threshold by the groom, have not been adopted at all by this group.

Some of the customs introduced in central Wisconsin were not even of Anglo-American origin. Such was the *"Shivaree,"* which was a custom of French and French Canadian origin.

Alongside the introduction of new customs, many traditional Polish elements have persisted to the present day. Examples of this are: the customary division of costs for the wedding, the celebration of a *"Poprawiny,"* the types of food served during the wedding, the overall character of the wedding dance, and the partiality for large, boisterous weddings. Other elements, although they have undergone change and their Polish character is not immediately apparent at first glance, also belong to this category. For example, it is my belief that the mixed-gender wedding showers, which are themselves like small wedding dances, are a transformed and renamed incarnation of the older custom of *"Zareczyny"* celebrations traditionally held before the wedding.

When confronted with this picture of central Wisconsin Polish weddings, one is compelled to ask: What then triggered these changes? Investigation revealed that a clear but limited influence on changes in wedding customs appeared to be stimulated by several key factors:

1.   level of education;

2.   type of ethnic environment at one's place of work;

3.   knowledge of the Polish language;

4.   parents' professions;

5.   place of residence of the newlyweds and their friends (i.e., on farm or in town);

6.   generational differences.

The level of education and ethnic character of the social environment (especially place of employment) seemed to stand out clearly as influencing factors. As outside contacts broadened, a greater tendency developed to introduce new elements or change old customs. Changes in the groom's customary clothing and that of his groomsmen, as well as customs such as the throwing of the bouquet, removal of the garter, and certain customs connected with the wedding night, may well have been introduced under the influence of the non-Polish environment in which some informants found themselves.

Certain elemental changes in wedding customs coincided markedly with the passing of Polish as a primary form of communication (even though it may have still been used exclusively in certain other circumstances). For instance, disappearance of the customary arrival of the groom at the bride's home before the wedding and a pre-wedding parental blessing, as well as, to a certain extent, changes in the make-up of the wedding party, took place at the same time one saw the disappearance of the daily, extensive use of Polish among those researched. The diminishing role of the mother tongue in their lives led to the weakening of bonds in the group to certain characteristically Polish traditions. This particular cultural threshold signifies a clear transition from a type of wedding ritual of predominantly Polish character, to a new form of Polish-American ritual.

The type of work the newlyweds' parents were involved in, as well as place of residence (on the farm or in town), appear to have had a significant influence on the continuity of traditional practice or the tendency toward change in primary elements of wedding customs. A number of elements within the traditional wedding cycle were connected more closely with the agricultural character of this community, and when this began to shift, certain customs began to change or disappear along with it. The consequence of this was the extinction of certain Polish "village" elements in the wedding.

Generational difference also played a role in the evolution of wedding customs, but its influence was neither strong nor all-pervading. It was most evident between the first and second generations.

It was not until the mid-1970s that brides began to use various published guides for wedding etiquette and fashion journals in planning the wedding. Some changes seen about that time were without a doubt influenced by such publications, but as a whole, that influence was quite small.

The bands that provided music for weddings came to exert an unusually large influence on customs. In the 1940s they began to play a dominant role in directing the course of events during the wedding dance. These bands travelled widely to both Polish and non-Polish celebrations throughout the region and new customs learned through these outside contacts were brought to the community, eventually becoming a part of the local repertoire.

Nonetheless, the above influences as a whole do not seem to account for the broader and more significant transformations of Polish American wedding customs in central Wisconsin. They led to modification of individual elements or parts of the wedding, but did not leave evidence of influencing the broader patterns of change seen within certain time periods. Therefore, other external factors had to be considered in trying to account for them.

The most significant and greatest number of changes in the wedding customs of Polish Americans in central Wisconsin took place during the periods directly following World Wars I and II—periods characterized by global cultural transformations, especially throughout America and Europe. Each of these brought many changes, new values, and customs. After the First World War, and especially after the Second World War, Western countries experienced periods of sweeping cultural change. These wars marked the end of an era, as well as a style of life.

In the United States, the post-World War II period, marked by prosperity and the expansion of industry, technology, and knowledge, was particularly intense. Changes across the country were intensified by the development of mass media, films, radio, and television. Many traditions were discarded, not so much because they were Polish, but because they were associated with a period of poverty and seen as "old-fashioned."

How then can we characterize the overall evolution of the Polish American wedding cycle in central Wisconsin through the course of this century? The years 1912-1942 were ones in which traditional forms of wedding customs—forms belonging to a Polish cultural heritage—could still clearly be seen. The weddings in this period were strongly dictated by custom, but were not as elaborate as in the Polish villages these people left. Following World War I they underwent some change. However, it was not until the years 1944-1958 that we see a period of rapid variation of the wedding scenario under the influence of broad cultural transformations taking place after World War II. By the early 1960s, wedding customs among the Polish American community of Portage County stabilized and retained that form into the 1990s.

During the course of seventy years—roughly three generations—wedding customs have changed several ways. Some elements have died, but among those a few have reappeared. New elements have appeared—some "American," some global, and many others which arose purely out of the internal cultural creativity of the community. In the midst of this, still other customs have persisted stubbornly over the entire seventy-year period and remain an organic part of the local culture in a form little changed from the way they were seen in 1916.

What clearly emerges is a continual unbroken progression of cultural changes, punctuated only by periods of greater or lesser intensity, presenting a complex picture of multi-dimensional evolution in a given set of practices of an ethno-regional culture which evolved according to the community's own needs, desires, and tastes.

Some of these customs today are Polish, some are Anglo-Saxon, some are French, some are Midwestern. But many are not American, but global. Ruth Benedict commented on this when she wrote: "In our civilization there is in the anthropological sense, a uniform cosmopolitan culture that can be found in any part of the globe, but there is likewise unprecedented divergence...."[14] When one looks close enough, this divergence can be seen between individual cultures within America. One of them is the Polish Americans of central Wisconsin.

The culture of central Wisconsin as reflected in its wedding customs is neither Polish nor American. It has changed no more than in many parts of rural Poland, where traditional nineteenth century customs no longer exist. Rather, they have evolved to create a new form—an ethno-regional cultural form, that will continue to evolve as the cultural needs of its people evolve.

Instead of looking within it and other American subcultures for disfunctionalism and polarization, we must begin perceiving them as living, autonomous organisms which are not governed as much by hostile outside forces as by their own internal mechanisms, which in each culture are unique and perfect in satisfying the intimate needs of its members.

---

[14]Benedict, p. 212.

Heroes and Aliens:
Everyday Life of Polish Refugees in France During the July Monarchy

by

Kenneth F. Lewalski[1]

When the Revolutionary Government in Warsaw collapsed on September 7, 1831, after a two-day siege by Russian General Paskiewicz, some 48,000 Polish soldiers found themselves outside the boundaries of the Congress Kingdom—in Austria or Prussia.[2] Although Austria and Prussia were not direct participants in the Russo-Polish War that resulted from the November Insurrection, they were clearly in accord with Czar Nicholas I's determination to crush the revolt and uphold the territorial provisions of the Congress of Vienna in what Polish patriots regarded as the Fourth Partition. Austria and Prussia established a military blockade to prevent outside support for the Polish rebels or the return to combat by troops that had been chased by the Russian army into their territories.[3] A medical *cordon sanitaire* to contain the cholera epidemic, which spread from Russia into Poland during the war, was also established in order to prevent

[1]Kenneth F. Lewalski is Professor Emeritus and Director of the Humanities Lecture Series at Rhode Island College.

[2]Lubomir Gadon, *Emigracya polska. Pierwsze lata po upadku powstania listopadowego* (Kraków, 3 vols., 1901-02), I, p. 7.

[3]R. F. Leslie, *Polish Politics and the Revolution of November 1830* (London, 1956), p. 223.

its advance to central and western Europe.[4] Faced with isolation and hostile circumstances, the stranded Polish Army had little choice but to accept the harsh provisions of Czar Nicholas' amnesty in October 1831 and return to the Congress Kingdom. All officers were expelled from the army; rank-and-file soldiers were conscripted into the Russian army and dispatched to the Caucuses.[5]

The amnesty excluded all leaders of the Revolutionary Government, members of the Diet, and all high-ranking officers. These were obliged to emigrate to countries outside the network of Russia and its Holy Alliance allies. As Norman Davies noted, this group comprised Poland's political, artistic and intellectual elite, giving the Great Emigration its highly articulate and influential character.[6] It has been estimated that 43% were intelligentsia or university students and that 53% were professionals of some variety.[7] The composition of the Great Emigration, however, shows that 70% were military personnel: lower-grade officers and enlisted men who rejected the amnesty and swore to continue the struggle for an independent Poland wherever they could find the means to do so.[8] Only 30% were civilians.[9] Most of them were from Congress Poland; male; Roman Catholic; in their twenties; unmarried; from minor *szlachta* or petty bourgeois families; moderately well educated, candidates for careers in the army or civil service; unfamiliar with other languages and cultures.

In all, some 10,000 Poles opted for political asylum in France, England, Germany, Italy or the United States between 1831 and 1863, the period of the Great Emigration.[10] Some went as far away as the United States and Chile.[11]

---

[4]"Circulaire du gouvernement national de Pologne relatif aux griefs contre la Prussie," Muzeum Czartoryskich (Kraków), 5306 IV fol. 625-37.

[5]Leslie, pp. 258-59; Norman Davies, *God's Playground: A History of Poland* (New York, 1982, 2 vols.), II, p. 331.

[6]Davies, II, p. 275.

[7]Alina Barszczewska-Krupa, *Reforma czy rewolucja: Koncepcji przekształcenie społeczeństwa polskiego w mysli politycznej Wielkiej Emigracji, 1832-1863* (Łódź, 1970), p. 16; Jerzy Zdrada, *Wielka Emigracja po Powstaniu Listopadowym* (Warszawa, 1987), p. 11.

[8]Józef Dutkiewicz (wyd.),*Wybór Źródel do Powstania Listopadowego* (Wrocław, 1957), p. 239.

[9]Gadon, *Emigracya polska*, III, p. 233.

[10]Sławomir Kalembka, "Polskie wychodzstwa popowstaniowe i inne emigracje polityczne w Europie w XIX wieku" in Stefan Kienewicz (wyd.), *Polska XIX wieku, Państwo-społeczęstwo-kultura* (Warszawa, 1977), pp. 195-252. For British policy and aid see Czesław Bloch, "Aid of the English People to Poland in 1831," *Acta Poloniae Historica,* Vol. XIII (1966), p. 117-123 and Norbert J. Gossman, "British Aid to Polish, Italian and Hungarian Exiles 1830-1870," *South Atlantic Quarterly* (Spring, 1969), p. 231 245. Norman Davies, "L'Echo Anglais de l'Insurrection Polonaise de Novembre" in Daniel Beauvois (ed.), *Pologne: L'Insurrection de 1830-1831. Sa réception en Europe* (Lille, 1982), pp. 237-233 plays down the contribution of England in the November Insurrection and the

Over six thousand, a substantial number for early nineteenth century demographics, sought haven in France. According to Michał Sokolnicki, this doubled the number of refugees (Spanish, Portuguese, Italians) already granted political asylum in France.[12] Prominent persons—Adam Mickiewicz, Joachim Lelewel, Adam Czartoryski, Władysław Zamoyski, Maurycy Mochnacki, Leonard Chodźko, Generals Karol Kniazewicz, Ludwik Plater and Roman Sołtyk—who had private resources, professional incomes, or wealthy patrons like General Lafayette or Count Montalembert, were free to locate in Paris without any special surveillance or accountability. The majority of refugees, however, were barred from Paris and were completely dependent upon the French government for subsistence. They were assigned to special barracks in provincial cities and placed under the strict surveillance of French ministerial and local authorities.

Polish refugees encountered contradictory and conflicting experiences in their treatment and status during the three decades of the Great Emigration: hailed as heroes in liberal circles throughout the world; showered with generosity by the general public in France, England and the German States. On the other hand they were regarded as a political embarrassment and a diplomatic liability by the July Monarchy; subjected to severe restrictions in punitive legislation against aliens; denounced by the Holy Alliance powers as a subversive element in league with secret conspiratorial movements in the German and Italian states. Finally, their original status as temporary refugees was eventually transformed into permanent emigrés when they sadly recognized that the hope of returning to an independent Poland was in vain.

Literature dealing with prominent individuals of the Great Emigration is substantive and rich in both primary and secondary sources. Their lives and activities have been well researched and delineated. This article deals with the experiences of lesser-known refugees—the common man, if you will—who are more representative of the Great Emigration as a whole. My focus will be on the material, psychological and moral aspects of their experiences in France from 1831 to 1848: where and how they were stationed and housed; how their material needs—food, drink, clothing, health—were taken care of; how they spent their leisure time; what psychological, emotional and moral stress they experienced; to what extent they adjusted to their refugee-emigré status; how they related to a

---

Great migration.

[11]For the role of the United States in the November Insurrection and Great Emigration see Joseph W. Wieczerzak, "The Polish Insurrection of 1830-31 in the American Press," *The Polish Review,* Vol. VI, No. 1-2 (1961), pp. 53-72; Jerzy J. Lerski, *A Polish Chapter in Jacksonian America: The United States and the Polish Exiles of 1831* (Madison, 1958); Florian Stasik, *Polska Emigracja w Stanach Zjednoczonych Ameryki, 1831-1864* (Warszawa, 1973) and Kenneth F. Lewalski, "American Responses to the November Insurrection in Poland," *Consortium on Revolutionary Europe: 1985 Proceedings* (Athens, Ga.: 1986), pp. 358-78.

[12]Michał Sokolnicki, *Les Origines de l'Emigration Polonaise en France 1831-32* (Paris, 1910), p. 97.

foreign land and culture; how they responded to the local citizenry; to what extent they integrated or assimilated into French society; to what degree they became self-sufficient through work and education.

Among the plethora of sources on the Great Emigration, we are fortunate that so many ordinary refugees left accounts of their experiences in diaries, letters, memoirs and autobiographies. My sampling is based on twenty-seven accounts; many of them are published, others are manuscript collections in libraries like the Biblioteka Polska and Bibliothéque Nationale in Paris, the Muzeum Czartoryski in Kraków, and the British Library in London. Each of these accounts has its own character and individuality. Jan Bartkowski's *Wspomnienie* is the most anecdotal and descriptive.[13] Aleksander Jełowicki is intimate and highly personal.[14] Wojciech Darasz's *Pamiętnik Emigranta* is detailed and episodic.[15] Jacenty Grabowiecki is the most optimistic and is strongest on constructive aspects of emigré life.[16] These rich sources complement the accounts we have from more famous and influential emigrés. Together with the research of scholars like Lubomir Gadon, Michał Sokolnicki, Sławomir Kalembka and Barbara Konarska, they create a vivid portrait of everyday life during the Great Emigration, especially the hardships and travails which the overwhelming majority of refugees encountered. My purpose is not to write a history of the Great Emigration, but to convey in highly personal terms the *experience* of being an ordinary emigré.

France, in spite of several unfortunate episodes, proved to be the most hospitable and generous to the Polish refugees.[17] The July Monarchy, however, found itself in a dilemma vis-á-vis the Polish Revolution.[18] Its own revolutionary origin placed it in a precarious position in international politics. In order to gain legitimization and allay the fears of the Holy Alliance powers, France declared its adherence to the principle of non-intervention during the November Insurrection. At the same time, it was conscious of France's traditional role as champion of liberal causes and movements, and particularly of its debt to the

---

[13]Jan Bartkowski, *Wspomnienia z powstania 1831 r i pierwszych lat emigracji* (Kraków, 1967).

[14]Aleksander Jełowicki, *Moje Wspomniena* (Kraków: 1891, 3 wyd.).

[15]Wojciech Darasz, *Pamiętnik Emigranta* (Wrocław: 1953).

[16]Jacenty Grabowiecki, *Moje Wspomnienia w Emigracji od roku 1831 do 1854 spisane w Marsylii* (Warszawa, 1970).

[17]Bolesław Limanowski, *Historia demokracji polskiej w epoce porozbiorowej* (Warszawa, 1946, 2 vols.), I, p. 286.

[18]Józef Dutkiewicz, *Francja a polska w 1831 r. La France et la Pologne en 1831* (Łódz;, 1950). For other international aspects of the Polish Revolution and Great Emigration see J.A. Betley, *Belgium and Poland in International relations, 1830-1831* (The Hague, 1960); Clive H. Church, *Europe in 1830* (London, 1983); Sławomir Kalembka (wyd.), *Wielka emigracja i sprawa polska w Europie 1832-1864* (Toruń, 1980); D. Beauvois (ed.), *Pologne*.

November Insurrection in Poland for having frustrated Czar Nicholas' plan to invade Belgium and then France to restore the "legitimate" rulers established by the Congress of Vienna. Officially, it defined its policy as the *juste milieu*, the middle path between revolution and reaction. At the popular level, in what Adam Mickiewicz referred to as *"France réelle"* as opposed to *"France officielle,"* there was considerable public support for active military and diplomatic intervention and for humanitarian aid to the Polish rebels as well. Lafayette and the radical opposition in the Chamber of Deputies relentlessly called for direct intervention. His *Comité Franco-Polonaise* and its branches throughout France contributed financial, medical, and humanitarian aid to the heroic Poles.[19]

The July Monarchy was frankly relieved when the Polish Revolution ended. Minister of Foreign Affairs Horace Sébastiani's unfortunate statement after the fall of Warsaw that "order reigns on the Vistula" was an insult to the Polish cause and its supporters.[20] It was also a harbinger of some of the hostility that was to come about between the refugees and the government over the next few decades.[21] Overtures for asylum for the Poles came from both sides. In the Chamber of Deputies, the pro-Polish Lobby proposed granting unconditional political refuge and emergency funds for their immediate material needs and passage through Germany and Austria.[22] Lafayette went a step further and proposed naturalizing all Polish refugees as French citizens.[23] This measure, however, was overwhelmingly rejected by the Chamber of Deputies.

The first governmental appropriation for refugee relief, a sum of 500,000 fr., was voted on October 26, 1831.[24] French Ambassadors and Consuls in Germany and Austria were also instructed to grant passports to Polish refugees. Travel money was provided by various French agents in Dresden, Hanover and other German cities.[25] Austria was ambivalent about the future of Polish prisoners in its custody and delayed implementing the French offer of asylum.[26] On

[19]Adam Lewak, *General M. R. Lafayette o Polsce. Listy, Mówy, Dokumenty* (Warszawa, 1934); Lloyd Kramer, "The Rights of Man: Lafayette and the Polish National Revolution, 1830-1834," *French Historical Studies*, XIV, No. 4 (1986), pp. 521-46; K. F. Lewalski, "The French Medical Mission to Poland during the Insurrection of 1830-31," *The Polish Review*, X, No. 2 (1965), pp. 44-58.

[20]Chamber of Deputies, *Archives Parlementaires*, 69, pp. 643-75.

[21]*Lettre d'un Polonais a' M. Sébastiani*, Bibliothèque Nationale Mp 4120.

[22]Chamber of Deputies, *Archives Parlementaires*, 69, pp. 494-523 and 70, pp. 2-28.

[23]Sokolnicki, p. 136.

[24]*L'Emigration Polonaise et le budget Français, 1831-1858* (Paris, 1869).

[25]Kazimierz Lewandowski, *Pamiętnik wychodźca polskiego* (Warszawa, 1977); Jan Nepomucen Janowski, *Notatki Autobiograficzne, 1803-1855* (Wrocław, 1950); Wiktor F. Szokalski, *Wspomnienia z przeszłości* (Wilno, 1921, 2 vols.); Sokolnicki, p. 98; and Lubomir Gadon, *Przejście Polaków przez Niemcy po upadku Powstania Listopadowego* (Poznań, 1889).

[26]Józef Mazurkiewicz, *Krotki rys pamiętników podróży z Galicja austriackiej*

the Polish side, the official Polish Mission in Paris, headed by Kniazewicz and Plater, held numerous audiences with Sébastiani to work out details of asylum.[27] Acting independently, General Bem appealed to the French Minister of War requesting haven in France and attempted to negotiate the incorporation of entire Polish units into the French Army under their own officers and under the Polish flag.[28] Bem's model obviously was the Napoleonic Polish Legion.

Once the preliminary details with the July Monarchy were worked out, the first detachment of refugees departed for France in October; others followed in November and December. The popular response to the Polish refugees as they crossed through German and Austrian lands on route to France was celebratory.[29] Jan Bartkowski (p. 145) describes the journey from Vienna to Strasbourg as a *"pochodem tryumfalnym"* [triumphal procession]. Not since the Greek Revolution in the 1820s was there such an outpouring of sympathy and support for a political cause. Hailed as "gallant symbols of a martyred nation," the refugees epitomized the struggle against the reactionary politics of the Holy Alliance powers.[30] While some of the enthusiasm, as Sławomir Kalembka and Norman Davies point out, was due to traditional Russophobia in central and western Europe, many actively identified with Polish national and liberal aspirations. As they passed on foot from town to town—altogether a forty to fifty day journey—they were clothed, housed, feted and entertained by the German populace. Even Prussian authorities—hardly sympathetic to the Polish cause, but relieved to see them leave Prussian territory—responded to their material needs and provided modest stipends for travel expenses. They also contributed a generous amount of clothing: 17,000 shirts, 1,200 coats, 9,200 pants, 450 hats and 19,000 pairs of shoes.[31] Often greeted by local bands as they filed into town, as Wojciech Darasz noted (pp. 11-23), the refugees were serenaded with songs especially written in their honor. A whole new genre of German literature, *Polenleider*, came into existence from these occasions.[32] Dresden and Frankfurt-am-Main were singled out by the refugees as the most friendly and hospitable cities. Evenings, they were treated to banquets and receptions; at theaters and concerts they were given standing ovations. Leon Drewnicki (p. 234) described a Fancy Ball given in their honor in Frankfurt-am-Main, in a hall decorated with

---

do Francji południowej w roku 1832, Biblioteka Polska (Paris), MSS 411.

[27]*Akta misja polskiej w Paryzæu 1831-32*, Biblioteka Polska (Paris), Rjeż 350-361.

[28]Gadon, *Przejście Polaków*, p. 24.

[29]Hans Henning Hahn, "Obraz Wielkiej Emigracji w niemckiej publicystyce sprzed Wiosny Ludów," in Kalembka, *Sprawa Polska*, pp. 65-87.

[30]Church, p.115.

[31]Gadon, *Przejscie Polaków*, p. 19.

[32]Liza Cukierman, *Polenfreundliche bewegung in Frankfort in jahr 1831* (Warszawa, 1926) and Hans Henning Hahn, "Stosunki miedzy polskim narodowym ruchem wyzwoleczym a liberalizmem niemieckiej w okresie przed Wiosna Ludów," *Rocznik Historyczny*, 42 (1976), pp. 139-163.

Polish flags, which lasted until four in the morning. Mothers and children embraced the Poles and invited them to their homes. Local fund drives contributed additional money and clothing. Shopkeepers gave them assorted goods without charge. Both Aleksander Jełowicki (p. 382) and Jan Bartkowski (p. 147) commented that they had no need for money since all their material needs were met.

This was an exceptionally cordial period in Polish-German relations at the popular level, strengthened even more by the direct involvement of Polish refugees in German liberal movements throughout the 1830 decade. But there were exceptions. Konstanty Gaszyński was stranded in Lithuania and held for fifty-three days in quarantine before he was allowed to proceed to Prussia. When they arrived at the Prussian border, he complained (p. 9), their wounds were not properly taken care of and they were given food and water only after they paid for it. In Austria the refugees encountered some hostility and indifference as well. Jacenty Grabowiecki, travelling through Galicia en route to France, tells us (p. 40) that Galician peasants were especially unsympathetic and declined to give them food even when they were willing to pay for it.

Legend has it that the first Polish refugee, bandaged and on crutches, arrived in Montmartre in Paris early in September 1831. A popular engraving of the incident was made and served to kindle pro-Polish sentiment throughout the Great Emigration.[33] The majority arrived, after an arduous winter sojourn, in January and February of 1832, in Strasbourg. As they entered, sometimes in columns of one hundred, they greeted France with shouts of *"Witaj Francja, Witaj Kraina."* They were immediately assigned to former Napoleonic Depots for prisoners of war along France's eastern border—*"zakłady"* as the Poles called them. Military personnel were sent to Avignon or to Besançon; civilians to Chateauroux. The largest depot was at Bourges, numbering over 1,600 in April.

Both sides—the French government and the Polish refugees—regarded their asylum as temporary. Most of the Poles believed that a general war was about to break out in Europe and that they would shortly return to a free Poland. Thus, they insisted on remaining with their regiments or companies, under their own officers and the Polish flag. The refugees, however, were far from homogeneous ideologically and politically. Most of the rank and file soldiers and subalterns followed the politics of their officers; some gave their loyalty to particular leaders like Lelewel, Czartoryski of General Józef Dwernicki; the radicals formed a separate faction, the Polish Democratic Society (*Towarzystwo Demokratyczne Polskie,* or TDP). Before long, the emigré camps became rife with personal recriminations, conflicts of loyalty and ideological controversies.

---

[33]A reproduction of this famous engraving can be seen in the one volume illustrated edition of Lubomir Gadon, *Wielka Emigracja w pierwszym latach po powstaniu listopadowym* (Paris: 1958, 2 vols.), p. 97 or in Jerzy Zdrada, *Wielka Emigracja,* p. 11.

The French government, faced with the assimilation of such a large number of foreigners, soon grew weary with their presence. At one point, an effort was made to enlist them in the newly created Foreign Legion serving in the recently acquired colony of Algeria.[34] The Algerian plan was violently denounced by Lafayette and the pro-Polish deputies in the Chamber, and even more vehemently by Joachim Lelewel and the radical leaders of the Government-in-Exile in Paris. Though enthusiastically supported by General Bem and some officers, efforts to recruit volunteers caused turmoil in the depots and yielded little response. Only about thirty refugees actually joined the French Legion, in spite of enticements of high pay and promotion in rank.[35] The large concentration of Polish refugees on France's eastern border also became a problem, especially when a large number of refugees left their assigned depots to participate in the abortive Frankfort revolution, the ill-fated Zaliwski Partisan movement in 1833, and the Mazzini-led Savoy invasion in 1834.[36] As a result, the government began dispersing the emigrés, transferring them from the larger camps to other depots in central and southern France: in remote provincial towns like Lunel, Salins and Bergerac or interior cities like Dijon and Nevers.

The most far-reaching measure of the July Monarchy, however, was the enactment of the Alien Bill of April 21, 1832 regulating the conditions of the Polish refugees in France.[37] This bill, sponsored by Prime Minister Casimir Perier—hotly debated in the Chamber of Deputies, denounced in the emigré press—dispersed and decentralized the Emigration. It appropriated a sum of three million francs for refugee relief, but prohibited subsidy holders from residing in Paris and transferred jurisdiction of the emigrés from the Ministry of War to the Ministry of the Interior. Notwithstanding several minor modifications by the Ministry of the Interior, the Alien Bill remained in force during the eighteen-year

---

[34]*Bulletin des Lois du Royaume de France*, IX ser., 23, No.88 (Paris): Ord. 52, No. 1313 (March 9, 1831).

[35]Gadon, *Emigracja polska*, II, 130. On the Algerian issue see Stefan Kienewicz, "Les Emigrés Polonais en Algérie (1832-1856)," *Acta Poloniae Historica*, XI (1965), 43-70 and Aleksandra Helena Kasznik, *Między Francja a Algieria. Z dziejów emigracji polskiej, 1832-1856* (Kraków, 1977). The refugees were all too aware of the unfortunate outcome of the Caribbean expedition under Napoleon: Jan Pachoński and Reuel K. Wilson, *Poland's Caribbean Tragedy: A Study of Polish Legions in the Haitian War of Independence, 1802-1803* (New York, 1986).

[36]Kenneth F. Lewalski, "Fraternal Politics: Polish and European Radicalism During the Great Emigration" in M.B. Biskupski & James S. Pula (eds.), *Polish Democratic Thought from the Renaissance to the Great Emigration: Essays and Documents* (New York, 1990), 93-108.

[37]Chamber of Deputies. *Archives Parlementaires*, 77, 354-81. The vote was 166 for and 99 against the measure. King Louis Philippe signed the Alien Bill on 7 November, 1831.

span of the July Monarchy.[38] Appropriations for emigré relief were renewed annually, the sum fluctuating depending on budget or political circumstances. The funds appropriated for Polish refugees were only partly a measure of largesse of the July Monarchy. For the most part it was due to powerful pressure from the parliamentary opposition, which demanded "national compensation" for having failed to provide direct military and financial assistance to the Poles during the November Insurrection. On average, emigré relief amounted to 2,500,000 francs annually; most of it went to the Poles, the rest to the other refugees in France.[39] As we shall see, this was hardly a sufficient sum to support the material needs of six thousand Polish exiles. Supplementary sums were frequently needed and authorized by the Chamber of Deputies. For example, extra travel funds were allotted when refugees were transferred to new depots or other towns.

The material welfare of the Polish refugees rested almost wholly on the monthly stipends from the French government. The Comité Franco-Polonaise and its local affiliates in the provinces provided small sums in particularly needy situations. Monetary and material contributions also came from local townspeople in depot centers and other refugee cities. The initial formula for allocating stipends to Polish officers was set at 50% of the salary of French military personnel: divisional generals were granted 150 francs per month; brigadier generals given 100 fr.; colonels, lt. colonels and majors allotted 60 fr.; captains received 45 fr.; non-commissioned officers and ordinary soldiers got 75 centimes daily, plus a bread allotment. Civilian refugees were granted 45 to 70 fr. monthly, depending on their social or professional status.[40] As the number of refugees swelled in 1832, however, stipends were reduced. In April 1833, clearly as a punitive measure against refugees who had participated in illegal expeditions, stipends were again reduced by 25% to 50%, depending on rank. While it is difficult to convert these sums to current equivalents, Kalembka points out that the average salary for a craftsman or factory worker in the provinces was around 2.75 fr. per day. He also notes that a kilogram of bread cost 28 centimes; a portion of beef, 96 centimes; and a liter of wine, 45 centimes. The Prefect of Bergerac estimated that a single man needed a minimum of 40 fr. per month (30 fr. for food and an additional 10 fr. for a room) in order to survive.[41] It is clear from these figures that the majority of refugees, especially those below the rank of captain, lived below national standards, on the margin of necessity.

Life—or perhaps one should say "internment"—in the depots was difficult and dispiriting. The barracks in larger depots were overcrowded and unsanitary.

---

[38]"Circulaires et Instructions Ministerielles," *Archives Nationales (Paris): FIA, 38-40.*

[39]The annual budget reports in *Bulletin des Lois* (IX serie), 1832-48.

[40]Gadon, *Emigracja polska*, II, 327.

[41]Sławomir Kalembka, *Wielka Emigracja: Polskie wychodźstwo polityczne w latach 1831-1862* (Warsaw, 1971), p. 276.

In Besançon, for example, five or six officers shared a single room and as many as fifty persons occupied the barracks for enlisted men. As mentioned above, the depots were initially under the jurisdiction of the Ministry of War with a French commander in charge. Each depot also had a Polish interpreter or "mediator" to negotiate their needs with French authorities. Regulations varied from depot to depot: in some, refugees were strictly prohibited from leaving their barracks; in others, they were allowed to go into town under certain conditions with special permission. Similarly, some depots required the refugees to muster for roll call daily, others weekly, still others only once a month when they got their stipends from the government. The Poles generally got along well with the French commanders. Bartkowski (p. 151) noted that his commander, General Jean Martin Pelet, was friendly and kind. Darasz (p. 65) tells us that the refugees at Le Puy presented a gold ring valued at 214 fr. to Colonel Duprat as a token of their appreciation.

At the outset, in the larger depots where whole units had been assigned, Polish officers generally retained their authority and maintained strict discipline over their men. In other cases, Grabowiecki noted, the refugees elected their own officers to keep order and harmony. But as internal problems and factionalism developed among the exiles, Grabowiecki reported (p. 57) that French authorities had to assert more authority over their lives. In Bourges, Bartkowski reports (p. 154), mornings were spent drilling and marching. Most of the rest of the day was idle, spent playing cards, smoking pipes and discussing politics.

Because of the growing number, the movement of refugees from one location to another was frequent. After the participation of the refugees in the Frankfort and Savoy Expeditions, the French government removed them from the depots along the eastern border and relocated them to interior cities and towns. Many were dull, dirty factory towns—as depressing as the depots. Darasz (p. 65) complained that Lunel was ugly, rundown and situated on a polluted canal. In some cases they had to find lodgings in private rooms, draining money from their already inadequate monthly stipend. Many were forced to borrow from friends, pool their money or take on small jobs to survive.

Three grievances surface in many of the memoirs and diaries. First was the indignity of incarceration and the loss of personal freedoms. Many said they were treated like prisoners and felt constantly harassed. They came to call France *"ciepła syberyja"* [a warm Siberia] because they were forbidden to move around freely.[42] Second was the constant movement from place to place. "Here today, there tomorrow, somewhere else next" wrote Kamil Mochnacki who found refugee life much too disconcerting and unstable.[43] The third complaint involved the difficult adjustment to the climate in France. Those in the south found the

---

[42]Gadon, *Emigracja polska*, III, p. 119.

[43]*Listy Maurycy Mochnackiego i brata jego Kamila wyszłych z wojskiem polskim do Francji w r. 1831. Pisane z Paryża, Metz i Avignon do rodziców swoich* in Mochnacki, *Dzieła* (Poznań, 1863, 5 vols.), I, p. 121.

heat and humidity oppressive, the air and wind unhealthy. Those in the north maintained that their rooms were too cold, lacking stoves or fireplaces, aggravating their already deteriorating health.

Another basic human need—clothing—was a continuing problem. To begin with, their uniforms—which they took great pride in—were worn, torn and stained from wounds even before the refugees arrived in France. Most of them were young, handsome and vain—anxious to make a good impression on the local girls and women. For noncommissioned officers and rank-and-file soldiers the cost of new clothing was prohibitive. Darasz stated (p. 68) that local merchants were advised not to give credit which exceeded the daily allowance of the refugees. At the end of the month when the stipends were distributed, local merchants swarmed around the refugees to collect their debts. Bartkowski, a second lieutenant, claimed (p. 155) that he could not afford to buy clothing replacements—even essential underwear. The only clothes Bartkowski had to his name were one jacket, one pair of trousers, three shirts and three pairs of stockings. He described that he had to shorten his trousers every couple of days. Before long, he wrote, they reached only to his calf. Fortunately, he received a gift of 12 fr. from a friend in Avignon which allowed him to buy a new pair of pants and some underwear. Grabowiecki (p. 75) also learned to repair, mend and restyle his uniform and clothing. According to Darasz (p. 63), the poorest soldiers whose allowance was completely inadequate, often obtained clothing from General Dwernicki and other high-rank officers. In Bourges, French authorities provided officers and soldiers with French uniforms (grey jackets and red trousers) from surplus infantry supplies. Bartkowski reported (p. 151) that the Poles found them unattractive and remade them in "Grand Duke Constantine style" in order to look "more Polish" and to improve their appearance in town and in parades. Eventually, as their military uniforms wore out, their appearance took on a hodge-podge character—half military, half civilian.[44] Leon Drewnicki (p. 252) lamented how poorly the refugees came to be dressed, mostly in discarded clothing from French veterans. Many items—shirts and shoes in particular—which were donated by local committees and townspeople were already used and worn when they got them, further contributing to the decline in their appearance and morale.

All the accounts I have examined addressed themselves to food, drink and the basic nutritional needs of the refugees. Here the major problems were the insufficiency of food, the non-nutritional nature of food, the poor quality of the food, and the unfamiliarity with French lower-class diet and eating habits. First, was the element of cost. The stipends of lower-rank officers and ordinary soldiers provided for only a subsistence diet. In depots such as Bourges, Drewnicki points out (p. 254) that they could only afford to eat once a day. Two officers were sent into town each day to buy bread and vegetables. Their daily diet became monotonous and dull: bread, soup, mushrooms and beets. Officers living

---

[44]Leon Drewnicki, *Za moich czasów* (Warsaw, 1971).

in boarding houses had to pay up to 35 centimes for a meager meal or around 20 fr. a month (almost half of their stipend) for meals which included "kasza" for breakfast, bread, wine, sausage and occasionally fish. Janowski (p. 462) found an arrangement in Poitiers where he could pay for meals on an individual basis rather than on a monthly pension. This type of accommodation was favorable to many refugees who were invited frequently to dinner at the homes of townspeople. In some circumstances, notably at Poitiers, refugees formed eating cooperatives consisting of up to sixty persons at a cost of 25 fr. per person per month.[45]

The Poles found it hard to get used to certain staples in French lower class diet and complained of its poor quality. Michał Podczasyński, in a letter to Maurycy Mochnacki (Dzieła I, 102), wrote that a doctor warned him against eating cheap cuts of meat and other fat products which were spoiled and adulterated with chemicals or fried onions to disguise its rottenness or rancidness. Drewnicki (p. 254) singled out "tête de mouton" and "tête de veau" as especially difficult to accept. Janowski (p. 344) found "pieds de mouton in white sauce" below human standards, declaring it suitable "for dogs rather than people." On the other hand, he came to like "moules" (mussels) and in general found the food in Normandy similar to that of Poland, especially cider and various apple products. For his part, Darasz stated (p. 39) that French food did not appeal to the Poles, and particularly criticized French soups as "too sweet" for the Polish palate. Refugees who were stationed in the south of France found the food there "too spicy" and were altogether unused to diets which consisted mainly of unfamiliar vegetables and fruits. What they missed most was Polish sausages, cabbage dishes and traditional recipes and modes of preparation.

The horrendous material and living conditions had a direct effect on the physical and mental health of the refugees. The memoirs, letters and diaries are filled with complaints and reports of sickness, deaths and suicides. Konstanty Gaszyński (p. 6) gives a graphic description of the physical and psychological condition of wounded refugees in Prussian detainment camps. In France, lung and skin diseases were rampant in the depots and in northern industrial cities and towns. Two of my principal sources, Janowski (p. 564) and Bartkowski (p. 191), report that they were sent to thermal baths in Vichy or Sens for treatment. In southern cities like Lunel and Avignon, refugees complained of fevers and stomach disorders. Since tuberculosis was virulent everywhere in the nineteenth century, there is no surprise, as Jełowicki reported (p. 423) that many refugees became infected. In his *Wspomnienie* Bartkowski quotes a letter (p. 409) from a friend in Montpelier informing him of the deaths of four friends from tuberculosis in 1833. Michał Podczaszyński published a monthly newsletter, *Pamiętnik Emigracja*, which carried regular reports of tragic happenings, especially deaths, in the emigré community.

---

[45]Kalembka, *Wielka Emigracja*, p. 279; Zdrada, p. 10.

We are familiar with the early, premature deaths of prominent emigrés like Frederic Chopin and Maurycy Mochnacki, but we should also take note of the untimely deaths of lesser known refugees. Kamil Mochnacki, younger brother of Maurycy died at age 29 in Avignon in 1833. Bonawentur Niemojowski, died at the age of 48 from a fever-induced madness. Jełowicki (pp. 423-424) discusses the large number of deaths in 1835 and 1836 and carefully provides specific names of the deceased.

Self-inflicted deaths—suicides—increased after 1835. Grabowiecki (p. 77) tells the sad story of a friend named Alojzy Manugiewicz who committed suicide on April 18, 1835. Grabowiecki found him in his room shot by his own hand and was puzzled and unable to explain what brought about his desperation. Manugiewicz had recently got a job at a local printing shop and only a few days before had ordered a new set of clothes from a tailor. There was no suicide note, only a copy of a poem in his pant pocket entitled "Un exile Polonais, une jeune anglais." Lacking any specific explanation, Manugiewicz' suicide was simply ascribed to the ever-increasing desperation of the refugees. Potrykowski relates another suicide—that of Second Lieutenant Stefan Sleszinger in March 1833. Shortly before his death Sleszinger purportedly gave his Silver Cross to a colleague, saying "I am not deserving to wear this."[46] Jełowicki (p. 427) and Bartkowski (p. 200) also call attention to the growing number of suicides and provide specific names of victims. Sławomir Kalembka counted fourteen officially registered suicides between 1832 and 1838.[47] Because of the stigma attached to suicide, perhaps there were even more unreported incidents. All told, Kalembka tabulated 550 refugee deaths in France between 1831 and 1842—almost 10% of the total emigré population.[48] Most were natural, some were suicides, as we have seen, and nine were in duels.

The psychological and mental health of the emigrés underwent a significant change during the course of the Great Emigration. At the outset, in 1832, bolstered by the enthusiastic welcome they received in Germany and France, spirits and morale were extremely high. Believing that their haven in France would be temporary and encouraged by the popular response to the Polish cause, they were convinced that a European-wide war against the Holy Alliance was immanent— enabling them to return home soon. Influential liberals in the Chamber of Deputies and Chamber of Peers applied relentless pressure on the French government to look after their material needs. Radical opponents of the July Monarchy outside parliament, like François Raspail, mounted a campaign of opprobrium against the regime, charging it with bringing shame and dishonor on France for its hostile treatment of the emigrés and for yielding to political pres-

---

[46]Józef Alfons Potrykowski, "Moje notatki i Wspomnienia emigracyjne z lat 1832-34, 1836 i 1840," MSS Muzeum Czartoryskich I 5349.

[47]Kalembka, *Wielka Emigracja*, p. 286.

[48]Kalembka, *Wielka Emigracja*, p. 56.

sure from Russia and Austria.[49] This kind of support, comforting and reassuring, lifted the spirits of the refugees.

Leon Drewnicki describes (p. 243) the mood in the depots in the early days as happy and carefree: the loud, boisterous atmosphere; friendly card playing; much smoking of tobacco; the singing of patriotic songs; reminiscing about incidents of the November Insurrection; the boastful re-telling of their war exploits. Within months, however, as idelness, boredom and homesickness set in, an element of anxiety and sadness began to intrude. Complaints about confinement in the depots and the lack of money for tobacco and wine show up in many letters and memoirs (Drewnicki, p. 243; Gaszyński, p. 4; Jełowicki, p. 423). Szymon Konarski, one of the most radical and restless of the refugees, revealed that he was so hungry and bored that he became unable to play cards or read.[50]

The camaraderie that marked the early months of exile soon gave way to bitter personal and ideological quarrels. Disputes often developed into duels. Gadon counted thirty-three duels in August 1833 alone.[51] French authorities resorted to strict measures against dueling. Darasz reports (p. 95) that the Prefect Villeneuve in Castres punished eleven refugees for participating in a duel. He also pointed out that a new law against dueling was passed, authorizing local authorities to confine or expel guilty persons.

In spite of economic hardship and poor social conditions, I found little evidence of crime. On the whole, the refugees were orderly and law-abiding persons—accustomed to military discipline and authority. They regarded themselves as ambassadors of Poland and recognized that its "good name" and reputation depended on their good behavior. To be sure, there were occasional brawls and rowdy incidents in towns from time to time. At Le Puy, all refugees found in town after 10:00 p.m. were arrested. According to Darasz (pp. 61, 70), the local commandant arbitrarily ordered three Polish officers to patrol the town in the evenings in order to prevent "adventurous incidents" on the part of the refugees. At a theater in Avignon, reported by Podczasyński in his newsletter (I, 21), a performance of a pro-July Monarchy play was interrupted by whistling and murmurs by Polish refugees in attendance. At intermission, they were locked out and prevented from reentering the theater.

Bartkowski describes (p. 156) one incident of theft: a watch stolen from a boarding house in Avignon, but clearly not by any of the three refugee boarders. Later, it turned out, a noncommissioned officer by the name of Stanisław Dylewski was identified as the thief. Gadon cited another instance of stealing—the theft of a silver spoon by Second Lieutenant Aleksander Gałecki.[52] Gałecki was arrested by the emigré council and turned over to the local authorities for

---

[49]F.V. Raspail, *De la Pologne sur les bords de la Vistule et dans l'Emigration* (Paris, 1839).

[50]Szymon Konarski, *Dziennik z lat 1831-1834* (Wrocław, 1973), p. 105.

[51]Gadon, *Emigracja polska*, III, p. 199.

[52]Gadon, *Emigracja polska*, III, p. 179.

trial. Although he was exonerated by a French court, he was retried by the *Rada Honorowa*, found guilty, and demoted two steps in rank. Kalembka claims to have found only one instance of murder by a member of the emigré community.[53] Thus, aside from dueling, leaving depots without permission, occasional town brawls, one murder, and a few cases of theft, no significant number of crimes were perpetrated by the emigrés.

After a few months in exile, many of the refugees grew listless. Some complained that they were unable to concentrate on reading or engage in any constructive activity. Many grew bored with obsessive card playing, frequenting theaters and drinking in cafes. Many expressed an eagerness to work, but were confined to depots and prohibited from doing so. Jerzy Zdrada stated that boredom "broke the spirit of those with weak character," especially those with poor educations or few intellectual interests.[54] Ideological quarrels within the depots—over Foreign Legion issues, among the followers of Adam Czartoryski and Joachim Lelewel, between the proponents and opponents of the Polish Democratic Society—turned the depots into serious turmoil, prompting French authorities to tighten restrictions and reassign many to new depots. The harassment of the refugees increased significantly. In Bergerac, for instance, Prefect Scipion Mourgue and Sub-prefect Taillefer engaged in a protracted jurisdictional dispute with a refugee officer, Lt. Colonel Roslakowski. Roslakowski was accused of ignoring French orders and of meddling in local politics.[55] In *De la Pologne*, Raspail reported that local officials at Poitiers, in a campaign directed against emigré radicalism, seized documents and papers of the *TDP* and arrested some of its members. Conflicts with local authorities steadily mounted. Alexander Jełowicki (p. 389) wrote that many refugees feared they would be expelled from France or forced to emigrate to Algeria. Pressure on the refugees to reconsider Czar Nicholas' amnesty and return to Poland also intensified. Those who participated in the Frankfort Expedition were refused reentry in France for over six months—left wondering whether they would have to seek permanent asylum in Switzerland. Thus, there is considerable evidence that 1832 to 1834 was the most critical period of the Great Emigration, the lowest point in the refugees' psychological and moral welfare.

While we know a great deal about the political passions of refugees—their intense patriotism, their nostalgia for Poland, their bonding and affection for each other—we know little about their intimate personal life, particularly their sexual lives. This is not unusual and is consistent with nineteenth century inhibitions and reticence to discuss sexuality in public discourse or even in private

---

[53]Kalembka, *Wielka Emigracja*, p. 286.

[54]Zdrada, p. 13.

[55]Marcel Bouteron, *Pologne Romantique* (Paris, 1937), pp. 197-201. Two similar regional studies of Polish refugees are J. Mathorez, *Notes sur les réfugies politiques polonais dans le Mayenne, 1833-1860* (Angers, 1918) and *Notes sur les réfugies politiques polonais dans le Sarthe et le Maine-et-Loire* (Angers, 1920).

writings. These were, however, young, handsome men—mostly in their twenties—highly visible in theaters and cafes in French towns. The accounts we have of their initial reception in German and French towns show that they were flattered by the adulation showered upon them by French girls and women. Only in Lunel, they complained, were the women unfriendly, refusing even to talk to them. Kalembka hinted that many refugees had amorous affairs, "few of them ending at the altar."[56] Gadon cites a case in Bourges where a refugee named Franciszek Dąbrowski, discovered in an affair with the wife of his host, was apprehended and evicted from the boarding house by gendarmes.[57]

As we have seen, there was little inducement for serious attachments since most of the refugees thought that their sojourn in France was only temporary. Moreover, confinement in the depots and the lack of spending money was not conducive to close relations with women and girls in town. The prospect of supporting wives and children was slim. Furthermore, the constant mobility from depot to depot, from town to town, did not favor the development of intimate attachments. Finally, some—but very few—were already married, with wives back in Poland. In one rare case described by Gadon, a twenty-two year old woman, identified only as Pani Babska, managed to join her emigré husband in France after an arduous three-month journey.[58] He also claimed that other wives of refugees managed to join their husbands in Avignon.

We do know, either by direct evidence or by inference, that many marriages took place. In Bourges, officials learned that Antoni Burnejko, a second lieutenant in the cavalry, secretly married a French woman named Emilia.[59] In another case a refugee named Franciszek Zakrzewski married a French woman, but soon abandoned her and subsequently escaped from the Avignon depot.[60] We know, by inference, that Jacenty Grabowiecki married, since he wrote his memoirs for his son. Kalembka estimates that, all told, there were several hundred refugee marriages, mostly between Polish officers and women from well-to-do families.[61] He also explained that when refugees were moved from one depot or town to new locations, those married to French women were allowed to stay behind. My research indicated that most of the marriages occurred during the later years of the Great Emigration, toward the end of the July Monarchy or after 1848 when most of the emigrés were in their late thirties, held jobs, or became naturalized French citizens. Barbara Konarska, for example, pointed out that eighty-seven emigrés who became doctors in France married: thirty to French women, eleven to Polish wives, the rest to women of German and other nation-

[56]Kalembka, *Wielka Emigracja*, p. 285.
[57]Gadon, *Emigracja polska*, III, p. 195.
[58]Gadon, *Emigracja polska*, III, p. 198.
[59]Gadon, *Emigracja polska*, III, p. 178.
[60]Kalembka, *Wielka Emigracja*, p. 43.
[61]Kalembka, *Wielka Emigracja*, p. 284.

alities.[62]

Although the early years of the Great Emigration were unsettling and disruptive, many refugees made productive use of their leisure. In Paris, several educational societies were founded in the very first months of the emigration: the *Towarzystwo Naukowe Polaków Tułaczów* founded by Joachim Lelewel in December 1831 and the *Towarzystwo Historyczne-Literacki* in 1832 headed by Adam Czartoryski.[63] Both were intended to preserve and disseminate knowledge about Polish history and culture. Refugees in the provinces placed a high priority on learning the French language in order to communicate with the local population and eventually to get jobs. Those who had even an elementary knowledge of French taught what they knew to others. Jacenty Grabowiecki knew some French before he came, but decided (p. 75) to hire a tutor for five francs a month to acquire a better command. Unfortunately his money ran out after two months. Wojciech Darasz, who was a university student before the November Insurrection, knew some German and Russian, but began studying French when he was transferred to Le Puy. In Besançon, a local citizen named Valentin d'André volunteered to teach French to the Poles and coopted three refugees to assist him.[64] Michał Podczaszyński, in the April 1833 issue of his newsletter (III, p. 8) recommended the publication in Bourges of *Grammatyka języka francuskiego dla wychodzców polskich* by Michał Pietkiewicz. At Dijon the refugees received permission to use the local libraries and reading rooms. In February 1833, the young academic refugees at the civilian depot of Chateauroux who had been university students at Warsaw, Kraków or Wilno created a Society of Mutual Enlightenment [*Towarzystwo Wzajemnego Oświecenia*] to promote intellectual activity.[65] The most widely read French book by the refugees is said to have been a popular history of the French Revolution by Albert Lapponneray.[66] Darasz mentioned that he read a local history of Velay-Massif Central by J. A. M. Armand in order to become better acquainted with France. Darasz also organized a subscription (p. 70) among the emigrés at Le Puy, ranging from two to two hundred sous per month, to create a library of books and a collection of French and Polish newspapers. One of the better educated emigrés, Jan Nepomucen Janowski, knew French well enough to translate François Raspail's *De la Pologne* for the benefit of his fellow refugees.

---

[62]Barbara Konarska, "Emigranci polscy z wykształceniem medycznym w życiu społeczeństwa francuskiego po roku 1831," in Kalembka, *Sprawa Polska*, p. 223.

[63]Maria Straszewska, *Życie literackie Wielkiej Emigracji we Francji, 1831-1840* (Warsaw, 1970); Lubomir Gadon, *Z Życia Polaków we Francyi. Rzut oka na 50-letnie koleje Towarzystwa Historyczno-Literackiego w Paryżu, 1832-1882* (Kraków, 1983).

[64]Gadon, *Emigracja polska*, III, p. 159.

[65]Gadon, *Emigracja polska*, III, p. 206.

[66]Adam Lewak, "Czasy Wielkiej Emigracji" in S. Lam, *Polska: jej dzieje i kultura* (Warsaw, 1934, 3 vols.), III, p. 231.

One way for the refugees to occupy their time constructively and to improve
their skills at the same time was to create their own schools within the military
depots. General Kniazewicz got permission from authorities in Besançon to
establish a school of artillery to teach fortification and weapon strategy. Townspeople in Besançon enthusiastically supported the project and contributed 196
books and twenty atlases.[67] The school officially opened on September 25,
1832. A few months later, in February 1833, a similar school was established
in the Bourges Depot. These schools proved to be short-lived, however. Preoccupation with emigré politics and participation in the Frankfurt, Zaliwski and
Savoy adventures interrupted the development of constructive activity within the
depots.

Since the refugees were stationed or moved to several different Departments
in France, they had many opportunities to visit various regions and observe local
customs and historic sites. Darasz, who moved around considerably, reveled in
his travels in France. He managed to obtain permission to visit Nimes, Arles,
Marseilles in the south and various cities in the north. He visited French cathe-
drals and commented on the quality of the architecture and stained glass. He was
greatly impressed (pp. 25-30) with Roman architecture, especially the Maison
Carrée and the Temple of Diana in Nimes. He marvelled at seeing the Mediterranean and Atlantic Oceans for the first time. He even described bull fights
(corrida) that he encountered in his travels. Jacenty Grabowiecki traveled a great
deal in central France, rode the railroad for the first time in his life, and recorded
(p. 58) his personal observations on the early stages of industrialization in
France.

Attending theaters and concerts was a popular activity among the refugees.
Darasz, who had broad artistic and cultural interests, was a particularly avid the-
ater-goer and astute critic. When he was stationed at Le Puy he remarked (p. 51)
on the absence of a resident theater and complained about the quality of traveling
companies. Many of the refugees possessed musical talent. At Bourges, the
largest depot, the refugees formed a chorus and small orchestra which performed
during the 11:00 a.m. mass in the cathedral. According to Bartkowski (p. 152)
townspeople began to flock to the "Polish Mass," creating such crowds that later
masses were delayed. The bishop eventually eliminated the special Polish mass
and forced the refugees to attend the other scheduled masses. The orchestra, however, continued to give concerts for the public, and became the core of the Fil-
harmonic Society of Bourges.[68] In the south, in Avignon and Lunel, local residents complemented the refugees on their musical talent and enjoyed Polish
religious and patriotic songs sung in church and at theatrical events.

The year 1836 was an important turning point in the Great Emigration. For
one, the failure of the revolutionary expeditions, the recognition that a general
European war was unlikely and the realization that the prospect of returning to

---

[67]Gadon, *Emigracja Polska*, III, p. 169.
[68]Gadon, *Emigracja Polska*, III, p. 198.

Poland was illusory, brought about a sober reassessment of their future. Furthermore, they recognized that they had lost some sympathy with the government and even the French public by leaving their depots without authorization and by other violations of their asylum. Moreover, with the death of Lafayette in 1834, they had lost their principal advocate in the Chamber of Deputies. Finally, the Minister of Interior reduced the monthly stipends for refugees in 1836 in order to encourage them to find jobs and to become at least partially self-sufficient. They were free now to look for work anywhere in France, providing they obtained permission to leave their assigned quarters. The Ministry also urged those whose educations had been interrupted by the November Insurrection to resume their studies in France.

Most of the refugees managed to find day-to-day jobs or seasonal occupations. Since many of the refugees were generally better educated than many local people in small towns, tutoring or teaching was one of the principal forms of employment. Janowski, for example, got a job (p. 565) in the town of Molinous as tutor for two sons of a French widow. Other refugees earned extra money teaching fencing, giving music lessons, or becoming waiters. Some painted signs or were hired as drivers of vehicles and wagons. A few were lucky to become apprentices in printing or craft shops. An enterprising person like Aleksander Jełowicki, started a subscription fund (p. 393) which allowed him to establish a bookstore and a small publishing shop [*Wydawnictwa na wygnanie*] in conjunction with another emigré, Eustacy Januszkiewicz. Those with engineering backgrounds were the most fortunate, finding jobs in railroad or canal construction.

The determination of Jacenty Grabowiecki to find work and become economically self-sufficient is a good example of the difficulties the refugees faced. Grabowiecki, bored in the depot at Salins, petitioned (p. 60) for permission to work in an armament factory in St. Etienne in the Department of the Loire. He began working in St. Etienne in early 1833 and remained there as an apprentice for three months. Finding the cost of living too high, however, he petitioned to move to another factory in Alsace, near Strasbourg. No sooner did he settle-in when he received a message from a friend urging him to return to Besançon in order to join the Frankfort Expedition. At first, Grabowiecki decided not to return because he did not want to compromise or implicate the director of the factory even indirectly by such clandestine activity. In the end, Grabowiecki's patriotism won out and he left St. Etienne, returned to Besançon and joined the expedition. When the revolution in Frankfort failed, Grabowiecki was stranded for ten months in Switzerland. After returning to France in January 1834, stationed at Chalons-sur-Marne, he looked for work around Reims. In March 1835 he managed to be taken on as an apprentice in a printing shop in Epernay. As an apprentice he received room and board, but no money. With the help of General Bem, Grabowiecki's stipend was restored (p. 79) to its pre-Frankfort rate of 60 francs per month, thus enabling him to remain in his apprenticeship.

General Bem, after abandoning the idea of creating a separate Polish Legion in France or in Portugal, sought other ways to help the refugees. In March 1835, he founded a Polish Polytechnic Society to help emigrés become economically independent. Bem's objective was to open a printing shop in Paris. Counting on the skills acquired by Grabowiecki, he invited him to become the director. Grabowiecki agreed without hesitation. His sponsor in Epernay, however, was displeased with the prospect of losing Grabowiecki since he had already made a considerable investment in him. In the end, Grabowiecki decided to go to Paris, but after several months found that General Bem was unable to raise sufficient money to sustain the printing house. After leaving Bem's shop, Grabowiecki worked at odd jobs in Paris for six months and eventually got permission to join friends in Toulouse where he found employment in another printing shop. Grabowiecki stayed in Toulouse for two years, from June 23, 1836 to June 5, 1838. In 1838, urged by two close friends who had obtained a certificate from the School of Mining in St. Etienne, Grabowiecki left Toulouse and went to Nimes to seek a job in railroad construction. By the time he arrived in Nimes, his friends had been reassigned. Grabowiecki, who relied too much on his friends and their promises, was again stranded—living on his meager stipend and odd jobs for several years. He eventually got a permanent post in Nimes (p. 93) with the Bureau of Railroads in November 1842, which he held for six years— until 1848 when he decided to return to Poland.

By a combination of necessity, perseverance and diligence, the majority of emigrés managed to find some form of remunerative work or profitable activity. By 1839, according to the statistics complied by Kalembka, 45% were in engaged in professional or intellectual work; some were students; 30% became craftsmen in small shops; 16% became factory workers; and 2.5% found jobs in agriculture. But 1,970 were still unemployed, he added, partly because they had not learned the French language, and 823 were disabled.[69] The number of refugees receiving government subsidies thus dropped to 4,974 in 1839; in 1845, there were only 3,770.

One of the most impressive features of the Great Emigration was the number of refugees who resumed their formal education in France and went on to launch professional careers in various fields. Before the November Insurrection, the majority of the refugees had a reasonably good education in a lyceum or gymnasium—many had attended universities. At the civilian depot of Chateauroux alone, there were sixty-five academics from the university at Wilno, plus another 40 from other Polish universities. Furthermore, a significant number of refugees in military depots had been students in various polytechnical institutes or were cadets in military academies. The desire to engage in some kind of intellectual activity and especially to resume their education was strong. Recognizing this as a healthy sign, the July Monarchy agreed to allow the refugees to resume or to begin studies in French institutions. The response on the part of

---

[69]Sławomir Kalembka, "Polskie wychodzstwa popowstaniowe" in Kienewicz, ed., *Polska XIX wieku*, p. 206.

the refugees, as Barbara Konarska discovered in her detailed studies of emigré education, was overwhelming. According to her calculation, 37% of the refugees pursued some type of educational study during the July Monarchy between 1832 and 1848.[70]

Requests to pursue formal study had to be processed through the Ministry of the Interior and applications submitted to the respective institutions. Passports and letters of travel [listy podróży] were issued to authorize a move to new locations. Students received a monthly stipend of 45 francs. Those who continued successfully were given a quarterly supplement of 100 francs for books and supplies.[71] Additional financial support for students was provided by the *Towarzystwo Naukowe Pomocy* in Paris headed by Adam Czartoryski. Some 25,000 francs was distributed in 1833 and in 1834, but only 8,000 in 1836.[72] Not all who began completed a program of study. Darasz signed up for courses at Montpelier and Bartkowski began studying law at Dijon, but both got caught up in emigré politics and dropped out. Darasz proudly noted (p. 70), however, that his older brother Paweł finished his studies at Montpelier and passed his medical exams in July 1834.

Applications to study in Paris were carefully screened: in 1833 only 32 were approved; 56 were allotted in 1834.[73] The majority of refugees attended schools in provincial cities: Montpelier, Dijon, Strasbourg, Poitiers, Bordeaux. As Barbara Konarska has shown, medicine was the most popular field of study: 405 refugees received medical degrees; 32 became pharmacists; fifteen obtained diplomas as sanitation officers. About 243 became independent physicians in various parts of France. Some of them—sixty-five—became naturalized French citizens. Nine went to Algeria. Twenty-two returned to Poland.

Engineering and other forms of technological study also proved attractive to the refugees. More than 300 studied engineering or mining at various polytechnical institutes. Lelewel's younger brother Jan finished an engineering degree in France and got a job as a quartermaster with an ordnance company. Several were admitted to ordnance programs in French military academies. Forty studied agriculture or veterinary science. Few ventured into the arts and humanities: fifty are said to have studied painting in art academies. One refugee by the name of Wojciech Każimirski took up the study of Eastern languages and became a distinguished orientalist later in life.[74] Legal studies, however, were relatively popular; approximately 120 completed degrees in law.

---

[70]Konarska, "Emigranci polscy" in Kalembka, *Sprawa Polska*, p. 212.

[71]Barbara Konarska, *Polskie drogi emigracyjne. Emigranci Polscy na studiach we Francji w latach 1832-1848* (Warsaw, 1986), p. 33.

[72]Konarska, *Polskie drogi emigracyjne*, p. 26.

[73]Konarska, *Polskie drogi emigracyjne*, p. 25.

[74]Gadon, *Emigracja polska*, II, p. 329.

Far from being a liability, at least at the intellectual and professional level, the Polish refugees in France more than compensated for the material assistance provided by the July Monarchy. Always conscious of being representatives of their nation abroad, the emigrés assiduously sought to create a positive image of Poland and managed in many ways to show their appreciation for the asylum and hospitality France had given them.

****

The Great Emigration is an important and significant phase of Polish history. The thousands who participated in it did so with the conviction that this was the best way to serve their country. Those who decided not return to Poland after the November Insurrection chose a path marked by many hardships and disappointments. After their initial reception as heroes, the harsh reality of protracted if not permanent alienation from Poland set in. Some succeeded in adjusting to emigré status and even found some degree of personal fulfillment in work or study. Others could only take comfort in the fact that they continued to serve their country by keeping the Polish cause alive in popular as well as diplomatic consciousness. The value of the memoirs, diaries and letters these refugees left behind lies in their very ordinariness. They invite us—even compel us—to experience exile: its material and moral conditions, its personal hopes and sacrifices, the poignant mixture of idealism and despair, dignity and humiliation.

"Nowa Emigracja" and "Stara Polonia": The Transformation of Social Relations and the Displaced Person Resettlement Program in the United States

by

Anna D. Jaroszyńska-Kirchmann[1]

"I work 5 days, earn about 40 dollars a week; I took a coat, a radio, and clothes on credit, not to look like a DP from Europe."

"One has to buy something to wear for family and oneself to look more like the people here so that they do not stare at you in the streets."[2]

These two short quotations from letters written by Polish displaced persons to their sponsoring organization are only modest examples of the intense feeling of alienation and distinctiveness experienced by many Poles who immigrated to the United States after World War II. Despite the fact that their group was relatively small in numerical terms, Polish displaced persons formed a significant

[1]Anna D. Jaroszyńska-Kirchmann is affiliated with the History Department and the Immigration History Research Center at the University of Minnesota.
[2]Letters of March 23, 1952, Immigration History Research Center, University of Minnesota (hereafter, IHRC) 84, Polish American Congress (PAC), Box 35, Fol. 260; *ibid.*, June 13, 1952, Box 35, folio 269.

and influential wave of Polish immigration to America. Their impact on the ethnic consciousness of American Polonia resulted in profound transformations of the construction of the Polish immigrant ethnic identity.

Displaced persons, DPs, or in Polish *"dipisi,"* and also *"wysiedleńcy"*—all these terms came to designate a specific group of people deprived of homes and normal lives for many years as a result of war and post-war political changes in Europe. Included among them were former prisoners of Nazi concentration camps, forced laborers of the Third Reich, civilian refugees who found themselves scattered around the world, as well as political refugees from countries which fell under Soviet domination. At the end of World War II there were several millions of them in Europe, representing all ethnic groups. By late 1946 about eight million had been repatriated with the United Nations Relief and Rehabilitation Administration's (UNRRA) assistance to their homelands,[3] leaving about a million of those, for whom such returns were either impossible or unwanted.[4] The group of Polish displaced persons amounted to, roughly, 275,000 persons, including a group of Polish Army veterans demobilized in the West, and was the largest among the European nationalities.[5]

International action to resettle European displaced persons resulted in various countries opening their doors to specific numbers of war refugees. Countries that accepted the largest contingents were Canada, Australia, Great Britain, and

---

[3]Malcolm J. Proudfoot, *European Refugees: 1939-52. A Study in Forced Popula-tion Movement* (Evanston, IL: Northwestern University Press, 1956), pp. 189-228, 275-292, 415-418; John George Stoessinger, *The Refugee and the World Community* (Minneapolis: The University of Minnesota Press, 1956), pp. 51-55.

[4]Stoessinger, pp. 55-58; Proudfoot, pp. 292-298. Between 1945 and 1948 approximately 315,000 of the "last million" of "unrepatriables" were already resettled throughout the world. An increase in the number of those who still waited for the resettlement was caused by a birth rate and influx of refugees from Eastern Europe. About 5,000,000 to 6,000,000 displaced persons lived in the camps and 400,000 outside them. Frank Auerbach, *Admission and Resettlement of the Displaced Persons in the United States. A Handbook of Legal and Technical Information for the Use of Local Social and Civic Agencies* (New York: Common Council for American Unity Incorporated, 1949), p. 8.

[5]Stoessinger, pp. 55-56. Determining precise numbers is not easy, since changes in population were happening rapidly. According to Proudfoot, in the peak period of 1945, Poles totaled 816,000 displaced persons which constituted 68% of the 1,202,000 in the western zones of Germany. Almost 700,000 were repatriated between 1945 and 1947. In December, 1946, 272,712 Poles remained in Western Germany as a part of the "non-repatriable" core. See Proudfoot, pp. 281-285, 291. See also Rene Ristelhueber, "The International Refugee Organization," *International Conciliation*, No. 470 (April 1951), pp. 186-187. Other numerous ethnic groups represented among the displaced persons were Jews, Lithuanians, Latvians, Estonians, Yugoslavs, and Ukrainians. See Proudfoot, p. 291; Auerbach, p. 8; Stoessinger, pp. 56-58.

France.[6] The United States Congress passed the Displaced Persons Act in June, 1948. It allowed 205,000 displaced persons to enter the country and start a new life in America. The law was safeguarded by a number of conditions and limitations which discriminated against certain groups of refugees and made the process of immigration to the United States particularly complex. The intense lobbying action undertaken by many ethnic groups in America, including Polish Americans, brought results in 1950 when amendments to the Displaced Persons Act were accepted prolonging the immigration deadline to June, 1952, and increasing the numbers of eligible immigrants to 341,000. The 1950 Amendments also contained a provision under which 18,000 Polish veterans in Great Britain could enter the United States.[7]

Rough estimates indicate that approximately 160,000 Poles came to the United States under the Displaced Persons Act of 1948 and its 1950 Amendments.[8] Those coming to America were considered lucky by the refugees still left behind, entangled in legal procedures, disqualified by health problems, or trying to emigrate from countries other than those specified in the Displaced Persons Act.[9]

The Polish displaced persons who did come to the United States faced the difficult task of establishing their new homes and putting together war-disrupted lives. Through ethnic sponsorship and kin and friendship networks, their first encounters with America usually took place within older immigrant communities. Those who found themselves far from large Polonia centers were, sooner or

---

[6]According to Proudfoot, between July 1, 1947, and December 31, 1951, the U.S. admitted 110,566 displaced persons whose principal nationality or last habitual residence was Poland. The U.S. was followed by Australia (60,308), Israel (54,904), Canada (46,961), the United Kingdom (35,780), France (11,882), and Belgium (10,378). Other destinations included the Netherlands and countries of South and Latin America. See Proudfoot, table 48, p. 427. For general IRO statistics for the period 1947-1951, see Proudfoot, p. 425.

[7]*Memo to America: The DP Story. The Final Report of the United States Displaced Persons Commission* (Washington, D.C.: U.S. Government Printing Office, 1952), pp. 9-41; Leonard Dinnerstein, *America and the Survivors of the Holocaust* (New York: Columbia University Press, 1982), pp. 137-182; Gil Loescher, John A. Scanlon, *Calculated Kindness: Refugees and America's Half-Open Door, 1945 to the Present* (New York: The Free Press, 1986), pp. 1-24.

[8]Although the precise number is hard to establish, statistics of the Displaced Persons Commission demonstrate that 34% of immigrants admitted under the Displaced Persons Act, as of May 31, 9152, indicated Poland as their country of birth. See *Memo*, tables 2 and 3, p. 366; Anna D. Jaroszyńska-Kirchmann, "Communications," *Polish American Studies*, Vol. 46, No. 2 (Autumn 1989), p. 90; Barbara Stern Burstin, *After the Holocaust, The Migration of Polish Jews and Christians to Pittsburgh* (Pittsburgh, PA: University of Pittsburgh Press, 1989), pp. 115-116. Burstin accepts 120,000 as a number of Polish Christians admitted to the United States under the Displaced Persons Act.

[9]Proudfoot, pp. 429-432; Stoessinger, pp. 139-140.

later, attracted to them in a natural way. For the first time in almost two decades, American Polonia was joined by a new and lively wave of Polish immigrants.[10]

The *"wysiedleńcy"* had many distinctive social characteristics, such as a prevailing middle class background and a relatively high educational level (including education acquired in Poland, in Great Britain, or displaced persons camps, or in the United States). While in America, the newcomers demonstrated rapid upward mobility and achieved noticeable socio-economic success.[11]

---

[10]Since the outbreak of World War II, the United States had become haven to a group of Polish refugees who arrived mainly through private channels. There were among them politicians, artists, scholars, writers, and representatives of the Polish governmental and social establishment. They settled mostly in New York and Chicago and formed there self-help organizations in order to relieve their harse economic conditions. See the records of the Executive Committee For Aid to War Refugees From Poland in the U.S., 1940-44; *Koło Uchodźców Polskich w Chicago, 1940-1942*, in the American Relief for Poland Collection, the Polish Museum of America, Fol. "Polish Refugees, New York Area," and "Polish Refugees, Chicago Area." Some became quickly involved in politics and in 1942 participated in establishing the National Committee of Americans of Polish Descent (KNAPP), one of the most influential and vocal Polish political agencies within American Polonia at the time. See Wacław Jędrzejewicz, *Polonia amerykańska w polityce polskiej. Historia Komitetu Narodowego Amerykanów Polskiego Pochodzenia* (New York: National Committee of Americans of Polish Descent, 1954). The remarkable achievements of this wave of immigrants included the founding of cultural institutions such as the Polish Institute of Arts and Sciences in America, the Polish American Historical Association, and the Józef Piłsudski Institute for Research in the Modern History of Poland, designed to support and facilitate further development of Polish culture and scholarship and represent them to the larger American society. See the following articles in Frank Mocha, ed., *Poles in America. Bicentennial Essays* (Stevens Point, WI: Worzalla Publishing Company, 1978): Frank Mocha, "The Polish Institute of Arts and Sciences in America. Its Contributions to the Study of Polonia: The Origins of the Polish American Historical Association (PAHA)," and Michael Budny, "Józef Piłsudski Institute of America for Research in the Modern History of Poland," pp. 709-724. Although not extensive numerically, those refugees helped to prepare Polonia for the arrival of a much larger wave of Polish displaced persons in 1948-1952. See John J. Bukowczyk, *And My Children Did Not Know Me. A History of the Polish Americans* (Bloomington: Indiana University Press, 1987), pp. 92-93; Stanislaus A. Blejwas, "Old and New Polonias: Tensions Within an Ethnic Community," *Polish American Studies*, Vol. 38 (1981), p. 62 ff; Richard C. Lukas, *The Strange Allies: The United States and Poland, 1941-1945* (Knoxville: University of Tennessee Press, 1978), pp. 107-116.

[11]Danuta Mostwin, "The Profile of a Transplanted Family," *The Polish Review*, Vol. 19 (1974), pp. 77-89; Danuta Mostwin, "Post World War II Immigrants in the United States," *Polish American Studies*, Vol. 26 (Autumn 1979), pp. 5-14; Rev. Stanislaus T. Sypek, "The Displaced Person in the Greater Boston Community," Ph.D. dissertation, Fordham University, 1955; Maria

First and foremost, however, the new arrivals belonged not to the category of voluntary migrants, as their predecessors from the turn of the century, but to the distinctive group of political refugees.[12] The psychological and emotional burden of the war, displacement, concentration camps, forced labor, and prolonged stay in the displaced persons camps while waiting for emigration, all contributed to the formation of very specific attitudes and psychological needs for the refugees. For many of them, the United States was not the first country of immigration. Some still counted on a return to Poland in a changed political situation. All felt a part of the larger Polish post-war diaspora and cultivated organizational as well as personal contacts with others resettled in various parts of the world. The loyalty toward the Polish government in London, participation in political parties in exile, and veteran bonds of combatant organizations, further strengthened the consciousness of Polish displaced persons as a separate and specific immigrant population.[13]

Barbara Korewa, "Casework Treatment of Refugees: A Survey of Selected Professional Periodicals for the Period from January 1, 1939 to January 1, 1956," Master's thesis, Wayne State University, 1957; Alicja Iwanska, "Values in Crisis Situation," Ph.D. dissertation, Columbia University, 1957; Danuta Mostwin, "The Transplanted Family; A Study of Social Adjustment of the Polish Immigrant Family to the United States After the Second World War," Ph.D. dissertation, Ann Arbor, University Microfilms, 1971; Sarah Van Atken-Rutkowski, "Integration and Acculturation of the Polish Veteran of World War II to Canadian Society," Master's thesis, University of Windsor, 1982.

[12]"In everyday speech, a refugee is any person who, as the result of some disaster, has been compelled to abandon his home.... Thus, in the generally accepted meaning of the term, a "refugee" is essentially someone without a home, someone who has been cast adrift.... This popular conception of a refugee includes an element of emotion of which the sociologist and jurist cannot but be aware.... In international law, the definition of a refugee is both narrower and stricter."

"First, a person can be considered a refugee only if, whether of his own free will or not, he has left the territory of the State in which he formerly resided either as a result of political events in that State, or for other political reasons."

"Secondly, the political events which are the cause of the refugee's leaving his country must be accompanied by persecution or the threat of persecution either against himself or—in our opinion—against some section of the population to which he regards himself as belonging. Persecution or the threat of persecution is an essential preconditioning." For the complete discussion of the concept of the "refugee" see Jacques Vernant, *The Refugee in the Post-War World. Preliminary Report of a Survey* (Geneva; 1951), pp. 3-16.

[13]Tadeusz Paleczny, *Ewolucja ideologii i przemiany tożsamości narodowej Polonii w Stanach Zjednoczonych w latach 1870-1970* (Warszawa: Państwowe Wydaw-nictwo Naukowe, 1989), pp. 233-242; Aleksander Hertz, *Refleksje Amerykańskie* (Paris: Instytut Literacki, 1966), pp. 90-98.

The year 1948 became the moment of the important encounter between the older American Polonia and this new group of Polish refugees. Both groups were looking forward to the meeting, and each formed its own image of the other, which did not basically match the reality. Displaced Poles knew next to nothing about American Polonia, its history, way of life, level of assimilation, and achievements. They tended to treat Polonia as "the fourth province of Poland," in accord with old nineteenth century concepts.[14] These assumptions were further supplemented by a traditional image of America as a Promised Land. The earlier immigrants, on the other hand, expected the newcomers to be their social replicas whom they would generously introduce into the Polish American world.[15]

In 1948 *Dziennik Związkowy* published a series of cartoons appealing to Polish Americans to support Polish war victims by welcoming them into the Polonia communities. They showed masses of poor, ragged people, crowding on the ships bringing them to American shores, as years before the first immigrants from Polish villages had arrived. Women in those pictures had plaid babushkas, men bushy mustaches, and everybody was carrying shapeless bundles with possessions rescued from the war.[16] A year later, in October, 1949, however, the same *Dziennik Związkowy* published another cartoon, announcing the opening of the *"Dom Wysiedleńców"* [The Displaced Persons House] in Chicago. In this picture, *"Chicagoska Polonia"* metaphorically shown as a beautiful woman draped in Greek style clothing, was handing to the representative of *"Polscy wysiedleńcy"* the traditional bread and salt, as a welcome taking place in front of the newly purchased house. The figure of a Polish displaced person did not resemble people from the harbor. He was a handsome, middle aged man, cleanly shaved and dressed in a suit and tie; a typical member of the class of Polish intelligentsia.[17] Within one year, the social image of Polish displaced persons underwent a complete transformation in the eyes of American Polonia, as the displaced Poles changed their image of the older Polish immigrants. The Polish American ethnic group was going through a period of crucial changes, charged with emotions, tensions, and negotiations which were to affect the future of American Polonia in the years to come.

---

[14]Hertz, p. 100; Blejwas, pp. 55-60.

[15]"While they (i.e. "old" immigrants) welcomed the displaced persons with material assistance, "old Polonia" also adopted a patronizing attitude toward Poland and the new immigrants because of its earlier arrival, economic success and assistance to the refugees. They expected to be looked upon as benefactors and experienced older residents, assuming that the displaced persons would be dependent upon them as they had been dependent upon family and friends. They also expected the displaced persons, whom they sometimes referred to condescendingly as the "Biedaki" [poor souls], to relive their early experiences, arriving poorly dressed and with no knowledge of English." See Blejwas, p. 76.

[16]See e.g. *Dziennik Związkowy* of June 23, 1948, October 29, 1948, and November 17, 1948.

[17]*Dziennik Związkowy*, October 15, 1949.

The formation of the social relationships between Polish displaced persons and the older Polonia took place in the worst possible conditions: during the difficult process of the displaced persons' resettlement in the United States between 1948 and 1952. In the atmosphere of the Cold War—economic hardship and chaotic and disorganized resettlement efforts by governmental and private agencies—the two groups were just beginning to get to know each other.

The resettlement process consisted of several steps. Each displaced person was required to possess a special assurance, guaranteeing a specifically identified job and housing accommodations. Sponsorship could be exercised either by an individual and a public or voluntary agency providing services in connection with migration and settlement, and which was recognized by the Displaced Persons Commission for this purpose.[18] Assurances, together with other required documents, were sent to Europe, where the eligible displaced persons were selected and their cases carefully processed. The International Refugee Organization (IRO) provided overseas transportation, but upon arrival at American ports, displaced persons did not obtain any further assistance.

The role of ethnic voluntary agencies was, therefore, twofold: obtaining sponsors and assurances for the displaced persons, and then assisting them after their arrival. They cooperated closely with many governmental, humanitarian, and other voluntary agencies in this respect, mostly exchanging information and providing various kinds of legal assistance. The Polish community was served primarily by three ethnic resettlement agencies: the Polish Immigration Committee (PIC) of New York, affiliated with the National Catholic Welfare Conference, and led by Father Colonel Felix Burant;[19] the American Relief for Poland, a major Polish charitable organization under the leadership of Francis X. Świetlik;[20] and the American Committee for the Resettlement of Polish Displaced Persons (ACRPDP), formed by and affiliated to the Polish American

---

[18]"The Displaced Persons Commission began formal operations on August 27, 1948, and continued in existence until August 31, 1952. During its four-year lifespan it helped resettle more than 339,000 DPs in the United States. Aided by a large number of social service agencies sponsored primarily by religious organizers and state governments, it was the first American immigrant resettlement agency established by the federal government." Dinnerstein, p. 183; *Memo*, pp. 48-55, 267-270.

[19]Thaddeus Theodore Krysiewicz, *The Polish Immigration Committee in the United States. A Historical Surve of the American Committee for Relief of Polish Immigrants: 1947-1952* (New York: The Roman Catholic Church of St. Stanislaus B. M., 1952); Burstin, pp. 78-82.

[20]Franciszek X. Świetlik, *Sprawozdanie a Działalności Rady Polonii Amerykańskiej odbyty dnia 4-go i 5-go grudnia, 1948 r. w hotelu Buffalo, w Buffalo, N.Y.* (Chicago: Rada Polonii Amerykańskiej, 1948), pp. 20-28, 30-35, 40-63; Burstin, p. 82; Donald E. Pienkos, *For Your Freedom through Ours. Polish American Efforts on Poland's Behalf, 1863-1991* (New York: 1991), pp. 89-98.

Congress.[21]

In New York and Boston harbors, representatives of those agencies received incoming displaced persons, took care of the necessary paper work, and directed their inland transportation to the places of their jobs and housing. Voluntary workers often served as interpreters and mediators between the immigrants and their sponsors or public agencies. They offered help with legal problems as well as information and advice for the newcomers. Both the American Relief for Poland and the ACRPDP developed a network of local committees in all large Polonia centers, which were supposed to receive the newcomers at their resettlement locations and aid them in their most immediate needs.

Since the majority of displaced persons were coming from Europe without any substantial financial resources, the American Committee for the Resettlement of Polish Displaced Persons loaned them money to cover their inland transportation within the United States. After settling down and starting a job, each displaced person was obliged to return the borrowed sum to the Committee. Both sides, therefore, exchanged correspondence related to financial matters. Many displaced persons wrote to the Committee asking for clarification of their legal status, requesting information about relatives and friends, or looking for assistance with numerous everyday problems. In addition, the Committee obtained letters from sponsors and employers, and correspondence from many individuals and organizations in various ways connected with the displaced persons resettlement.

The ACRPDP sources constitute, therefore, an interesting and valuable body of records which document the first experiences of Polish displaced persons on American soil, and also their first encounters with older American Polonia. A close examination of these sources sheds more light on different aspects of an "uneasy co-existence" of the two distinctive immigrant groups in the United States in the immediate post-World War II years.[22] The resettlement process significantly shaped the social environment of the "Stara Polonia—Nowa Emigracja" relationship, producing both positive and negative experiences which were to weigh heavily on the future interactions between the two immigrant groups.

The first American experiences of the Polish displaced persons were intimately related to the rules and laws of resettlement. In many cases it meant

---

[21]Anna D. Jaroszyńska, "The American Committee for the Resettlement of Polish Displaced Persons (1948-1968) in the Manuscript Collection of the Immigration History Research Center," *Polish American Studies*, Vol. 44 (1987), pp. 63-73; Donald E. Pienkos, "Communications" [response], pp. 87-93; Pienkos, *For Your Freedom*, pp. 122-130.

[22]The term "an uneasy co-existence" was first used by Blejwas, p. 72. Other authors also discussed the problem of tensions between both groups in Polonia, e.g. Hertz, pp. 99-104; Bukowczyk, pp. 93-96; Helena Znaniecki Lopata, *Polish Americans. Status Competition in an Ethnic Community* (Englewood Cliffs, NJ: Prentice Hall, 1976), pp. 26-27; Paleczny, pp. 226-242; Burstin, pp. 126-137.

meeting with long-unseen relatives or relatives whom they had never met. In the letters to the Committee written from the displaced persons camps in Europe, refugees often asked to locate their family members, distant cousins, friends, or acquaintances who might become sponsors. More often than not, however, sponsors and displaced persons were not blood related. In spite of being strangers, initial relationships between them were, many times, favorable for both sides.

A good example of harmonious relations can be found in a letter from a young electrician who came to a small town where he could not find a job. He was living at his sponsor's expense: "My sponsor is very good for me and shows me an honest Polish hospitality. ... Staying with this patriotic Polish man without a job is for me a psychological torture."[23] Some sponsors loaned money to help the displaced persons start their own businesses.[24] One seventy-three-year-old retired miner was offering to sell his life-time collection of 7,000 stamps to get money for the displaced persons' needs.[25] Neighbors wrote to the Committee requesting that it extend the term of loan payment for a female displaced person living in hard conditions.[26] Many other such heartwarming examples of compassion and friendship were probably never reflected in any correspondence, although there exist numerous letters from the resettled Poles expressing to the Committee and the entire Polonia gratitude for help in their immigration to the United States. Some of those letters were also published in the Polish American press. "We are surrounded by truly good people here," reads one of those letters, "and they are so nice to us. ... We are very grateful to Ladies and Gentlemen from this organization, and God bless you that you helped us to get out of that German hell."[27]

But cases of hostility between displaced persons and their sponsors were also frequent. Police had to intervene in an argument between a female displaced person and her sponsor—the owner of a gift shop. The woman claimed that her sponsor was exploiting her work; the sponsor accused her of ingratitude, slovenliness, and theft.[28] Another female displaced person wrote to the ACRPDP looking for help against a Polish American farmer from Oregon who tried to harass her sexually, threatening to send her and her son back to Europe.[29]

---

[23]Letter of October 4, 1949, IHRC 84, PAC, Box 33, Fol. 247. The majority of letters quoted here were written in Polish. Translations are provided by the author.

[24]Letter of March 10, 1955, IHRC 84, PAC, Box 37, Fol. 273.

[25]Letter of August 1949, IHRC 84, PAC, Box 33, Fol. 251.

[26]Letter of May 20, 1952, IHRC 84, PAC, Box 37, Fol. 272.

[27]Undated letter to the ACRPDP, IHRC 84, PAC, Box 33, Fol. 249.

[28]Correspondence of December 10-17, 1951. IHRC 84, PAC, Box 26, Fol. 199.

[29]Letters to the ACRPDP, IHRC 84, PAC, Box 37, Fol. 272 and Box 35, Fol. 260.

Many serious problems were caused by misinterpretation or violation of laws pertaining to sponsorship. Displaced persons, being often unaware of their rights, were easy victims of dishonest sponsors who used them financially and exploited their work. There are many examples of sponsors who required gratuitous work, refunds for nonexistent costs, or who refused to allow the displaced persons to change their jobs.[30] On the other hand, sponsors were disappointed by the displaced persons, who, after coming to America, were choosing different destinations and either never showing up or almost immediately leaving jobs and housing prepared for them by sponsors. Many displaced persons, misunderstanding the law, expected sponsors to provide them with care and financial support. Such problems between newcomers and older Polonia badly hurt mutual relationships and caused a reluctance on the part of Polish Americans to sponsor new displaced persons.[31]

There were also other sources of conflict. One Polish displaced person complained about mistreatment and harassment by his Polish American sponsor because of his German wife whom he married in the displaced person camp.[32] Some Polish Americans, who had to work hard in America to achieve economic security, resented the newcomers for their easier successes: newly-purchased houses, cars, television sets, radios, and even bicycles for their children. Polish Americans also criticized the displaced persons for going to the movies as a form of entertainment.[33] The ACRPDP was advised to show more firmness and less compassion in the action of collecting refunds for transportation. Addresses of firms where the displaced persons worked were sent to the Committee in order to locate some indebted displaced persons. The author of one of the letters, after describing the wealth and newly-purchased possessions of a family of displaced persons, added: "From disease, hunger, and war, and such DPs, save us Lord."[34]

One Chicagoan in a letter to the ACRPDP told the story of his conflict with a family of Polish displaced persons. The author of the letter suggested that

---

[30]IHRC 84, PAC, Box 28, Fol. 218. Such problems were experienced by all resettlement agencies. See Pennsylvania Commission on Displaced Persons, the *Third Annual Report* (1951), *passim*; also paper clippings in IHRC 115, American Relief for Poland, District 33 (ARP) Dis. 33, Box 2.

[31]The Displaced Persons Commission's report of 1952 pointed to several reasons for both successful and unsuccessful resettlement of the displaced persons. The following general observation may as well relate to the Polish ethnic group: "It appears evident that the misconceptions of both sponsors and displaced persons were in many cases responsible for the breakdown of a resettlement. As several of the case histories have pointed out, much of the fault seemed to lie in the lack of orientation given the displaced person before he left Europe and of the even more substantial orientation of sponsors." *Memo*, p. 241.

[32]Letter of November 17, 1949, IHRC 48, PAC, Box 33, Fol. 248.

[33]Letter of May 8, 1942, from Chicago, IHRC 84, PAC, Box 35, Fol. 260; letter of October 20, 1952 from Lowell, Massachusetts, IHRC 84, PAC, Box 28, Fol. 218; letter of August 27, 1955, IHRC 84, PAC, Box 27, Fol. 209.

[34]Letter of October 20, 1952, IHRC 84, PAC, Box 28, Fol. 218.

his displaced person friend join the Polish Army Veterans Association of America to which he belonged. The displaced person refused fiercely. Later on, the same displaced person refused also to apply for U.S. citizenship, and his sponsor demanded the whole family move out of his house.[35]

Those displaced persons who found themselves in areas deprived of any Polish population felt the need for activity and relations with their own ethnic group. An author of a letter to the ACRPDP, resettled with his family in a small town without any Polonia community, tried dramatically to plug into the mainstream of the Polish American life. "Remember once and forever that people like me, though arriving here not a long time ago, are not savages...—but are such people like you all...," he wrote to the Committee. Moreover, the tragic experiences of the war were interpreted by him as improving the survivors' character and making them more altruistic than "millions of US citizens, also of Polish background, living only for themselves and their businesses."[36] That displaced man, requesting addresses of the nearest centers of "some Polish Associations," wanted to break out of his isolation, so deeply experienced also by other displaced persons.

Those who were resettled on the farms, felt especially lonely and embittered by the necessity of accepting occupations below their qualifications. "I can speak English with a dictionary," wrote a thirty-seven-year-old radio electrician from a farm in Indiana. "In Europe I was advanced in English; unfortunately here, by the cows, I forgot more than learned during seven months. I spent six years in German captivity but I felt morally better."[37]

Due to the Displaced Persons Act of 1948, the priority in immigration was granted to farmers and farm laborers who could work in American agriculture.[38] Therefore, many job offers sent to the ACRPDP were coming from Polish American farm owners in need of help. Farmers were usually willing to sponsor

---

[35]Letter of May 8, 1952, IHRC 84, PAC, Box 35, Fol. 260. The conflict among veterans went even further. "In 1952, the Association of Veterans of the Polish Army ..., representing the members of General Haller's Army in World War I, held its convention in Utica, New York. The delegates adopted a new rule requiring candidates for district or central offices to be American, Canadian or Cuban citizens who had belonged to the Association for at least five years. Additionally, all members were to wear the Association's traditional 'Blue Uniform.' These rules were directed against the 'new arrivals' and led ultimately to the formation of a rival organization, the Association of Polish Combatants (Stow. Polskich Kombatantow, or SPK) for Polish World War II veterans. The split was provoked by the fear of the old Polish American veterans that the 'new arrivals' would seize control of their group, and, indeed, by the desire of some former Polish politicians and soldiers to do just that and establish themselves as commanders of American Polonia." See Blejwas, p. 71.

[36]Letter of July 8, 1952, IHRC 84, PAC, Box 37, Fol. 272.

[37]Letter of May, 1952, IHRC 84, PAC, Box 26, Fol. 199.

[38]This provision was dropped in the 1950 Amendments to the Displaced Persons Act. *Memo*, p. 38.

either young single men or young married couples. Many letters addressed the
displaced persons issue as a job market for cheap labor; few of them contained
remarks about feelings of loneliness and desire to have fellow-countrymen
around. Numerous displaced persons, in order to qualify for immigration, provided false data on their professions and claimed extensive agricultural experience. As the young electrician, whose letter was quoted above, those displaced
persons wanted to leave farms as soon as possible and find jobs in the city.[39]

There were also some single Polish American farmers who looked forward
to meeting Polish displaced women. Among several letters with offers of marriage, correspondence from Joseph A. from New York state, is especially
remarkable. Joseph wrote to the Committee: "It is hard for me on my farm
without a landlady. When the first transport comes from Germany, please,
choose for me a pretty lady, because I want to marry her. I am enclosing three
photographs of me and my farm." In another letter (all of them left without a response by the Committee), Joseph expressed willingness to come to New York
to get introduced to the right candidate for a wife. "I would marry a Polish
woman," he added, "or a Lithuanian one if you ran out of Polish."[40] This example is, of course, extreme, but in the face of shrinking ethnic communities,
some Polish Americans gladly welcomed a new influx of native Poles, counting
on establishing their families within their own ethnic group.[41] Many American
Poles, as well as Americans of different ethnic background, sought also information on the ways of adopting Polish orphan children. This program was,
however, conducted separately under the auspices of the United States Committee
for the Care of European Children in New York.[42]

An especially dramatic situation faced those of the displaced Poles who
could not find jobs matching their education and previous profession. According
to John J. Bukowczyk, "heavily middle-class in background those refugee Poles
who did make their way into better paying factory jobs, the only employment
for which many were suited because they lacked English-language skills, now
felt declasse."[43] A good example could be that of a married couple looking in
vain for jobs other than those of a house maid and a factory worker. Both of
them were renown scholars and impressive lists of scientific publications in for-

---

[39]Bukowczyk, *And My Children*, pp. 94-85. The trend of migration from
farms to the city was characteristic for the displaced persons from all ethnic
groups. *Memo*, pp. 257-258.

[40]Letters of September 22, 1948, and November 1, 1948, IHRC 84, PAC, Box
41, Fol. 289.

[41]In one author's words, with the coming of "the fresh wave of refugees,
exiles, and immigrants ... new matrimonial frontiers were opened up for some of
the second generation girls." Joseph A. Wytrwal, *Behold! the Polish Americans*
(Detroit: Endurance Press, 1977), p. 429.

[42]*Memo*, pp. 206-209.

[43]Bukowczyk, *And My Children*, p. 95.

eign languages were enclosed in each of their resumes.[44] Similarly, many officers and soldiers of the Polish Army from Great Britain had to accept low-paying factory jobs as unskilled workers.[45]

Another initially unpredicted aspect of the Displaced Persons Commission's propaganda resulted in suspicion towards the displaced persons in many ethnic groups. In order to evoke sympathy among the potential sponsors, the displaced persons were often portrayed as victims, and their war and post-war experiences depicted in the gravest terms. It contributed to the opinion that refugees consisted of an element depraved and dehumanized by the war and subsequent sojourn in the displaced persons camps. Sentiments about the "low quality" of people immigrating to America under the Displaced Persons Act were widespread. The Citizens' Committee and the Displaced Persons Commission together with other charitable and ethnic agencies devoted a great part of their effort to convince American society that the displaced persons would be valuable and hard-working citizens.[46] It cannot be denied, however, that the war experiences left profound emotional wounds on many displaced persons.[47] Some of them could not easily deal with adjustment to the new environment and went through breakdowns not always registered in medical statistics.[48]

---

[44]Letter of September 3, 1949, IHRC 84, PAC, Box 33, Fol. 251,

[45]See for example a letter of February 22, 1952, IHRC 84, PAC, Box 35, Fol. 260. A report of the Pennsylvania Commission on Displaced Persons reveals a number of reasons for which employers only reluctantly hired displaced persons: "Approximately 250 employers have been appraised of the displaced persons program as a source of labor by our local offices. Reaction was one of indifference due to: No critical need, language barrier, time lag in recruiting workers, interpretation of government security regulations in defense plants, and unfavorable experiences of employers with displaced persons mainly due to improper placement resulting in displaced persons working in jobs far below skill or social level. Also, tendency to 'job hopping' after arrival in this country." *The Third Annual Report*, p. 26. Resettlement of intellectuals remained one of the unsolved problems of IRO. See Stoessinger, p. 139.

[46]William S. Bernard, "Refugee Asylum in the United States: How the Law Was Changed to Admit Displaced Persons," *International Migration*, Vol. 13, No. 1/2 (1975), pp. 9-10, 11-15.

[47]Stoessinger, pp. 188-196; Licucija Baskauskas, "The Lithuanian Refugee Experience and Grief," *International Migration Review*, Vol. 15, (Spring/Summer 1981), pp. 276-291; Burstin, pp. 120-121.

[48]Cases of alcoholism were also noted. The ACRPDP records contain correspon-dence with the Immigrants' Protective League about a neglected Polish child whose parents—displaced persons—were reportedly having drinking problems. A pastor from one of the Southern states wrote about two Polish displaced persons employed by the parish for the maintenance of church property. "Both of these men are industrious, capable and personable and have done well the tasks assigned to them," the pastor commented. After some time in Texas, both displaced persons started to drink and provoke fights. The pastor, asking for help, recommended for the two men a change of environment to a place where

There is no firm evidence what dimensions this problem had among Polish displaced persons. The ACRPDP correspondence with displaced persons contains only a few letters relating to this question. In one of them a displaced person from Chicago asked the Committee to provide him with some kind of security, because of an alleged communist conspiracy against his life. Another letter was written by a patient of a psychiatric hospital who claimed that American physicians held him there in order to carry out experiments on his body. The third letter was from a thirty-five-year-old man who, after coming with his family to America, allegedly murdered his wife. Initially, the man was put in jail, but then he was placed in the psychiatric ward. From there he wrote to the Committee requesting legal help, money, and cigarettes.[49] One report of the Committee includes a brief mention of the problem: "We had also several persons who after arriving to this country broke down and became mentally ill. Due to our efforts, those people were placed in psychiatric hospitals. After adequate treatment, some of them regained their health and now work and live a normal life."[50]

Both the Polish press and the resettlement agencies tried to deal with this situation by presenting positive success stories about displaced Poles, and patiently pleading on their behalf. For example, one of the articles published in the *NFD Bulletin* [National Fund Drive] aimed directly at revising misunderstandings about a "DP problem" within Polonia. "There is still another mistake...," the author argued, "Here a displaced person did something wrong, there he behaved wrong, and the news that a DP is so and so, that a DP did this or that, spreads among Polonia faster than a lightning. A DP got drunk ... more, a DP cheated or stole. So a wrong behavior of one DP is transferred on all DPs, the door is closed in front of thousands of innocent victims because of the wrong behavior of that one."[51]

The striking feature of the displaced persons' experience during the resettlement period were continuous economic problems. War wounds, malnutrition, and general physical exhaustion were collecting their toll. Sickness in the family was the most frequent reason for delays in repaying loans to the ACRPDP. Accidents at work disabled temporarily or even permanently men and women employed in factories. The unstable post-war economy did not offer many jobs, and strikes and lay-offs happened repeatedly.[52] The conditions of everyday struggle to make both ends meet, further contributed to the tensions within the Polish

---

they could live among their countrymen and avoid loneliness and despair. IHRC 84, PAC, Box 27, Fol. 207 and Box 28, Fol. 218.

[49]Letters to the ACRPDP, IHRC 84, PAC, Box 36, Fol. 270; Box 29, Fol. 225; Box 27, Fol. 208.

[50]"Sprawozdanie ACRPDP" [1955?], IHRC 48, Box 6, Fol. 32.

[51]"O Wysiedleńcach" from Pittsburczanin. NFD [National Fund Drive] Bulletin, No. 2, July 31, 1949, IHRC 48, American Committee for the Resettlement of Polish Displaced Persons (ACRPDP), Box 6, Fol. 34.

[52]Displaced Poles were also participants in some strikes. Letter of 1952 and September 22, 1953, IHRC 84, PAC, Box 35, Fol. 263 and Box 28, Fol. 216.

American community.

Polish displaced persons influenced the ethnic consciousness of American Polonia in many significant ways. Probably the most important was the increased politicization of the entire group resulting from the displaced persons' intense involvement in the political parties in exile and their ardently hostile attitude against the Communist regime in Poland. The political situation in Poland, as well as international circumstances which could condition it, became the focus brought to the constant attention of the entire Polish American community. This new mass of immigrants exerted an impact also on Polish organizational life in the United States through the creation of new, and reinforcement of old Polish American organizations. Moreover, the presence of Polish displaced persons in the United States became a reminder of the existence of the broader Polish diaspora in the world and contacts with Polonias in other countries increased. Last but not least, the new arrivals visibly influenced the development of Polish cultural and artistic life in America and Polish participation in American arts and sciences.

The history of American Polonia cannot be complete without the story of this significant immigration wave and the mutual interactions between older immigrants and refugee newcomers. This essay focused mostly on the influence of the resettlement process on the initial interactions between "Stara Polonia" and "Nowa Emigracja" in the United States. There remains, however, much more unknown than known about this period of Polonia's history. Many aspects which remain hidden in the shadows include the life and organizations of Poles in European displaced persons camps; Polonia's lobbying effort to change the immigration law; experiences of various resettlement programs (for example, group resettlement; special projects for Polish orphans; and resettlement in the plantations of the South); adjustment—success or failure—of displaced Poles in America; their impact on the shape of Polish American ethnic life; their own organizations and participation in older associations and fraternals. Many questions regarding older Polonia could be raised in this context, e.g. the role of ethnic organizations and parishes in facilitating the displaced persons' adjustment; the involvement in the resettlement process on the rank and file level; competition between major Polonia resettlement organizations; the struggle for the leadership over Polonia between newcomers and Polish Americans, and many other problems.

Understanding the process of formation and transformation of social relationships within Polonia in the post-World War II years is even more important in the light of future developments in the Polish community, namely the arrival of subsequent waves of immigrants, out of which the post-Solidarity group seems to be the most numerous and vocal.

The split into "Stara Polonia" and "Nowa Emigracja" subsided throughout the years but never disappeared. With the arrival of each new wave of immigrants and refugees from Poland, all groups were forced to re-define their ethnic identity against each other, as well as against the larger American society. The formation of social relations between the old Polonia and Polish displaced persons was probably the most difficult and emotional process. Many of the initial conflicts and tensions have their roots in the early period of the resettlement in the United States. The imperfect and often simply chaotic resettlement program too often conditioned first encounters and influenced the construction of relations between the two groups. The more we know about this process and its consequences, the closer we can get to understanding the specific experience of Polish displaced persons in America and mutual interactions of "Stara Polonia" and "Nowa Emigracja" within Polish American immigrant community in the United States.

America, Poland and the Polish American Community: Defining and Preserving Polish Ethnicity in the United States

by

Donald E. Pienkos[1]

In 1879, Agaton Giller, a participant in the insurrection of 1863 against tsarist Russia and an exile in Switzerland for his efforts, published his thoughts about the character and concerns of the Polish emigration of his day. More than a century later, these thoughts remain a useful starting point for one who wishes to study the largest of all concentrations of Poles and people of Polish heritage living abroad, the Polish Americans.

Giller's essay came in response to activists in the still small Polish emigration in America who had written to him for advice on how to best proceed in mobilizing their countrymen to work together for the old homeland. In part, Giller (1831-1887) told them:

> Because the Polish emigration in America constitutes an undeniably great force, it should be the task of those who are motivated by true patriotic feelings to direct this force so that our Fatherland's cause will be presented to its best advantage.... In what way can we best direct the realization of Poland's cause? Through organization, we reply, since it is only through organization that our scattered immigrants can be uni-

---

[1]Donald Pienkos is a member of the Political Science Department at the University of Wisconsin-Milwaukee.

fied. Only organized work will enable us to channel their concerns so that individual efforts will not be wasted, but rather consolidated for the good of our Fatherland....

Having become morally and patriotically uplifted by the fact that we have unified ourselves, the major task before a Polish organization must be to help our people attain a good standard of living in America. For when the masses of Poles, simply by their presence in the country, reflect the good name of Poland to all whom they meet, they will be providing an enormously important service to Poland. In time, this service will be even greater as Poles begin to exert influence upon the political life of the United States.[2]

Giller could not have imagined that the Polish population in America, which in 1880 was estimated at about 500,000 persons (then less than 1 percent of the U.S. population) would number at least 9.5 million (or 3.8 percent) by the early 1990s. Still his observations are deserving of some comment here.[3]

---

[2]The full test of Giller's essay, in the Polish language, is in Stanisław Osada, *Historya Związku Narodowego Polskiego 1880-1925* (originally published by Alliance Printers and Publishers in Chicago, 1905, reprinted in 1957, and originally subtitled "the rise of the Polish national movement in America"), pp. 97-108. Excerpts in the English language can be found in Donald E. Pienkos, *PNA: A Centennial History of the Polish National Alliance of the United States of North America* (New York, 1984), pp. 52-54; and Frank Renkiewicz, compiler, *The Poles in America 1608-1972* (Dobbs Ferry, NY, 1973), pp. 64-65.

[3]Andrzej Brożek, *Polish Americans 1854-1939* (Warsaw, 1985), pp. 36-39; Helena Znaniecka Lopata, "Polish Immigration to the United States of America: Problems of Estimation and Parameters," *The Polish Review*, 21, No. 4 (Winter 1976), pp. 85-108.

According to its 1990 survey of the ethnic ancestry of the American population, the U. S. Bureau of the Census reported that 9,366,106 persons identified themselves as of Polish heritage (3.8% of all those identifying their heritage), placing Polish Americans seventh among all such population "groups" after persons of German, Irish, English, Italian, "American" and Canadian heritage (African Americans and Mexican Americans also placed higher in total numbers although these groups' size was ascertained from Census Bureau questions on the racial composition of the U. S. Population).

In the 1980 Census, the first to survey ethnic heritage beyond enumerating the number of immigrants and their offspring, Polish Americans were estimated at 8,228,037, of whom 3,805,740 (46.3 percent) reported only Polish as their ancestry, with the rest identifying themselves as being of multiple ancestral heritages, including Polish. Between 1980 and 1990, the number of Polish Americans rose by 13.8 percent (the total U. S. population increased by 9.8 percent), with the Polish Americans' rise apparently due to increased immigration and a more adequate surveying of the total population and perhaps to a greater sense of positive ethnic feeling on the part of some Polish Americans.

The ten states having the largest population of persons with Polish ancestral heritage were: New York (1,178,173), Illinois (892,009), Pennsylvania

Over the span of ten decades and more, the Poles in America have indeed focused a great deal of attention upon the building of organizations to meet their needs and advance their interests, just as Giller had counseled. Moreover, the organizations they built, whether local, national, religious or secular in character, have in fact tended to blend agendas aiming to both unite the ethnic community in support of broadly appreciated social causes and to meet the individual interests and ambitions of their members. Through more than six generations, the Polish American community or "Polonia," has been notable for its highly organized character. At its height, Polonia included as many as 800 local and ethnically based parishes, thousands or neighborhood fraternal societies (most of them linked to one another into fraternal federations having a national or at least a regional scope of operation), hundreds of daily, weekly, monthly and more occasional newspapers and magazines published in Polish, English or in both languages, and uncounted numbers of other societies having some cultural, recreational, professional, political or humanitarian rationales for their continued existence.[4]

Giller argued too that Polonia's organizational agendas involved at one and the same time its' members advancement in American society and strengthened their ability to rally both the Polish ethnic population and the broader American community behind its concerns over Poland. And here, while one might doubt his underestimation of assimilation's effects on the ethnic consciousness of the

---

(840,741), Michigan (824,721), New Jersey (592,172), California (465,677), Wisconsin (462,145), Ohio (403,768), Massachusetts (337,518), and Connecticut (287,016).

The ten states with the highest proportion of persons of Polish heritage were: Wisconsin (10.3 percent), Michigan (9.6 percent), Connecticut (9.5 percent), Illinois (8.4 percent), New Jersey (8.1 percent), Pennsylvania (7.4 percent), New York (6.6 percent), Massachusetts (6.0 percent), Delaware (5.7 percent), and Minnesota (5.4 percent).

In all, the number of foreign born Poles in America was 397,014, 4.2 percent of the total population of Polish Americans and 1.8 percent of the 21,631,601 foreign born persons in the United States in 1990. In 1930 there were more than 1,268,000 Polish foreign born and in 1960 about 747,000.

The largest concentrations of foreign born Poles were in the states of New York (89,874), Illinois (82,211), New Jersey (40,280), Connecticut (21,091), Michigan (19,160), Pennsylvania (14,667), and Massachusetts (13,229). No other state claimed as many as 10,000 Polish-born respondents.

In 1990, Polish Americans comprised 53.7 percent of all Americans of Slavic ancestry, but less than 40 percent of the foreign born of Slavic origins.

[4]On the character of organized Polonia, see Brożek, *Polish Americans*, pp. 43-96; Pienkos, *PNA*, pp. 3-16; Helena Znaniecka Lopata, *Polish Americans: Status Competition in an Ethnic Community* (Englewood Cliffs, NJ, 1976); Frank Renkiewicz, "An Economy of Self-Help: Fraternal Capitalism and the Evolution of Polish America," in Philip Shashko, et al., *Studies in Ethnicity: The Eastern European Experience in America* (Boulder, CO, 1980).

immigrants and their descendants, it should be appreciated that for all his enthusiasm about Polish organization Giller strongly opposed Polonia's isolation from American society. For him, it was for the members of members of Polonia to strive to be good Poles and good Americans at one and the same time.[5]

From Agaton Giller's time to present, there have been other efforts to define a rationale for Polish ethnic life in the United States. The classic formulation propounded by the World War I era scholars William Thomas and Florian Znaniecki, for example, saw Polonia as a kind of vestigial link with the "old country" the immigrants had left behind. From their analysis the long term prospects of the community could not be regarded as bright, given their conclusion that within a generation or so the population of Poles in America would be largely absorbed into the national cultural community that was the United States.[6]

A much more recent redefinition of Polonia's role and functions has been presented by the American sociologist Helena Znaniecka Lopata. Lopata has characterized the Polish community as a kind of arena in which ethnic activists competed for status and prestige, objectives apparently denied them in the larger American environment in which they found themselves rather marginal participants. Lopata's analysis, to be questioned as defining something unique to Polonia (in fact status competition may be a behavioral characteristic found in all ethnic communities), does provide a good explanation nonetheless of the gradual absorption of better educated and better-off Polish Americans into American organizational life and their consequent withdrawal from Polonia.[7]

Still other depictions of Polish ethnic organization have tended to regard them as manifestations of community activity that are essentially the same in function as those to be found in non-ethnic communities. Here Polish American involvement in civic associations, labor unions, political organizations or neighborhood pursuits are seen as no different from the involvement by Americans of other cultural, religious or racial origins in similar kinds of groups serving their needs. Accordingly, the "Polish" rationale for people to participate in such organizations is thus regarded as more of an accident of birth or residency than something rooted in their ethnic heritage.[8]

---

[5]On the Polish Americans' economic success, see Harriet O. Duleep and Hal Sider, et al., *The Economic Status of Americans of Southern and Eastern European Ancestry* (Washington, DC, 1986); and Lopata, *Polish Americans*. On the limits of Polish Americans' professional advancement, at least into the 1980s, see Russel Barta, *The Representation of Poles, Italians, Hispanics and Blacks in the Executive Suites of Chicago's Largest Corporations: A Progress Report 1972-1983* (Chicago, 1984).

[6]William I. Thomas and Florian Znaniecki, *The Polish Peasant in Europe and America*, 2 volumes (New York, 1958).

[7]Lopata, *Polish Americans*.

[8]Two examples of this approach include Paul Wrobel, *Our Way: Family, Parish and Neighborhood in a Polish-American Community* (Notre Dame, IN,

Here I would like to make state proposition that Polonia's existence, dynamism and persistence for the past century may be better understood as a manifestation of its members' continuing interest in achieving three interrelated goals, the advancement of their own well-being in America, their concern for the Polish homeland and its people, and their consequent interest in preserving a general sense of respect in the United States for the Polish cultural heritage, both among people of Polish descent and Americans in general.[9] Furthermore, these objectives have, for more than 125 years, served to animate the organizations of the Polish ethnic community and to largely define their missions as Polonia organizations. However, a look at the past shows that Polonia has been more successful in realizing its first two objectives than its third.[10]

From the existing research on Polonia's history, we can learn a great deal about the evolution of ethnic organizational life in the Polish community from the 1860s (when the first enduring groups formed) to the present time. From this substantial body of information, one may categorize Polonia's own development as falling into two distinct phases, with World War I and the years immediately afterward serving as a dividing line in its history.

In its first phase, mass migration to the U.S. was the central reality for the still fledgling, if rapidly growing, Polish community. In this era, the Polish parish stood out clearly as the dominant social institution servicing the needs of the waves of newcomers entering this country in ever growing numbers in each decade after 1870 up till the outbreak of World War I in 1914 (when unrestricted migration to the U.S. came to a permanent halt.)

The fraternal societies were at first marginal factors in the community, at least until the 1890s and for the most part their programs had them endorsing the work being performed by the parishes, that of helping the immigrants to survive and advance in the new land. Significantly, the fraternals would not attract a substantial following from the burgeoning immigrant population until the new-

---

1979); and Thaddeus Radzilowski, "The Great Depression and Mobilization of Second Generation Polish American Women in Detroit, 1930-1937," a paper presented at the Fiftieth Anniversary International Congress of the Polish Institute of Arts and Sciences of America, Yale University, 1992. An attempt, largely unsuccessful, to synthesize the various approaches to the analysis of the Polish experience in the United States is that of John J. Bukowczyk, *And My Children Did Not Know Me: A History of the Polish Americans* (Bloomington, IN, 1987).

[9]Donald E. Pienkos, *For Your Freedom Through Ours: Polish American Efforts on Poland's Behalf, 1863-1991* (New York, 1991); Victor Greene, "Poles," in Stephen Thernstrom, editor, *Harvard Encyclopedia of American Ethnic Groups* (Cambridge, MA, 1980) pp. 787-803.

[10]Two examples of such activities include those of the Kościuszko Foundation, headquartered in New York City and in operation since the 1920s, and more recently Witold Płonski, director of several federally sponsored projects in the 1980s to promote the enlightenment of the general public about Poland's history, culture, politics and the Polish American experience.

comers were able to meet two essential conditions of membership, namely, a commitment to remain permanently in America and thus become willing to throw their lot in with friends of a similar mind (rather than returning to Poland after having saved enough money in this country to establish themselves back in the homeland) and their attaining of more than minimal income status so they could pay for the costs of fraternal membership. Only after American Polonia had existed for a generation or so (till around 1900) were a sufficient number of immigrants able to meet these two critical conditions; once this had happened, however, they way was open for the fraternals to succeed in greatly expanding their mass memberships and their role in the community.[11]

In some of the fraternals, most notably the Polish National Alliance (founded in 1880 and formally rechartered as an insurance provider in 1896) the Polish Falcons of America (organized in 1894, re-established in 1912 and chartered as an insurance society in 1926), and the Polish Women's Alliance (founded in 1898-1899), an interest in assisting in the rebirth of an independent Poland would complement the benefits programs each organization offered its members. This "patriotic" concern in turn led them, often in concert with allies in the Polish American clergy and sometimes in league with such political groups as the small but influential Polish Socialist Alliance, to push for the creation of an all Polonia federation to reach Pole outside their formal memberships. Activists in the Catholic fraternals (most notably the Polish Roman Catholic Union in America that had formed in 1873) at first resisted the "nationalists" as a threat to their work; indeed, Polonia's history before 1914 is marked by a series of failed attempts by partisans of each camp to organize a universal federation to advance their aims at the expense of their rivals. However, by the time of the First World War, the entire fraternal movement, whatever its members' varied ideological roots, had united behind the cause of partitioned Poland's reunification and independence as a democratic political entity.

Early after the outbreak of the War, the main nationalist and clerical groups did succeed in making Poland's independence a unifying cause for the community; already in 1914 most of the organizations of Polonia had gotten together to promote humanitarian activities on behalf of the devastated homeland by creating the Polish Central Relief Committee (*Polski Centralny Komitet Ratunkowy*, PCKR). In 1916 the same organizations established a political federation which argued, with some justification, that it reflected the thinking of the whole community. This body, the Polish National Department (or *Wydzial Narodowy*) of the PCKR, enjoyed good relations with pro-independence activists in France who

---

[11]Pienkos, *For Your Freedom*, pp. 40-44. Interestingly, the social and economic conditions presently facing a large proportion of the Poles who have come to the United States since the 1970s are in some way very similar to those of the pre-1900s immigration, and this fact alone provides a fairly satisfactory explanation for the generally limited degree of interest among these "newcomers" thus far in joining existing Polonia societies, particularly the fraternal insurance associations.

were in operation as the Polish National Committee and were led by Roman Dmowski and Ignacy Paderewski. It was the Committee's aim throughout the War to gain the status of a kind of Polish provisional government in exile and to this end, its leaders strove to establish good relations with the Western democracies, the United States, France and Britain, against Germany.

Not all of Polonia backed the PCKR or its National Department; another federation, the Polish National Defense Committee (*Komitet Obrony Narodowej*, KON) had actually formed earlier, in 1912, with the aim of uniting the emigration. Indeed, at first KON had seemingly succeeded in bringing together all of Polonia under its wings. But internal ideological differences soon surfaced and caused the conservative groups headed by the Catholic clergy and the Polish Roman Catholic Union to exit from KON in June 1913, only a few months after its creation. Their withdrawal led to others by the nationalist groups, including the P.N.A., the P.W.A and the Falcons Alliance. And while KON would continue to exist throughout the War and for several years after, it no longer possessed the mass base it needed to rally Polonia and had to rely upon the small and controversial Polish Socialist Alliance and the schismatic Polish National Catholic Church for its survival.

The National Department's record of wartime activity can be measured in terms of its three key achievements. These involved the formation, in September 1917, of a Polish military commission in New York to recruit Poles in America into an army fighting under Polish colors on the side of the Western Allies; U.S. President Woodrow Wilson's declaration of support, in his "Fourteen Points" speech of January 8, 1918, for an independent Poland in line with the ideas promoted by Dmowski and Paderewski; and the Department's convocation of a massive Congress of the Polish Emigration in Detroit in August 1918 in support of Poland's rebirth.

Eventually more than 38,000 young men volunteered for duty in the Polish Army from America. Nearly 21,000 of them saw action in France and most of these individuals later served in Poland. A total of 1,832 lost their lives in the conflicts and 2,0111 were wounded.

Wilson's statement was not his first public pronouncement in favor of Poland's independence; in fact he had already done so nearly a year previously on January 22, 1917 in a speech in which he had offered to serve as a mediator in ending the War. His support was viewed in Polonia as crucial to the cause of Poland's restoration and was judged by many to have been made in response to the appeals of Paderewski and the leaders of the National Department.

The 1918 Congress of the Polish Emigration proved to be the last major manifestation of the National Department's ability to mobilize Polonia behind the independence cause. The Congress was attended by more than 900 delegates from around the country as well as by both Dmowski and Paderewski. At the event, plans were also laid to transform the Department into a permanent Polonia political federation working in support of Poland following the War.[12]

But this was not to be. The National Department would disappear within a few years after the War's end as most of its member organizations opted to focus their attentions on Polonia's domestic concerns (and not those of the new Polish state that came into existence in November 1918). Significantly, only a relatively small number of Polish immigrants actually returned home following the War; most by their determination to remain in the U.S. demonstrated that their priorities were focused more upon achieving their aims as an element of American society that as part of some vague "fourth partition of Poland." And while the Polish America community remained ethnic in practically all its salient characteristics, it was not until the outbreak of the Second World War in September 1939 that its members would unite on behalf of Poland, this time a Poland subjected to invasion and partition at the hands of Nazi Germany and Soviet Russia.

Once again, as in World War I, America's initial neutrality in the conflict meant that Polonia's early efforts to organize on behalf of the homeland would be in the humanitarian realm. This time the work was performed by the Polish American Council (*Rada Polonii Amerykańskiej*, RPA), later known as the American Relief For Poland), a federation of Polish fraternals working closely with Polonia's network of Roman Catholic and National Catholic parishes and their leaders in the two churches. Supported in both Polonia and the American general public, the RPA in the next decade would deliver more than $150 million in clothing, medical supplies and foodstuffs to Polish refugees and prisoners of war, making its effort the most successful in Polonia's history to that time.[13]

On the political side, Polonia would again organize only later, again as had been the case in World War I. And once more, as in the earlier period a certain division would mark the efforts on behalf of Poland's restoration. First to act after the U.S. entered the war as an ally of Britain and the Soviet Union were pro-Soviet sympathizers of Polish heritage who formed the American Slav Congress and the American Polish Labor Council. Claiming to speak for millions of Slavic and Polish Laborers and trade unionists, these groups won some credibility with President Franklin D. Roosevelt due to their assertions of fidelity to his wartime leadership and by staunchly supporting his 1944 campaign

---

[12]On the National Department, see Louis Zake, "The Development of the National Department as Representative of the Polish American Community, 1916-1923," Ph.D. dissertation, University of Chicago, 1979. For the activities of K.O.N., see the contributions by M. Drozdowski and by M. Francič, in H. Florkowska-Francič, et al., editors, *Polonia Wobec Niepodleglości Polski w Czasie i Wojny Swiątowej* (Wrocław, 1979); on the formation and services of the Polish Army raised in the United States, see Donald E. Pienkos, *One Hundred Years Young: A History of the Polish Falcons of America, 1887-1987* (Boulder, 1987), pp. 91-112. For an overview of the period, see Pienkos, *For Your Freedom*, pp. 45-72.

[13]See Francis X. Swietlik, *Rada Polonii od 1939 do 1948* (Chicago, 1948); and Pienkos, *For Your Freedom*, pp. 73-104.

for an unprecedented fourth term in office.[14]

Worry over Polonia's passivity in the face of the threat to the country's postwar fate at the hands of the U.S.S.R, led to the creation of another political organization, the National Committee of Americans of Polish Descent (*Komitet Narodowy Amerykanów Polskiego Pochodzenia*, KNAPP), which eventually succeeded in linking up with the Polonia fraternals to form the Polish American Congress (*Kongres Polonii Amerykańskiej*, KPA) in May 1944. Initially viewed with distrust by a White House concerned over the slightest criticism of its war policies, the Polish American Congress did become the unquestioned voice of the ethnic community in opposing Poland's post war re-establishment as a Soviet-dominated, communist run dictatorship.

Unlike the National Department, whose work was seen as having been completed in the 1920s after Poland's rebirth, the PAC remained an uncompromising foe of communist rule over Poland, though its stand initially placed it in opposition to the Roosevelt administration. In time, however, the Congress would see a number of its objectives realized. Thus, by 1948 the U.S. would adopt a new foreign policy to contain Soviet aggression in Europe (while accepting the reality of its control over Poland and its neighbors). Washington would also approve extraordinary legislation backed by the Congress enabling more than 120,000 Polish refugees and war veterans to enter the country and a Federal investigation of Soviet responsibility for the World War II era Katyn massacre. Yet another PAC priority, winning U.S. recognition of Poland's western border with Germany, would be far more difficult to achieve. But this objective too was realized as early as 1975, when the President Gerald Ford signed the multilateral Helsinki Accords.

In the early 1970s, the PAC would establish a separate charitable agency under its direction, the Polish American Congress Charitable Foundation, to carry out the work of the by then defunct *Rada Polonii*. The PAC Charitable Foundation was particularly active after 1980 in delivering more than $170 million in medical and material goods to a Poland whose deteriorating economic conditions were only made worse by the Communist regime's decision to suppress the Solidarity labor movement instead of responsibly confronting the country's problems.[15]   That action was followed by the U.S. decision to impose economic sanctions on Poland, a move the PAC originally supported out of a belief that tough measures by Washington would lead the Polish regime to move to re-establish a dialogue with the nation's representatives in the Church and Sol-

---

[14]Louis Gerson, *The Hyphenate in Recent American Politics and Diplomacy* (Lawrence, KS, 1964); and Charles Sadler, "Pro-Soviet Polish Americans: Oskar Lange and Russia's Friends in Polonia, 1941-1945," *The Polish Review*, 22, No. 4 (1977), pp. 25-39.

[15]Wacław Jędrzejewicz, *Polonia Amerykańska w Polityce Polskiego: Historia Komitetu Narodowego Amerynaków Polskiego Pochodzenia* (New York, 1954); and Richard C. Lukas, *The Strange Allies: The United States and Poland, 1941-1945* (Knoxville, TN, 1978).

idarity.

It is an interesting question, although thus far one that has not received much investigation, whether this move by the PAC (as well as other decisions by its leadership over the years) have always enjoyed the full support of Americans of Polish origin. On the organizational level, it is a fact that no significant Polonia group has directly opposed its policies since the Second World War, although there have been occasions when individual Polish Americans have taken issue with the PAC's sometimes highly militant positions. What seems to be beyond much doubt is that events in Poland over the period between 1945 and 1989 demonstrated that the Polish American Congress' stance about Communism's political illegitimacy was a correct one. Not only was communism overturned and ousted from power as soon as the Polish population was at last given the opportunity to freely vote on who should govern the country (in the June 1989 elections to the country's national assembly and senate); in the early 1990s the very party of Polish communism simply disappeared from the country's political life.[16]

Important to understanding the role of the PAC and its predecessor federation as factors in Polonia has been the close association between them and the mass membership organizations in the ethnic community, namely the fraternals and the parishes (and in the case of the Polish American Congress, the office of president has been invariably headed by the president of the largest of Polonia fraternals, the Polish National Alliance). Moreover, the Congress' remaining executive offices have nearly always been filled by the heads of the other large fraternals, the Polish Roman Catholic Union, the Polish Women's Alliance and the Polish Falcons of America. Similarly, the Polish American clergy has traditionally played a visible role in Congress, even as the character of priestly leadership in its activities has grown more symbolic than instrumental over the years.

If Polonia has experienced some substantial achievements in realizing its first two objectives, it has met with less success in its third area of concern, the maintenance of widespread interest in, and commitment to, the preservation of the Polish heritage in the U.S. The era of greatest activity in this realm came in the decades ending in the early 1920s, when the community focused on the objective of building Polonia. It was in that period, from the 1860s up to the years immediately following the First World War, that the Polish community was essentially comprised of immigrants and their children (the "first" and the "second" generations in the U.S.) During these years, the community rapidly expanded in size and institutional complexity, incorporating into the mix the systems of parish activity, the fraternals, a vital Polish language mass media and

---

[16]Pienkos, *For Your Freedom*, pp. 105-217; also Richard C. Lukas, "The Polish American Congress and the Polish Question, 1944-1947," *Polish American Studies*, 38, No. 2 (Autumn, 1981), pp. 39-54; and Romuald Bilek, *Jak Powsta Kongres Polonii Amerykańskiej* (Chicago, 1984).

a host of auxiliary societies and voluntary associations. By the mid 1920s, immigration to the United States diminished to a trickle as a consequence of restrictive Federal legislation; that action also reduced the need to maintain a system of distinctly Polish, as contrasted to Polish American or native voluntary associations, to serve the population of Polish origin. With Poland's independence regained after 1920, so also was there a decline in Polonia interest in the affairs of the old country.

World War II brought a renewed concern by Polonia over the fate of a Poland under Nazi and Soviet occupation, of course. Still it should be noted that a primary stimulus for the KNAPP organization came from a group of highly motivated Polish emigres and it was this rather small group that would play a significant role in the later formation of the Polish American Congress. Similarly, in the years and decades following the War, the Congress' own vitality would be closely tied in with the role played in its leadership by highly politicized newcomers to the U.S., many of whom had refused to return to Poland after 1945 and to accept the legitimacy of the communists' domination of their country.[17]

Here, one can hardly but compare conditions in the Polish American Community of the interwar years with those of contemporary Polish America in the wake of the collapse of communism in 1989. Thus, today, without the cause of anti-communism and opposition to the Soviet Union to help energize public opinion, a general pre-occupation with America's domestic fortunes has signalled a much lowered interest among Americans about international matters, including those facing post-communist Poland.

Yet, while there are comparisons to be made between the current situation facing American Polonia and those of the interwar years, there are differences to be acknowledged too. And recognizing these differences tells us a lot about the serious challenges that Polish America faces in the 1990s.

For one thing, the Polonia of the 1920s and 1930s was still composed mainly of immigrants and their children; furthermore, the ethnic community was still relatively homogeneous in terms of its members' incomes, occupations and educational attainments. Too, the Polish Americans of the Depression years of the 1930s shared a highly homogeneous set of political attitudes. For example, in their voting behavior they supported Franklin Roosevelt and the Democratic party by margins of 9 to 1 in the elections of 1936 and 1940.

In the 1990s, Polish Americans constitute a far more heterogeneous collection of people which cannot be readily lumped together on the basis of national origins, style of life, income, educational and professional attainment or inter-

---

[17]Pienkos; Stanisław Brodzki, editor, *Rada Koordynacyjna Polonii Wolnego Swiata, 1978-1992* (Toronto, 1992). See also Jędrzejewicz, *Polonia Amerykańska*; and the comments of Casimir Lukomski on the disproportionate role in Polonia played by the "new emigration," in Pienkos, *For Your Freedom*, p. 569. Also, Stanislaus Blejwas, "Old and New Polonias: Tensions Within an Ethnic Community," *Polish American Studies*, 38, No. 2 (Autumn 1981), pp. 55-83.

ests. Indeed, one might even question whether the very term "Polonia" can even be applied with much accuracy to characterize the interests and activities of Polish Americans. Certainly, judging by membership in secular Polish American organizations, one finds only a fairly small fraction of the total population of Polish Americans actually enrolled any longer in fraternals and/or ethnic parishes. And the once powerful Polish ethnic press is today but a shadow of its former self; indeed where once as many as nine Polish language daily papers operated as recently as the early 1950s, in 1992 only two such publications remained in business. Similarly, the proportion of the foreign born Polish population is smaller in relation to the number of native-born persons who identify with their Polish heritage than at any time since the 1850s, approximately 400,000 out of 9.5 million or 4.2 percent in all.[18]

Given these realities and the lessened capacity of Polonia to communicate with persons of Polish heritage through ethnic radio and television programming, the key question for contemporary Polish American organizations is one of finding the means through which they might motivate potentially receptive persons to identify in some fashion with their concerns and possibly join their ranks. First and foremost among the issues before Polish Americans is that of devising programs aimed at preserving a widely shared ethnic memory of their heritage among the millions of people of Polish ancestry around the country. Without such an effort, the very future of Polonia's present day organizational network is likely to be bleak.[19]

It is clear that the Polonia of the 1990s must focus its attentions upon better identifying and propagandizing knowledge of Polish heritage, values and traditions, if only because no other institution in America will perform this work on Polonia's behalf, neither the public or private school systems around the country not the mass media.

Still, to accomplish this task Polonia does have some real assets at the community's possible disposal, assets which were not in existence in the 1930s. One includes the existence of several thousand well trained specialists in Eastern European and Russian-area studies, most of whom teach in America's colleges

---

[18]See *The American Agenda*, circular 4 (August 24, 1992), a recent series of publications of the Washington Metropolitan Area Division of the Polish American Congress under the editorship of veteran Polonia activist Alfred Bochenek. In a piece titled "Membership Changes in Major Polish American National Organizations, 1978-1992," membership in thirteen major Polonia associations, Bochenek noted that involvement in the groups had declined from 746,000 to 554,000, or 26 percent during the years under review. Also note Duleep and Sider, *Economic Status of Americans*.

[19]The Płonski-led effort to secure continued federal support for his efforts to promote the Polish ethnic heritage met a devastating reversal in 1988 following the death of Aloysius Mazewski, President of the Polish American Congress and the Polish National Alliance, until his passing an influential backer of the plan in Washington, D.C.

and universities. Many if not most of these persons have a substantial degree of knowledge about Polish history, culture, literature, language and Poland's contemporary experience. Some are expert about the Polish ethnic experience in the United States. All need to be enlisted into serious collaborative relations with local and national Polonia organizational activists, for the purpose of developing courses, lectures and exhibitions whose aim is to enlighten interested members in the Polish American and broadly American communities about the Polish heritage. A far larger number of individuals of Polish heritage can be found teaching in America's secondary and primary schools; ways must be identified to make it possible for more of them to use their skills in developing appropriate kinds of educational programs that will include "Polish studies" into the countless "multi-cultural studies" activities that are being promoted throughout the land. For Polish Americans, indeed, "multi-culturalism" should not be restricted to include racial and minority studies alone but can be readily expanded to cover the experiences of all peoples who have migrated to the United States during its long history, including the Poles.[20]

There is a second and equally significant asset of potentially great value to Polonia in its revitalization of interest in the Polish heritage in America beyond that of this country's teachers. And this asset is Poland itself, a Poland that in the early 1980s is at last an independent and democratically governed nation possessing a substantial intellectual population of its own, a population capable as never before possible to exert a positive and invigorating impact upon the Polish ethnic communities outside of the country.[21]

In the past, this was not possible. Poland, under foreign oppression, could not serve as a major regenerative asset to Polonia (aside from providing the emigrant communities with a steady stream of newcomers who of course did possess a vivid awareness of their own nationality and language). Rather, through most of Polonia's history Poland was to be seen more as an object of political concern and charitable assistance than as a partner in the work of preserving life abroad. Even worse, during the period of communist rule between 1945 and 1989, Poland's own cultural efforts to reach the United States were generally regarded in Polonia as but cynical and politically-motivated attempts by an illegitimate regime to corrupt and manipulate Americans' appreciation of the actual Polish

---

[20]Membership in scholarly and professional societies of Polish Americans and persons interested in Polish affairs, most significantly the Polish Institute of Arts and Sciences of America and the Polish American Historical Association, is a significant base for such activity. In the two organizations are to be found at least 1,500 individuals, most of them educators, and many of these are open to cooperation with Polonia organizations in promoting greater awareness of Polish culture.

[21]See Casimir Lukomski's comments on "Polonia's 'Domestic Agenda,'" originally published in the October 1990 issue of the *Polish American Journal* (Buffalo, New York) and reprinted in *For Your Freedom*, pp. 423-425; and Pienkos' recommendations in the same work, pp. 238-244.

conditions. Obviously, the situation has radically altered since 1989. The time is therefore ripe for the beginning of a serious and systematic effort by Polonia, the Polish educational establishment and Poland's government to begin the expansion of popular knowledge about Poland's culture in America.[22]

Over the past 130 years or so, the organizations of Polonia have in fact accomplished a great deal in creating among countless Polish Americans a positive sense of identification with their own heritage based upon a pride in their material achievements in America and a concern for the fate of their ancestral homeland. It is now time for them to better use the available resources, in the United States and in Poland, to work consistently to enable more Polish Americans to better understand who they are and thereby, as Agaton Giller predicted in 1879, to better "reflect the good name of Poland to all whom they meet ... simply by their very presence in this country."[23]

---

[22]Thus, at the World Congress of Polonia and Poles from Abroad held in Kraków in August 1992 under the sponsorship of the Polish government and its newly formed agency to deal with the Polish communities abroad, *Wspolnota Polska*, the focus of attention was on the question of whether or not the Polonia communities would unite with *Wspolnota* to form a permanent international organization to coordinate relations between Poland and its diaspora, both in the West and in the lands of the former Soviet Union. The failure to accomplish this aim was, consequently, seen by many as a replay of the Congress of 1934 in Warsaw, when American Polonia's representatives refused to join the World Union of Poles from Abroad (*Swiatpol*). Unfortunately, relatively little attention was given to matters pertaining to the question of Poland-Polonia cooperation in the cultural area. See Donald Pienkos, "Rola kultury w utrzymaniu polskości wsród Polonii Amerykańskiej," a paper presented at the meeting of the World Congress of Polonia and Poles from Abroad, Kraków, August, 1992 and published in *Dziennik Związkowy* (Chicago), September 20, 1992. Also the article on the results of the Kraków congress that appeared in the New York-based Polish language daily, *Nowy Dziennik*, October 15, 1992.

Significantly, the future of American Polonia was the central issue before the Polish American Congress as it gathered in October 1992 in Washington, D.C., to hold its first national convention in sixteen years. Notably, the convention featured a special one-day session dealing with Polonia's "American agenda." Even more important, the resolutions its participants unanimously adopted at the conclave signalled their deep concern about focusing new energies upon the preservation of the Polish cultural heritage in the United States now that Poland's independence had at last been regained. Hilary Czaplicki, Donald Pienkos, Ewa Gierat, John Olko and Frank Milewski, Resolutions of the Eleventh National Convention of the Polish American Congress, Washington, D.C., October 17, 1992.

[23]Giller, in Renkiewicz, *The Poles in America.*

The Polish American Historical Association

by

John J. Bukowczyk[1]

The year 1992 marked the fiftieth anniversary of the Polish Institute of Arts and Sciences of America. The same year also marked the fiftieth anniversary of the Polish American Historical Association, and considering its early history as an outgrowth of PIASA, some mention of PAHA in this book of proceedings is especially appropriate.[2]

The story perhaps rings familiar, but it is worth reviewing, at least in outline, nonetheless. The germ of what would become the Polish American Historical Association was organized in 1942 as one of PIASA's original four "Scholarly Sections" on the "Historical and Political Sciences."[3] At the first meeting of the Historical and Political Sciences Section, Professor Oskar Halecki, the renowned Polish historian who headed the section (and who by the early 1950s would inherit the presidency of the entire PAHA organization), "proposed to create a special Committee for the study of the history of Poles in the United States" and, upon approval of his proposal, enticed Mieczysław

---

[1]John Bukowczyk is Professor of History at Wayne State University, Detroit, Michigan.

[2]Considering the co-mingling of Polish Christians and Jews in the migration stream that emitted from Poland's partitions, perhaps it should also be noted that 1992 also marked the one hundredth anniversary of the American Jewish Historical Society.

[3]Frank Mocha, ed., "The Polish Institute of Arts and Sciences," *Bicentennial Essays*, pp. 709-710.

Haiman of the Polish Museum in Chicago to chair it. Christened the Commission for Research on Polish Immigration at its first conference and meeting (held December 2, 1942, in Chicago), that committee would soon find quarters in the Polish Museum. Incidentally, the papers from the first conference were assembled and published successively in PIASA's new journal, the *Bulletin of the Polish Institute of Arts and Sciences in America.*[4]

Historian Frank Mocha, reviewing the early activities of the Commission, found first, that scholarly activity—in history and in sociology—burgeoned immediately after its founding and, second, that work on Polonia spilled beyond the Commission proper, as Polonia-related research popped up regularly elsewhere in PIASA.[5] By 1944, the Commission for Research on Polish Immigration had begun to meet annually at different Polish-American colleges and universities, had elected its own five-member board, and had begun to discuss starting its own journal, eventually named *Polish American Studies.* The establishment of *Polish American Studies* at this time was perhaps fortuitous, because it came about just as PIASA activities in this area were coming to a halt, owing to Allied withdrawal of recognition and support for the Polish Government-in-Exile in London, hitherto PIASA's main source of funding.[6]

At the second annual meeting of the Commission for Research on Polish Immigration, held at Orchard Lake Seminary on October 27-28, 1943, the organization changed its name to the "Polish-American Historical Commission." According to Mocha, "The new Commission differed from the former in that it was more egalitarian and had more members," within three years in excess of one hundred.[7] Though founded as "an independent scholarly society" and now possessed of its own journal, *Polish American Studies,* whose first issue was subvened by both the Polish Roman Catholic Union of America and the Polish Women's Alliance of America, the Commission retained links to the Polish Institute.[8] As Mocha pointed out, both Haiman and *Polish American Studies* editor Konstanty Symonolewicz belonged to PIASA. Symonolewicz's co-editor (and the treasurer of the Commission), however, was Rev. Joseph Swastek of Orchard Lake Seminary.[9]

The dual point I wish to draw from this perhaps overlong narrative is, firstly, that these two scholarly organizations—PIASA and PAHA—shared a common early history and, secondly, that this fiftieth anniversary congress offers a rich opportunity for both groups to assess the current state of affairs and to reconsider their relationship to each other and to other independent scholarly organizations here and abroad—which is, after all, why we are here.

---

[4]*Ibid.*, p. 710.
[5]*Ibid.*, p. 711.
[6]*Ibid.*, p. 712.
[7]*Ibid.*, pp. 713, 722 n. 29.
[8]*Ibid.*, p. 713; *Polish American Studies*, Vol. 1 (1944), p. iii. *Polish American Studies* was also subsidized by the *Polish American Congress.*
[9]*Ibid.*, pp. 713-714.

As we also well know, when Polonia's organizational leaders set to taking stock of their organizations' respective health and accomplishments, those leaders typically tell a tale of woe, sounding not unlike my late maternal grandmother's constant lamentation: "*O, Boże. O, Boże. O, Boże.*" And in the last years of her long life, "Everything is going down, down, down." About their successes, in contrast, our organizations usually beat a boastful drum. I have no doubt that somewhere in the distant marches of worldwide Polonia, some tiny Polish cultural club, altar society, or even historical association has taken credit for bringing the Evil Empire to its proverbial knees.

When I now set to considering PAHA and Polonia—whence and whither—I therefore should do a little bit of boasting and a little bit of moaning—and the reader should take both with several grains of salt. On the positive side, this fiftieth anniversary sees our own organization in a remarkably vital state: we publish a quarterly newsletter and continue an unbroken run of our scholarly journal, *Polish American Studies*, which stretches back fifty years. PAHA has nearly $60,000 in assets (with an annual operating budget of around $13,000), has converted its cumbersome membership records into a computerized database, and continues to sustain a membership of over a hundred institutions and over five hundred individuals (in various membership categories). PAHA continues to sponsor an assortment of scholarly projects—principally in the area of publication and public history—and offers several annual prizes—soon to be funded by endowment—for scholarship, service, and civic achievement. Finally, and of some especial charm and one might say human interest, in 1991 PAHA received its first significant bequest, a gift in excess of $20,000 from the estate of the late Stanley Pachon. It might be noted in passing that Mr. Pachon, whom none of us ever met but whom apparently we somehow served, amassed this small fortune, perhaps even inadvertently, by collecting old comic books—proverbial treasures in the attic.

But countervailing signs are worrisome, both for our organization and for its ability to carry on a program here and abroad. Perhaps I describe a situation also familiar to my fellow panelists. From a peak of around 750 in the 1970s, for example, PAHA's membership has fallen to just over 600 (actually, a slight improvement over the past few years). Annually, we need to enroll over a hundred new members in order to offset membership losses from non-renewal and other causes. Much of our membership, I believe, is heavily skewed toward middle-aged and elderly persons. About ten percent of our members purchased "life memberships" at very low prices many years ago; because they receive PAHA periodicals published at current, inflated prices, these Life Members are now maintained on our books at a loss. We have fewer than fifteen student members. What can I say but: "*O, Boże.*"

Certainly, organizations such as PAHA need to reassess their relationship to their existing membership, to their mission, and to their prospective clientele. Recent events in Eastern Europe especially offer opportunities for scholarly collaborations, exchanges, mutually beneficial projects, etc., but PAHA can seize upon—and realize—none of these without concentrating attention and energy—at least in near term—on organizational modernization and development.

Like Piłsudski's army on the Wisła, however, we might suggest under these trying circumstances, first, that the best defensive posture lies in attack, and, second, that the best attack falls on the flank. For PAHA—and, by extension, for other Polonian scholarly and cultural organizations—perhaps the appropriate course is not to shrivel, retreat, regroup, nor especially to plan for our eventual demise, but rather to look beyond some of our own, often rather tawdry, administrative and bureaucratic difficulties, to larger projects and plans. Perhaps the time has come, for example, for Polonia's diverse intellectual, academic, scholarly, and cultural organizations—The Kościuszko Foundation, The Polish Institute of Arts and Sciences of America, the American Council of Polish Cultural Clubs, the Polish Genealogical Society, the Commission on History and Archives of the Polish National Catholic Church, and, of course, PAHA—to form themselves up into an umbrella group—in some ways, the scholars' analogue of the Polish American Congress. Perhaps the PAC might properly sponsor such a liaison, but perhaps it might be PIASA—and thus we return to the theme.

Of course, there is something preposterous about suggesting that a handful of groups, many struggling to survive, join together, with no greater resources than before, and form a big group, also perhaps struggling to survive, and one that probably would exist largely on paper. There is likewise something almost offensive about suggesting that one group "absorb" others and thereby grow—we do, after all, proudly possess the *liberum veto* as one of our historical traditions. Yet, considered more optimistically, the group—actually, a federation of independent groups—could prove a ready resource for Polonia (and, indeed, even for the work of the PAC which, with a few notable exceptions, has to date not mobilized Polonia's academic community). In the short-run, such a group—perhaps it would be a council of presidents from the Polish-American academic and cultural community (COPPACC?)—might write letters in support of Polonian positions (writing long, elaborate letters is certainly something at which scholars like myself, for better or for worse, excel). With a relatively small amount of money—someday Polonian institutions might mobilize the appreciable financial resources of the members of this ethnic group—it might be able to support a modest, part-time Washington, D. C., presence, alongside the PAC and other Polonian representatives. With more still, it could become the Polish American counterpart of the American Enterprise Institute, the Heritage Foundation, or the Brookings Institute, that is to say, an intellectual "think-tank" group, though certainly of vastly more modest ambitions, resources, scope, and importance.

Clearly, I have run on too long. I look forward to any comments that these suggestions might prompt.

The Polish Press in Australia as a Link Between Polish Emigrants and Their Homeland, 1949-1980

by

Jan Lencznarowicz[1]

This article will examine the role played by Polish language newspapers published in Australia (1949-1980) in maintaining close ties between the Polish emigrant community in Australia and Poland. However, it is impossible to conduct a readership survey and thus determine the actual social role played by the press. Today we are not able to quantify precisely how readers related to news stories published forty years ago, or how such news shaped their opinions and behavior. In such circumstances the purpose of this paper is to present the changing content of Polish newspapers and point to some social functions to which this content was adapted. It is also intended to assess attitudes and the prominence given to particular topics. In particular, much attention is devoted to the picture of post-war Poland as portrayed in the Polish language press in Australia and its attitude towards the political situation in the homeland. The historical and quantitative analysis reveals both political attitudes and ideological values present in the Polish group, or at least the attitudes and values held by its leadership and the most politically active members.

---

[1]Jan Lencznarowicz is affiliated with the Jagiellonian University in Kraków, Poland.

The first Polish community in Australia was established at Polish Hill River near Sevenhill in South Australia in the 1850s. However, until the late 1940s Polish emigrants formed only a small section of the Australian population. In 1947 there were 6,573 Polish-born persons in Australia, and about 80% of them were of Jewish background. Between September 1947 and October 1948, 1,457 Polish ex-servicemen landed in Tasmania. Also in 1947 Australia signed an agreement with the International Refugee Organization (IRO) and consequently received over 170,000 Displaced Persons, of whom about 60,000 were Polish. It is estimated that about 65,000 Polish refugees came to Australia between 1948 and 1951. However, the exact number of Poles resettled in Australia at that time is difficult to ascertain. From 1951 to 1979 over 17,000 Polish-born immigrants arrived. According to the 1981 census there were 59,441 Polish-born persons, of whom 12% stated their religion as Hebrew. In 1983 the total number of Polish immigrants (including those of Polish-Jewish background) was estimated at 80,000 and, together with subsequent generations could be viewed as constituting the Polish-Australian community. At the beginning of the 1980s this community was estimated between 122,000 and 180,000, and amounted for about one percent of the total population of Australia.[2]

On the whole, Polish immigrants were characterized by strong national and religious identity, while their homeland's situation, as well as their personal experiences, gave them a firm anti-Communist stance. Despite the existence of some frictions within the community, the Poles displayed strong political cohesion, formed many political and social organizations and vehemently opposed Communist power in Poland and Soviet domination in Eastern Europe.

Throughout the period under consideration the following weeklies were published regularly: *Wiadomości Polskie* [Polish News] in Sydney and *Tygodnik Katolicki* [Catholic Weekly] in Melbourne, the latter being renamed *Tygodnik Polski* [Polish Weekly] in 1965. These two were the most accessible and widely read Polish periodicals published in Australia. Their circulation fluctuated, but never surpassed 5,000 copies. In Adelaide *Nasza Droga* [Our Way] was published every two weeks from 1952 until 1980 with a circulation of fewer than 1,000 copies. However, in the 1970s its readership declined significantly and only eleven issues were printed annually. In addition to these three the following weeklies were published in the early 1950s: *Echo* in Perth, *Głos Polski* [Polish Voice] in Melbourne and *Forum* in Sydney. In 1965-66, also in Sydney, *Polonia* was published monthly and the emigré political journal *Nurt*

[2]Department of Immigration and Ethnic Affairs, Profile 81, 1981 Census Data on Persons Born in Poland; J. Jupp, ed., *The Australian People. An Encyclopedia of the Nation, its People and Their Origins* (Sydney, 1988), pp. 102, 734-747; E. Kunz, Displaced Persons. *Caldwell's New Australians* (Sydney, 1988), pp. 78-85; C. Prince, "The Demography of Polish Settlers in Australia," in R, Sussex and Jerzy Zubrzycki, *Polish People and Culture in Australia* (Canberra, 1985); Jerzy Zubrzycki, "Foreword" in Lech Paszkowski, *Poles in Australia and Oceania 1790-1940* (Sydney, 1987), p. xiii.

[Current] appeared erratically in the 1960s. In the following decade *Panorama*, Sydney-Canberra, and *Kurier Polski* [Polish Courier], Sydney, were issued irregularly. Moreover, there were dozens of mimeographed newsletters published by local Polish clubs and organizations as well as news sheets, bulletins or tabloids published by ex-servicemen, scouts, educational associations and churches.[3]

Quantitative Analysis

For purposes of this study quantitative content analysis was conducted on samples from *Wiadomości Polskie* [Polish News], *Tygodnik Katolicki* [Catholic Weekly; later named *Tygodnik Polski* (Polish Weekly)], and *Nasza Droga* [Our Way] for the following years: 1953, 1965 and 1977. From each of the newspapers published in these three years, twelve issues (the last issue from each calendar month) were drawn, giving 108 issues in the whole sample. The recording unit used in this study is the news item, i.e. "the whole 'natural' unit employed by the producers of symbol materials."[4] However, as news items differ considerably in their length, it seems necessary to measure their space as well. This allows for the comparison of a number of news items and the space devoted to particular categories and makes it possible to present, with a relatively high degree of precision, the main areas of interest covered by the Polish press and the changes taking place in them over a selected period of time. Measurement of the area, amount of news items and page numbers will allow assessment of the prominence given to particular content categories by editors. Identified sources of information and reprinted articles will help illuminate the information channels used by the Polish press in Australia.

News items concerning the content category *Poland* constitute 11.1% of all news items in the sample and take up 10.9% of the whole space, while 27.9% of news items and 26% of the area were devoted to the category "Polish community in Australia and in other foreign countries" or "Polonia." However, only 4.4% of news items and 3.6% of the space were related to the category "Australia." There was a strong connection between the category "Poland" and two other categories: "Cultural tradition" and "Foreign affairs." The latter category was generally presented from a Polish perspective. Finally, advertisements frequently related to

---

[3]Jan Kowalik, *World Index of Polish Periodicals Published Outside Poland Since September 1939* (Lublin, 1976), p. 1988. See also M. Gilson and Jerzy Zubrzycki, *The Foreign-Language Press in Australia 1848-1964* (Canberra, 1967); M. Kałuski, "Polish Press in Australia," in A. Wate Ata and C. Ryan, eds., *The Ethnic Press in Australia* (Melbourne, 1989), pp. 170-189.

[4]B. Berelson, *Content Analysis in Communication Research* (Glencoe, Illinois, 1952); M. Tenezakis, *The Neglected Press. A Study of Arab and Greek Newspapers and Their Sydney Publics* (Canberra, 1984); C. Young and J. Taylor, *The Turkish and Yugoslav Press. A Survey of Content and Readership of Ethnic Newspapers in Melbourne* (Canberra, 1985).

the homeland were tabulated.

The percentage of news items devoted to the category "Poland" in samples from the years 1953, 1965 and 1977 varied slightly and amounted respectively to 11.2%, 11.6% and 10.4%. The space covered by this category increased from 9.4% in 1953 to 12.4% in 1977. As collected data show, the case of the Polish press in Australia does not support the hypothesis about gradual decline in space devoted to homeland affairs and the increase in space given to Australia.[5]

Table 1
Percentage Allocation of News Items and Space in the Whole Sample

Content Categories	News Items	Space
Advertisements	31.1	26.5
Australia	4.4	3.6
Cultural Traditions	4.2	14.6
Foreign Affairs	13.5	10.9
Miscellaneous	7.8	7.5
Poland	11.1	10.9
Polonia	27.9	26.0

Table 2
Percentage Allocation of News Items and Space
for the Years 1953, 1965 and 1977

Content Categories	1953		1965		1977	
	News Items	Space	News Items	Space	News Items	Space
Advertisements	25.3	20.4	35.6	31.7	31.0	25.8
Australia	4.3	3.9	3.4	3.2	5.6	3.9
Cultural Traditions	6.4	22.2	8.2	15.4	2.1	6.8
Foreign Affairs	20.0	16.3	8.9	8.1	13.2	9.4
Miscellaneous	7.6	7.8	8.2	6.5	7.4	8.2
Poland	11.3	9.4	11.6	10.7	10.4	12.4
Polonia	25.1	20.0	27.9	24.7	30.3	33.5

---

[5]M. Gilson and Jerzy Zubrzycki, *The Foreign-Language Press*, p. 63; Victor Turek, *Polish-Language Press in Canada* (Toronto, 1962), pp. 88-89.

Division of the content category "Poland" into detailed sub-categories allows us to pinpoint the main fields of interest of the Polish press in Australia in homeland affairs. Out of 1,168 news items, 216 relate to internal politics in Poland, 146 to Poland's international standing, 132 to economic and social situations, and 136 to religious and church affairs, which were usually presented in connection with the political situation. Other frequently covered topics included, cultural life and scientific development (155 news items); "human interest" including everyday life, crime, gossip, inclement weather, natural disasters and other accidents (134 news items); and sporting news from Poland (120 news items). The space devoted to the Polish internal political situation takes up over one quarter of the whole area covered by news on Poland. Together with news items on the social and economic situation, foreign policy and church affairs, political materials make up over half of space given to the category "Poland." Issues related to the Polish-German border, the situation in former Polish territories east of the Bug river, and emigration and defection to the West are less frequently mentioned, but their presence evidences the interest of the Polish-Australian press regarding the political situation in the homeland. Although news items on cultural life and scientific development, "human interest" and sports appear regularly, they are usually brief and the space taken up by each of these categories is less than 10% of the area given to the category "Poland."

Among newspapers included in the sample, the *Tygodnik Katolicki/ Tygodnik Polski* had the smallest percentage of news items and devoted the least amount of space to homeland affairs, respectively 8.4% and 9.1%. The *Wiadomości Polskie* consisted of 12.4% news items, with 12.2% of its space devoted to Poland, while the *Nasza Droga* was tabulated 13.9% and 11.5%, respectively.

Among journalistic genres, short news or reports constitute 52.7% of all news items on Poland, while longer news or reports (usually accompanied by commentary) comprise another 34.9% of news items devoted to this content category. However, these data cannot be explained only by pointing to the informative function of the Polish press in Australia. Indeed, weeklies and even biweeklies had to fulfill this function due to the lack of interest of the mainstream Australian press in East-Central European affairs, especially in the 1950s and 1960s. Inadequate knowledge of English among Polish immigrants at the beginning of their settlement contributed to the fact that they looked for information to Polish-language newspapers. However, the Polish press, as well as many ethnic newspapers in Australia, tended to interpret events, rather than simply report the news. It represented the European style of journalism (which is more "formative") as against the Anglo-Saxon style of journalism (which is more "informative").[6] It manifested itself in the constant efforts of the majority

---

[6]P. Bosi, "Ethnic Press. A Question of Survival," *Media Information Australia*, No. 15 (February 1980), p. 35; A. Nasielski, "Australia," *Kultura*, No. 5/295 (1972), p. 124. A. Nasielski, "Początek końca," *Kultura*, No. 5/320 (1974), p. 103.

of Polish periodicals to form and maintain a hostile attitude towards the Communist regime in Poland and to combat its propaganda. This was evident not only in articles, editorials, speeches, and letters to the editors, but also in the selection of news.

Materials concerning the category "Poland" were concentrated on the front and last pages, as well as the most popular sections in the paper. A considerable amount of space allocated to Poland was presented on the first page (19%). With the exception of foreign affairs (23% of space devoted to this category was on the first page), coverage of other stories, although extensive, was usually hidden inside the newspaper.

The Image of Poland in the Polish Press in Australia

While at the end of the 1940s, mass immigration was shaping a new Polish community in Australia because news arriving from Poland was very limited and dated. The iron curtain was hermetically isolating Poland from the West. Additionally, the Poles who had settled in distant Australia were separated from the large Polish centers in Europe and America, which were relatively well-informed about the Polish domestic situation. Apart from a small group of war and pre-war immigrants, the Polish refugees were largely newcomers taking their first steps in Australia. In this rather insular existence, the emigrants lived scattered and had neither vital organizations nor immediate contact with Poles in other countries. However, by taking advantage of their former connections from their military service or displaced persons camps, they were creating new ties, especially with Polish centers in Great Britain and the United States, from which news about Poland was more easily available.

At that time news from home was obtained from the radio and services of the Free Europe Press (FEP) agency, the American Inter-Catholic (IC) agency, the United Polish Press in America (*Zjednoczona Prasa Polska w Ameryce*, ZPPA) as well as other agencies. Editors looked for news about Poland in the world press; first of all they would read emigré newspapers, mostly *Dziennik Polski* [Polish Daily] published in London and *Kultura* [Culture] published in Paris, as well as Polish-American newspapers such as *Dziennik Związkowy* [Polish Daily Zgoda] based in Chicago. From Western agencies they quoted from newspapers published in Poland, for example, *Tygodnik Powszechny*, *Przekrój*, *Dziennik Polski* (Kraków) and later *Odrodzenie*, *Po prostu* and *Ekspres Wieczorny*. At times they published letters from Poland sent to relatives or acquaintances in Australia.

Home columns were usually filled with short news items compiled in special sections. However, quite a considerable number of news items concerning home affairs were also found in sections dedicated to political, cultural and sports news of the world.

In the first half of the 1950s, concise yet recurrent reports of repressive measures, the increasing control of the authorities over all spheres of life, the domination of Communist ideology, the "bolshevization" of the education system, the collectivization of the Polish villages, and complete subordination to the Soviet Union were predominantly featured. They detailed the political trials, the activity of the Secret Service, the labour camps, censorship and the persecution of the Catholic Church.

At the same time, they called attention to even the slightest indications of social resistance, reporting on the dissatisfaction of farmers, workers and young people. "The desperate fight is going on," they reminded Polish emigrants, instructing them that while growing rich in their new country of settlement, they should not forget their oppressed homeland.[7] A motif of the emigrants' duty to come to their countrymen's aid in their struggle with the Communist system in Poland would recur throughout the whole period being researched. At the same time, they referred to expectations on the part of Poland, from which, came appeals imploring: "Liberate us from the regime!"[8] Polish journalists in Australia repeatedly emphasized the political character of the post-war emigration. "Our whole country is looking at you," announced a widely distributed declaration of fugitive Polish sailors, "it expects from you political aid, the political fight for freedom, for our country's right to freedom."[9]

Text presented in English (required by the Australian law to constitute 25% of each issue at that time) was also instrumental in illuminating the political situation in Poland and Eastern Europe.

The "Sovietization" of Poland and the imposition of the Communist ideology or "the nonsense of the materialist theories" filled emigré journalists with anxiety. With real concern they wrote about indoctrination of the young generation, its scale and intensity which they thought to be a threat to the continuity of the national culture so deeply rooted in Christianity and Western European culture.[10] They estimated that the fight for the Polish culture "is becoming more and more fierce year after year, is taking place in all the spheres of social life and will reach its peak in the regime's brutal eagerness after taking possession of the young people's minds, extorting their faith in God from them, extorting the principles of Christian ethics, love of freedom and even their homeland from them." Simultaneously, newspapers appealed for contacts with Poland which would be expressed as protests against the destruction of a thousand years of tradition. Important here was the maintenance in exile of Polish national culture, whose existence was endangered in the homeland itself. "Under such gloomy circumstances, our role as a free people living in a free country becomes

---

[7]*Echo*, February 3, 1951.

[8]*Wiadomości Polskie*, March 7, 1954.

[9]*Nasza Droga*, December 24 and 31, 1955.

[10]*Wiadamości Polskie*, October 1, 1950, October 8, 1950, October 28, 1950, and January 11, 1953.

particularly significant. As the fight for culture and education is a real fight for national independence, we have to preserve the enduring treasures of Polish culture in our souls and entrust them to the young generation [in Australia]."[11] The sense of this mission, although weaker than among emigrants from countries directly annexed by the Soviet Union, was still very conspicuous among Poles. It helped Polish newspapers play a role in maintaining the Polish language and culture in Australia.

Apart from political oppression and ideological pressure, the papers focused on the difficult living conditions. They systematically reported on the scarcity of basic goods and services, of low salaries and wages, and deteriorating condition of the community's health. Nationwide poverty was contrasted sharply with the prosperous life of the Communist Establishment as well as with the conditions under which Poles lived and worked in Australia. The journalists emphasized the exploitation of employees by the Communist authorities, the tightening of discipline at work, and the absurdity of the Stakhanovite competitions. They briefly commented on a new housing law: "No Communist act can do without robbery."[12] Analyzed newspapers stressed the contrast between the official propaganda and reality, revealing the nonsense, disorder, overgrown bureaucracy and waste. Entire columns were dedicated to the above-mentioned problems, for instance, "Delights of the regime paradise—pictures of the life in Poland" or "Propaganda versus reality."

Was the image of the situation in Poland painted only in black? Indeed, such a negative portrayal predominated. However, positive or at least neutral materials, were presented, namely news of the restoration of cities, historical monuments (churches in particular), of archaeological discoveries, and achievements in sports and, at times, in science. Only very seldom was news about the development of industry and social changes accompanied with any favorable comments or presented in any positive context.

Although rarely voiced in the columns, opinions were heard, criticizing this narrow, entirely negative image of contemporary Poland. "Poland is not a gang of secret service sleuth-hounds."[13] "Do we, who know best what Soviet Russia is like, need to be trained to be anti-Communist?" a reader of *Nasza Droga* asked. He continued, "I stress the fact that I believe every word you write in your newspaper, but this is just one side of the coin. You never mention other.... Obviously, our emigrant newspapers cannot compete with the Warsaw *Trybuna Ludu* [a leading Communist daily], but please give us some positive news from the homeland now and then." An editor, who by publishing the above letter had already violated a taboo, replied that he would wait for further opinions on this matter. He commented, "we may diverge from our policy in favour of the matters you have taken up only in the event that the majority of our readers demand

---

[11]*Wiadomości Polskie*, November 10, 1951.

[12]*Tygodnik Katolicki*, April 5, 1951.

[13]*Nasza Droga*, June 19, 1955.

this of us."[14]

The year 1956 not only marked changes in Poland which resulted in a growing openness toward Western countries, but also brought the Olympic games and Polish athletes to Melbourne. A period of visits and re-established contacts with family and friends followed, precipitating a new "post-October" emigration in Australia. Subsequently, this promoted an increase in the amount of news about Poland and enriched, as well as complicated, its image in the press.

Polish newspapers in Australia barely kept pace with the course of events in the summer and autumn of 1956. Already before that time "a return to a recent heresy—the views of Gomułka" and changes within the government were observed very closely. Nevertheless, the journalists were quite reserved in their comments. They instructed readers to warn their families in Poland for Communist tricks aimed at exposing opponents of communism at home and attracting emigrants from abroad. The events in Poznań shook the hopes for a "thaw" in Poland. Importantly, it resulted in a new emphasis on the duties of political exiles, expressing solidarity and furthering contacts with countrymen in the homeland.

Newspapers gave detailed, though usually much delayed, accounts of the October changes in Poland and of the Hungarian uprising. Not only printed newspapers such as *Wiadomości Polskie*, *Tygodnik Katolicki*, or *Nasza Droga* but mimeographed local bulletins as well were filled with home news. Again hopes for a decisive turn in Polish politics re-emerged, yet fear of the Soviet threat and lack of hope for full and lasting liberalization persisted.[15]

News from the following years reported on the retreat from the policy of liberalization. "Stalinism (is) inseparable from communism," "Kadarization of Poland," "Gomułka returns to Stalinism," "Good-bye to October 1956," were titles announcing news from Poland. It might be of some interest to examine to what extent news from Polish-language newspapers, the main source of information on Poland for many Poles in Australia, influenced Poles' attitudes towards naturalization. Initially a relatively small number of Poles, especially those with secondary and university education, became naturalized as Australians in 1956. However, disappointment with the situation at home led to a rapid increase in naturalization between 1957 and 1959. The comparison with other groups of refugees from Central and East Europe, Hungarians in particular, illustrates this phenomenon. As Egon Kunz points out, a reduction of the naturalization figures among Poles in 1956 can be explained by the fact that the recent events in their country inspired their hopes and directed them towards Poland. In the following years, as hopes for an early return to Poland faded, there was a marked increase in the trend of naturalization. Through its endeavor to attract readers' attention to the situation in Poland and intensify their emotional en-

---

[14]*Nasza Droga*, January 31, 1954.
[15]*Wiadomości Polskie*, November 11, 1956; *Nasza Droga*, October 21, 1956; *Tygodnik Katolicki*, November 3, 1956 and November 17, 1956.

gagement in the affairs of the homeland, the Polish press in Australia strengthened the "second push." This was brought about by political events in Poland,
and contributed to the fact that Poles acquired Australian citizenship on a mass
scale, a phenomenon defined by Kunz as "catharsis naturalization."[16] I have analyzed the role the researched press might have played in the political integration
of Polish immigrants in Australian society in another paper.[17] Here I would only
like to mention the contradictory tendencies of the emigrant press, which on the
one hand provided information and promoted ties with the homeland. At the
same time, it promoted emigrants' adaptation to the country of settlement.

Although a large number of texts published at that time state that Stalin's
principles seem to have returned, even a quick glance at Polish-language newspapers shows a much wider range of information from Poland, and indeed more
numerous and vivid contacts than ever. The sources of information were broadened, yet still much of the news or reprints on Poland could have been obtained
from the Polish press published in exile. News items were reprinted from *Kultura*, from *Dziennik Polski i Dziennik Żołnierza* [The Polish Daily and Soldier's
Daily], *Orzeł Biały* [White Eagle], *Na Antenie* [On the Air], *Tydzień Polski*
[Polish Week], *Trybuna* [Tribune] and in the 1970s, from New York's *Nowy
Dziennik* [Polish Daily News]. The press services of the Warsaw *Krajowa
Agencja Infromacyjna* [Home Information Agency], although not always admitted, were widely used. A large number of newspapers from Poland was also
available. More often than before, editors quoted or even reprinted contents of
newspapers published in Poland, and many of the homeland papers were received
by Polish readers in Australia. To a certain degree, they were competitive in
providing news from Poland, forcing emigrant newspapers to diversify and
broaden their domestic sections. Toward the end of 1970s the Polish underground press became an important source of news and reprints. Frequently
quoted were *Biuletyn Informacyjny* of the *Komitetu Samobrony Społecznej
KOR* ["Information Bulletin" of the Committee of Social Self-Defence KOR],
Opinia [Opinion], *Głos* [Voice] and many others. *Wiadomości Polskie* published the column "Out of the Polish Free Press" and, using the same source, a
second one titled "Resistance in Poland."

Travel to Poland, which grew more and more frequent might have played an
important role, too. Editors had to take into consideration the fact that a growing number of actual and potential readers visited Poland and thus formed an
opinion on the post-war reality. The schematic, and limited portrayal of Poland
was anachronistic for readers who came to Australia after 1956, who had been
brought up under the Communist regime. Soon accounts of visits to Poland

---

[16]E. Kunz, "Political Events at Home and the Concept of Catharsis
Naturalization Among Refugees," *International Migration*, Vol. 9, No. 1/2 (1971),
pp. 55-67.

[17]Jan Lencznarowicz, "The Polish Immigrant Press in Australia and Australian
Politics 1949-1979," *Znanstvena Revija*, Vol. 3, No. 2 (1991), pp. 415-427.

appeared in the Polish press in Australia. At first, there appeared accounts written by old, pre-war emigrants, and among them, Stanisław Robe or Fryderyk Goldschlag. Later, a whole series of articles from such journalists as Irena Gronowska, Krystyna Gwizdała, Tomasz Ostrowski, and Eugeniusz Bajkowski were published. There were good writers among newcomers as well, namely, Leszek Szymański, Jerzy Steinmetz and Maria Boniecka. Steinmetz wrote to the editors of *Wiadomości Polskie*: "if you found yourself at home [in Poland], today, you would feel as strange and ill at ease, as I feel here in Australia."[18]

Disputes with the press published in Poland, especially with the newspapers meant for emigrants, had been recurring since the controversy between *Tygodnik Katolicki* and *Biuletyn Rozgłośni "Kraj"* [Bulletin of Broadcasting Station "Homeland"] in 1956. It was an example of confrontation with Communist propaganda, which increased considerably since the second half of the 1950s and aimed at the Polish emigrant centres in the West. As a result of their conflict with the official Communist press in Poland, Polish newspapers in Australia brought the domestic affairs of Poland even closer to their readers.

Consequently, the reader was provided with a richer, more diversified image of Poland. Although this tendency survived until the end of the period under scrutiny, it never significantly changed the picture presented of contemporary Poland. Journalists concentrated on political problems, continued the existing trends which contrasted the Communist regime and Polish society, reported on the repressions of the authorities against social resistance. This perspective was present during the whole period under discussion, but it was particularly conspicuous during political crises in 1956, 1968, 1970-71 and especially after 1976. On the one hand there was *Polska Zjednoczona Partia Robotnicza* [Polish United Workers' Party] with its helpless leadership, corrupt government and well developed machine of repression. On the other hand, there was initially the spontaneous, and in the second half of the 1970s better organized and alleged mass social resistance. The dependence of the Polish People's Republic on the Soviet policy, the inefficiency of the Polish economy controlled by the communist party, shortages in the market, and low standard of living were all strongly emphasized. Polish society was presented as being for the most part hostile to the regime. This allegedly resulted in both passiveness and active resistance to the government and spurred defection and emigration from Poland. Nevertheless, apart from demonstrating a principally anti-Communist attitude of the majority of Poles living in homeland, at times the press would touch upon the problem that Polish society was shaped by the socialist ideology and everyday life in a Communist state. For instance, in polemics on the attitudes of the latest emigration, some contributors readily resorted to an argument that these recent arrivals from Poland were *"skomunizowani"* [communized], which, they maintained, provided an explanation for their conflicts with earlier emigrants.

---

[18]*Wiadomości Polskie*, August 10, 1958; J. Steinmetz, *Pół życia na obczyźnie* (Warsaw, 1990), pp. 39-40.

Newspapers like *Polonia* or *Panorama*, and especially *Kurier Polski* introduced a sort of a departure from the point of view presented above. *Panorama* provided a rather neutral image of Poland and moderately, without unequivocal criticism, reported of the political situation in Poland. From the columns of the propagandist, pro-Communist *Kurier Polski* emerged an image of Poland as a dynamically developing country with no major domestic conflicts, only some "growing pains." "Contemporary Poland, although it is still far from ideal, is a modern, highly cultural country respected world-wide in trade and politics."[19] These words were supported by news items about numerous achievements, social security and a safe future for Poles at home. Frequent photographs showed the leaders of the Polish People's Republic, as well as "prefabricated beauties"— modern blocks of flats. Included also were the Central Railway Station—"the pride of inhabitants of Warsaw"—and even *"czyn społeczny na Wisłostradzie,"* a collective social action participating in the construction of an important highway in Warsaw. However, the above-mentioned periodicals, compared with the mainstream Polish press in Australia, were peripheral phenomena and could not counterbalance the image of Poland promoted by the most significant newspapers.

Naturally, the above image not always and not in all main newspapers corresponded with the above-mentioned stereotype. *Nasza Droga* edited by Jerzy Dudziński and Władysław Romanowski paid closer and more sympathetic attention to the situation in Poland than when the paper was later edited by Jan Sobolewski. The editor of *Wiadomości Polskie*, Jan Dunin-Karwicki, attempted to present an image of Poland of that time relatively more complete than the one which appeared in other newspapers, thus facing criticism and even accusations of having diverged from the line of the Polish political emigration. Roman Gronowski in *Tygodnik Katolicki* and *Tygodnik Polski* gave an equally precise, yet more schematic, black and white image of the situation in Poland. The fact was noticed in Warsaw as well. According to authors of an internal Communist party analysis of *Instytut Badań Współczesnych Problemów Kapitalizmu* [the Institute of Research on Contemporary Problems of Capitalism], prepared in 1975, *Wiadomości Polskie* was "a more flexible newspaper, efficiently adjusting its contents to its readers' expectations, needs and mentality. By publishing 'objective,' although tendentiously selected news items on Poland, it seems to be a newspaper conveying a more complete image of life in our country than *Tygodnik Polski*. Nevertheless, these are only appearances," warned the authors.[20] In the second half of the 1970s new editors of *Tygodnik Polski* introduced a different emphasis upon the presentation of homeland affairs.

[19]*Kurier Polski*, May, 1971.
[20]Z. Kacpura and A. Kowalski, *Prasa Polonii i polskiej emigracji politycznej* (Warsaw, 1975), p. 284.

A significant place in the image of Poland reconstructed here was taken by Polish Western and Northern territories acquired after the war, their integration and development. Not only mainstream, but also such varied periodicals as *Nasze Wiadomości* [Our News] published by the Carpathian ex-servicemen and *Wiadomości Handlowe* [Commercial News] took up the issue as well. No less importance was attached to the Eastern borderlands occupied by the Soviet Union. Even as early as in the 1950s any available information on the situation in Wilno (Vilnius) and Lwów (Lviv), at times imprecise or incorrect, was printed by the Polish-language press in Australia. As access to these territories became less restricted, the news service grew more and more complete. Marian Kałuski showed the strongest commitment to providing information on the Eastern borderlands, stressing their Polish character. He published *Merkuriusz Ziem Wschodnich Rzeczypospolitej* [Courier of the Eastern Territories of the Polish Republic], as Kałuski put it himself, "a private paper, dedicated to problems of the Eastern Territories illegally torn away from our Mother Country."[21] Later, while editing *Tygodnik Polski*, he also published a regular chronicle dedicated to problems in the Eastern territories.

The Catholic Church was another, very important element of Poland shaping the image presented by the Polish press in Australia. Characteristically, *Przegląd Katolicki* [Polish Catholic Review] published by *Towarzystwo Chrystusowe* [Society of Christ], which had its headquarters in Poland, concentrated on strictly religious matters and did not cover the church affairs in the homeland extensively. Nevertheless, the other newspapers, particularly *Tygodnik Katolicki* and its continuation *Tygodnik Polski*, as well as *Nasza Droga* (when published by "Caritas") did inform quite regularly on church affairs. The problems grew in importance at such times as repressions during the Stalinist period, celebration of the Millennium of Poland, and the election of Pope John Paul II. Cardinal Stefan Wyszyński was seen as the only great authority in the country and a counterbalance for the Communist government. His statements were quoted extensively and with utmost respect. The personage of Cardinal Karol Wojtyła, although respected and quite popular after his visit to Australia in 1973, had been kept in the background of Primate Wyszyński until his election as Pope. The issue of the Church and Catholicism in the Polish People's Republic was touched upon in the majority of newspapers, firstly from the point of view of the Church's and Catholicism's political significance, and in particular, their role in anti-Communist resistance. It was especially visible in the case of *Wiadomości Polskie*. At one point this weekly was criticized for being too lenient in its presentation of the repression of the Church and for publishing articles which allegedly hurt religious and patriotic feelings.[22]

---

[21]*Merkuriusz Ziem Wschodnich Rzeczypospolitej*, Vol. I, No. 1 (November-December, 1965).

[22]*Wiadomości Polskie*, July 4, 1965 and October 10, 1965; *Nurt*, December 1964/January 1965.

The image of contemporary Poland in the Polish press in Australia was con-
structed, chiefly, from materials of political character, even when they directly
referred to cultural issues or church affairs. Neither sports news, which quite
often revealed the sentiment of solidarity and pride regarding the achievements of
Polish athletes, nor "human interest" news, which flavored domestic sections,
counteracted the political emphasis. Naturally, political attitudes of disposers of
newspapers played a role in shaping such an image of Poland under Communist
rule.

The Attitude of the Polish Press in Australia Toward the Communist Regime in Poland and Poland's International Standing

The viewpoint of the analyzed newspapers was affected by the following factors: international situations, changes in the homeland and, above all, the origin
and political character of the war and post-war emigration (which was especially
evident in the case of the majority of publishers and editors). Opposition to the
Communist system and the domination of the U.S.S.R., as well as attachment
to the idea of an independent and democratic Poland, made it impossible to accept
the post-war *status quo* and even its more liberal versions. The authorities in
Warsaw were quite aware of this fact. In 1975 an analysis of the Institute of
Research on Contemporary Problems of Capitalism stated: "The Polish newspapers in Australia are among the most reactionary in the whole Polish press in
exile. First of all, they systematically demonstrate, as a rule, a negative attitude
towards the Polish People's Republic.... The Polish press existing at the moment in Australia is a reflection of the political character of the Polish emigré
centres in Australia.... The Polish organizations are under control of 'intran-
sigents' [*niezłomni*], that is, of representatives of the war emigration who do not
accept the changes which took place in Poland following World War II. This
decided on the fact that the Polish press is the main platform for promoting slogans with claims concerning Poland's 'independence,' liberation from the 'dictate
of Bolsheviks,' etc."[23]

The opinion that the attitude of the Polish press in Australia to the post-war
political reality in Poland was decisively hostile, although true with reference to
the majority of the newspapers, does not take into consideration a large number
of important variations, and can even be misleading. First of all, the opposition
to the political system imposed upon Poland did not imply the propagation of a
return to the pre-war conditions. In 1953, the author of the article "Away with a
Dream!" published by *Forum*, just arrived from Poland, attempted to persuade
emigrants that the dreams of those expecting to restore the previous system were
bound to fail. He argued that the people of Poland, although in the majority
hostile to the regime, are proud of their recent achievements. Importantly,

---

[23]Kacpura and Kowalski, p. 283.

"they, and not we, reside there, and they, not we, will shape the future of Poland." The editor of *Forum* expressed the hope that this opinion would help "correct a large number of notions which had become distorted by our separation from the homeland."[24] *Wiadomości Polskie* also referred to this idea. In 1955 Bolesław Korpowski and in 1958 Jerzy Malcharek and others discussing the attitude towards Poland emphasized the magnitude of changes taking place there. General Juliusz Kleeberg, President of the Federal Council of Polish Associations in Australia, underscored their irreversible character, admitting that "it is very hard for us here in Australia even to keep pace with [the profound ideological and structural transformations in the homeland]. Today's Poland is entirely different from the one we left sixteen years ago."[25]

The thaw of 1956 and the first years of Gomułka's rule brought about some changes in emigrant attitudes toward the situation in Poland. "Until Gomułka's days," as a publicist of *Wiadomości Polskie* observed, "the problem seemed to be clear and simple: each and every thing coming from our homeland or connected with it was, in plain terms, condemned altogether as being of Communist origin, whether it was good or bad.... It was enough simply to perceive everything coming from Poland as being red.... Together with the meandering of Gomułka's 'own way [to socialism]' the political line of emigration and its attitude toward the homeland started, in a strange way, to grow more confused."[26] Changes taking place in Poland, more frequent and easier contacts with the mother country, as well as the offensive of the Polish People's Republic's propaganda aimed at the Polish diaspora, all required a reconsideration of the totally negative attitude, but also suggest a limit to a potential compromise. Transgressing this line of compromise would imply a renunciation of Polish political emigrants' ideals. The editors, publicists, and political and social activists attempted to define a model policy regarding emigration-homeland relations, which would neither threaten the emigration by maneuvering it into cooperation, nor pretend to approve of the political system in Poland. On the other hand, it should enable the emigration to have the broadest possible contact with Poles at home, provide support for them, and as much as possible weaken the communist system, and thus bring the idea of an independent and democratic state nearer.

A dichotomous division of the regime and the nation, which was already visible in this description, formed a basis for such a model. At the same time, both of these elements, the regime and the nation, contrasted very sharply. Often the newspapers emphasized this difference and warned emigrants against transposing their critical opinions of the regime onto the nation. They pointed out that their views were critical toward Poland's regime and not to its people. As *Nasza Droga* wrote: "We are all aware, I think, of the fact that the interests of the Polish nation have nothing to do with the interests of the regime. Indeed,

---

[24]*Forum*, March 8, 1953.
[25]*Nasza Droga*, May 20, 1956.
[26]*Wiadomości Polskie*, June 14, 1959.

the regime and the nation are two entirely unrelated bodies. Unrelated and hostile."[27]

The above-mentioned differentiation opened up relatively broad prospects for contacts with the country of origin on a private and informal basis. However, it did not prevent troublesome situations, which could result in conflicts and sharp divisions within the Polish community in Australia. This was all the more so as in many contacts, even private ones, it was very difficult to avoid the element of formality, quite often intentionally provoked by the Polish authorities. On the other hand, even contacts with individuals and institutions identified with the policy of the Polish People's Republic might provide an opportunity for valuable, informal meetings.

Opinions differed, for instance, as to what extent cultural, educational and sports cooperation with Poland could be developed, who could visit Poland, and under what circumstances Poles in Australia should cordially welcome artists or sportsmen from Poland. The propaganda and policy of the Warsaw government with reference to Poles abroad, including actions undertaken by the Polish Consulate in Sydney, prompted various reactions on the part of the Polish centres and papers and even resulted in internal divisions among them. An analysis of the political situation, especially on the international scene, led some authors to accept certain elements of Warsaw policy, particularly the question of the Polish-German borderline.

A detailed analysis of various attitudes toward the Communist system in Poland and the Warsaw government's infiltration among Poles in Australia exceeds the framework of this article and requires a separate elaboration. My purpose is only to point out the fact that apart from a predominant, yet internally diversified attitude of anti-Communist, pro-independent circles, there emerged, especially in the 1970s, a policy of cooperation with the authorities of the Polish People's Republic, as evidenced in the editorial line of the *Kurier Polski*.

I would like to emphasize the fact that the position of the most active Polish centres in Australia, as expressed in the newspapers, were to a considerable degree shaped by influential emigré circles in other countries, Great Britain in particular. Attitudes towards Poland reflected this dependence to a larger extent than could, for instance, be observed in the Polish-language press in the United States.

As has already been remarked, Polish affairs in the newspapers under consideration cannot be analyzed without reference to the coverage of international politics which constituted a background indispensable for understanding the situation in Poland. Of course, the background itself was considered from the point of view of the Polish interests as perceived by the disposers of the newspapers. On the whole, the sample materials analyzed with respect to the content category "foreign affairs" amount to 13.5% of all news items and take up 10.9% of the printed space. An overwhelming majority of these refer to political problems.

---

[27]*Nasza Droga*, July 5, 1959.

This fact is quite obvious in the newspapers published by political emigrés who envisioned the future of Poland in an environment of radical change in international politics. Their interests concentrated upon West-East relations, since in them Polish publicists sought a decisive factor for the fate of their homeland. They placed particular emphasis upon the policies of the United States and the Soviet Union, and persisted in following tensions as well as rapprochements between these two world-powers. This explains why Polish publicists focused so much attention upon such events as the wars in Korea, Vietnam, and Afghanistan. They perceived these events as elements of the same process upon which depended the future of Poland: a confrontation between the Kremlin-controlled Communist system and the democratic world led by the United States. If they criticized the West it was only for the lack of determination in its fight against communism as well as for its reluctance to make difficult decisions. "A disturbed world is a feeding ground for communism," wrote the editor of *Wiadomości Polskie,* who stressed the fact that "one cannot buy the world's freedom for American dollars" or "at the cost of one's friends."[28] Most of all, however, the attention of the Polish press was drawn by the situation in Europe, especially in the neighborhood of Poland. They criticized the post-Yalta order and the Soviet domination over Central and Eastern Europe. They deplored Poland's integration into the system of communist countries, as well as its political dependence and economic exploitation by the U.S.S.R. Since during the Cold War the Polish press sought a change in the post-war *status quo*, the news about its stabilization was bitterly received. They also reacted very critically against the policy of détente and the Conference on Security and Cooperation in Europe because they thought it symbolized a confirmation and consolidation of the "dictate of Yalta" as well as of the division of Europe. Only from time to time did opinions emerge pointing out prospects of changes the détente policy brought about for Poland.

The questioning of the Yalta order was directly associated with the problem of Polish borders. Newspapers, whose readers often came from the Eastern territories of pre-war Poland, did not approve of the Soviet Union's annexation of Eastern Poland. At the same time, almost unanimously these newspapers defended the Oder and Lusatian Neisse border and warned against German revisionism. Nevertheless, a constant opposition to the loss of the Eastern territories stood in the way of understanding and agreement with both the nations bordering with Poland in the East and their emigrants in Western countries, with whom the Polish leaders in Australia made an endeavor to cooperate, particularly in the Assembly of Captive European Nations (ACEN). The idea of cooperation and even the notion of federation of the Central- and East-European nations as the best guarantee against Soviet or German domination was promoted with a particular intensity by *Wiadomości Polskie.* "The sovereignty of the Ukraine, Byelorussia and Lithuania is a guarantee of the sovereignty of Poland," stated a

---

[28]*Wiadomości Polskie,* May 25, 1958 and June 15, 1958.

headline, accurately representing the editorial policy of this weekly.[29] The paper also promoted close cooperation of the Polish opposition and emigré circles with their Czechoslovak and Hungarian counterparts. On the other side, those in favour of an unconditional return to the pre-war borders in the East sharply rejected any concessions.[30] The polemics over this issue continued through the end of the researched period.[31]

The press frequently spoke of the moral aspects of the Polish cause, recalling at the same time the Polish contribution to the fight for freedom of other nations as well as disloyal allies abandoning Poland and leaving it subject to its own fate. Condemnations of Yalta ("this infamous agreement") were accompanied by appeals for a renewal of moral values in politics. Polish emigré publicists were attacking their main enemy—the Communist East. Yet they were referring to Western democracies with regrets and reproach. The image of the West defending its security but indifferent to the fate of nations behind the iron curtain included: selfish public opinion, cynical politicians motivated by short-sighted temporary interests, and decline of the spiritual element in life and morality in politics. "Under such circumstances, Poland," as Władysław Romanowski wrote in 1958, "is a standard of political honesty and judging by an attitude towards our Cause, we can tell the factors of disintegration from the ones sincerely aiming at building a better Tomorrow."[32]

However, this was exactly the attitude of various Western politicians to the situation in Poland and other countries under Communist rule that Polish observers found so disappointing. For instance, Polish newspapers protested against the reception that Khrushchev and Bulganin received in London in 1956. They were upset by President Ford's statement during a television debate in 1976 which alleged that Central and East Europe was not dominated by the Soviets. They also demanded a boycott of the Olympic games in Moscow in 1980.

The Polish emigré press was dissatisfied with the indifference of West public opinion toward the situation in Central and Eastern Europe. Consequently, they expressed a conviction that one of the main emigrants' objectives should be to inform the world of the real situation under Communist rule, to mobilize resistance against it and to create a favorable atmosphere for Poland. The press' role was to assist in fulfilling these aims. The major papers of the Polish community in Australia made attempts to realize these goals, particularly in their English sections. However, their actual capacity could not match their declarations. Although the Australian government and opposition sometimes noticed views expressed by Polish newspapers, they principally provided the politically active Polish élite with an instrument of publicizing its perspective

---

[29]*Wiadomości Polskie*, February 12, 1978.

[30]*Nurt*, December 1965/January 1966 and June 1966; *Tygodnik Polski*, November 13, 1965, February 5, 1977, February 12, 1977, and July 16, 1977.

[31]*Tygodnik Polski*, October 18, 1980 and November 1, 1980.

[32]*Nasza Droga*, December 28, 1958.

on international politics among a wider group of readers. The papers persuaded Polish emigrants that their leaders were still in command and that "the Polish Cause" was still alive.

Maintaining Links with Poland

Numerous and regular news about Poland's situation was certainly a fundamental element which determined the function of maintaining ties with the country of origin adopted by Polish newspapers in Australia. As mentioned earlier, the question of what extent they actually performed this function cannot be answered in this paper. Nevertheless, the press also published a number of additional materials—advertisements, announcements, appeals, letters, proclamations and poetry which reinforced its role of a link with Poland. Several important examples of this are presented in the following paragraphs.

Numerous advertisements of travel and trade agencies run by Australian Poles encouraged emigrants to send to Poland and "Polish occupied territories (beyond the Curzon Line)" food, drugs and other articles which were unavailable there, and to purchase by PKO S.A. apartments, cars, agricultural machines, etc., for themselves or their relatives at home. Such advertisements amounted to 4.7% of all news items and occupied as much as 6% of the space of the entire sample. From 1949 until the end of the period under scrutiny, advertisements of this sort were always present in newspapers and bulletins and they offered a wider and wider range of services. At times publishers would also run mail-order firms. However, in the majority of cases newspapers would confine themselves to publishing advertisements and encouragements. The editor of *Tygodnik Katolicki* determined, on the basis of a questionnaire filled in by the weekly's readers during a very severe period of unemployment for all immigrants (1953-54), that "it is sure that 83% of all Poles in Australia send parcels to Poland."[33] Advertisements of parcels and money orders frequently referred to the feeling of emotional ties with relatives and friends in the homeland and of the duty to help them. At the same time, these advertisements reinforced this feeling. "Remember your near and dear in Poland!" was the most common of these slogans, especially popular during the time preceding Christmas or Easter, and usually accompanied by concrete commercial suggestions. Apart from advertisements, newspapers published detailed information on changes in customs regulations and tariffs. During the 1970s, offers directed toward people leaving permanently for Poland started to appear, namely estate services concerning houses and apartments in Poland, travel services, money order and baggage shipment services, as well as safe deposit services.

Following October 1956, individual and group trips to Poland became more popular. Newspapers and bulletins printed not only travel agency advertisements

---

[33]*Tygodnik Katolicki*, April 23, 1955; *Echo*, February 24, 1951.

providing tourist services and assisting in bringing relatives to Australia (they amounted to 3.1% of all news items in the sample and covered 3.7% of the whole printed space), but they also published photographs and impressions about visits to Poland.

The Polish press in Australia also performed a considerable function in searching for families and friends, especially during the second half of the 1950s. They published lists of people sought by PCK (Polish Red Cross), appealed for assistance in finding particular persons and described happy family reunions. Letters from Poland intended for Poles living in Australia were often addressed in care of Polish newspapers. Offers to enter into correspondence came quite frequently, mainly from young people in Poland. At times, they were accompanied by more or less explicit marital offers, which drew the attention of single men, who were abundant among the Poles in Australia. The editors informed readers of the possibilities of bringing relatives and fiancées to Australia and even gave advice in this matter. Usually they warned against hasty decisions. It appears that in a number of cases editorial offices of the main newspapers served as contact points, even though this fact was not always reflected in their columns. However, as a rule, they showed a considerable restraint in the martial question. Despite this, they tried as much as they could to make individual contacts easier.

At the end of the 1950s, Polish artists made their way to Australia. Mieczysław Fogg, enthusiastically greeted by the Polish papers, was the first one to arrive. "No use talking, Mieczysław, you brought us a piece of Poland and may God bless you for this," wrote emotional reviews.[34] Performances by such folk-dance ensembles as *Śląsk* and *Mazowsze,* as well as by Polish theater troupes and symphony orchestras, resounded throughout Polish Australia. These performances were frequently involved in political conflicts and there was no doubt that "the regime ... never sends anybody over here without any control of the Communist party members."[35] Still, guests from Poland were most often met with great hospitality. Performances of Polish artists were usually advertised in newspapers by travel agencies who were organizing these artists' tours in Australia and, later on, related in detail. The more popular artists were interviewed, with their photographs printed. If they visited any small Polish centres, local bulletins wrote about it immediately. Social meetings with visitors from Poland, in as much the same way as their performances, provided an opportunity for contacts with contemporary Poland and its culture.

As films from Poland arrived, the newspapers announced the time when they were to be shown, with the exception of those films organized by agencies of the Warsaw government. Advertisements of films were also published by local bulletins such as *Polak w Newcastle, Biuletyn Polonii w Geelong* or *Biuletyn Organizacyjny Millennium* in Adelaide. In addition, the weekly and fortnightly publications reserved more space for reviews. The newspapers advertised records

---

[34]*Wiadomości Polskie*, November 2, 1958.
[35]*Tygodnik Polski*, June 8, 1963.

and books imported from Poland, but never advertised, for political reasons, the press that was published officially in Poland. In 1950 *Wiadomości Polskie* announced that "the first freight of *wódka wyborowa* from Poland arrived in Sydney."[36] Advertisements of this product appeared many times throughout the entire period in question.

Organized campaigns, mostly by the major papers but also by local bulletins in the support of their countrymen in Poland, were another element maintaining ties with the homeland. They published letters of request and collected money for individual Poles. Such was the case with *Echo-Opowiadania*, whose readers sent drugs to Warsaw to a student ill with tuberculosis.[37] In addition, they also organized relatively large campaigns, especially during political crises after 1956, 1970, 1976 and 1980. The editors set up special benefit funds for Poland to which readers sent offerings which later were transferred to Poland. Both *Wiadomości Polskie* and *Tygodnik Katolicki* organized a wide benefit campaign for the poor and the repatriates in 1957. Money, medicine and shoes were sent overseas to the secretary's office of the Primate of Poland. Following the events of 1970 and 1976 the aid was directed toward the victims and the families of the repressed. The newspapers published lists of donors, appealed for participation in collections and presented accounts of their progress. Nevertheless, as a person collecting in Hobart said, the mount of money collected "would have been many times smaller had we not knocked on and called up houses of Polish families or had we not reminded them that it was I who collected the money.... You could count on your fingers how many people turned to me on their own account."[38] The author blamed the lack of initiative on the fact that these people never or seldom read Polish newspapers.

It is difficult to determine the actual influence of these publications on the Polish emigrants' commitment to the affairs of their country of origin and its scale, expressed at least by the size of the material aid. However, this element of ties with Poland was reflected in the Polish press in Australia in a very explicit way. The newspapers, while heading material aid campaigns for Poles in the homeland and organizing the Polish community in Australia in order to fulfill this objective, acted for the benefit of the community's integration. They drew Polish emigrants closer to Poland's domestic problems and, at least partially, gave patriotic value to their activities, which for some Poles was more substantial than emigré politics.

Religious affairs in Poland were not confined merely to information or comments. The newspapers printed pastoral letters and statements of Polish bishops, especially the sermons and letters of Primate Wyszyński. Many of these were directed specially at Poles in Australia and emphasized not only the religious but also national ties with Polish society in the mother country. Detailed

---

[36]*Wiadomości Polskie*, January 1, 1950.

[37]*Echo-Opowiadania*, No. 5.

[38]*Komunikat Informacyjny Związku Polskiego w Hobart*, November ,1979.

accounts of Polish church leaders' visits and their addresses to their countrymen in Australia played a similar role. A visit of Cardinal Wojtyła and visits of general superiors of the Society of Christ always gave occasion for emphasizing the link between faithfulness to the ancestors' religion and loyalty to the country of origin, its language and culture.

We should also remark that the organ of the Polish Catholic Mission in Australia and New Zealand, *Przegląd Katolicki* [Polish Catholic Review], published a number of texts written in Poland. These texts presented the problems of upbringing and morality, with a strong reference to this situation in contemporary Poland. In this way the paper provided its readers with a knowledge of this sphere of life in Poland, and endorsed certain patterns of behavior which were very different from ones predominant in Australian society.

During the first years of the post-war immigration Polish publications in Australia included texts emphasizing loyalty toward Poland as the principal question. Any connection with the country of settlement was seen as a temporary stage, a stop on the exiles' journey. A motif of returning to liberated Poland emerged at that time as well and should be distinguished from the controversy aroused by the question of returning to the Polish People's Republic after 1956. A paper entitled *Polonia* (a predecessor of *Biuletyn Stowarzyszenia Polaków w Queensland*) was established in 1951 in order, as they wrote, to "give us strength to survive, to accompany us along the way and to lead us intact past the threshold of our homeland."[39] The publicists agreed then that "had it not been for the political situation in post-war Poland, the emigration as a whole, with few exceptions, would come back home, as everyone misses his Homeland equally, except for some of the youngest generation."[40]

At the beginning of the 1950s the international situation encouraged hopes of coming back. In 1950 Tadeusz Naklicki wrote, "Today a new storm is brewing slowly over the world, and as a result of it Poland will regain its independence."[41] But even then there were observers who did not believe that the political changes in Poland desired by Polish emigrants would compel everyone to return. "Many of us will not come back to Poland," stated Jan Hempel, Chairman of the Polish Colony in Brisbane, who appealed for acquiring a strong social standing in Australia.[42] The Polish periodicals took up these problems and discussed such issues as becoming nationalized as Australians or the policy of assimilation. Despite this, hopes of return to Poland and symptoms of dominant loyalty towards Poland kept surfacing in the press throughout the first half of the 1950s. However, the political situation in Poland and the duration of settlement in Australia made even the most patriotic circles change their point of view. In 1955 during the Congress of the Federal Council of Polish Associa-

[39]*Polonia*, November, 1951,

[40]*Nasze Wiadomości*, May, 1949.

[41]*Wiadomości Polskie*, October 8, 1950.

[42]*Tygodnik Polski*, supplement to *The Catholic Leader*, April 17, 1952.

tions in Australia, the ex-Consul General of the Polish Republic in Sydney, Sylwester Gruszka, after an analysis of the international situation, came to the conclusion that "the period of our national misery," and along with it being in exile, "can last far longer than the worst pessimists might have ever assumed. This imposes upon us a duty, first of all, to thoroughly think our situation over..., to seriously revise our objectives and methods of working."[43] A columnist for *Wiadomości Polskie*, Jacek Suski, confirmed this opinion by saying, "We have been hoaxed for quite a long time that we are coming back to Poland tomorrow, the day after tomorrow, in the springtime. Let's mentally unpack our suitcases and live realistically. Let's unite and take root in this soil, we, Polish willows on the Australian Seine. What would be the significance of the Polish Americans, had they lived out of a suitcase [maintaining thoughts of returning to Poland]?"[44]

The issue of coming back to free Poland was put off to the distant and unspecified future and statements on the topic disappeared almost completely. Still, apart from a confrontation with the post-war reality in Poland, which included discussions on trips and cases of coming back to captive Poland—the Polish People's Republic, a motif of happy and complete repatriation kept recurring, manifesting itself in daydreams, memories and poetry. A number of memoirs, poems and occasional articles express one of the most severe experiences of Polish emigrants longing for their homeland, their country of childhood memories. Authors and readers kept trying to return via the pages of the newspapers to well-known landscapes, hometowns, their families and friends. Poems, memoirs and photographs were instrumental in fulfilling this desire. This can be seen in the literary output of Andrzej Chciuk, Zygmunt Przybyłkiewicz, Władysław Romanowski, Andrzej Gawroński and many others. The ideal Poland which they created (which does not mean that all the authors idealized the image of pre-war Poland) was particularly significant for those who refused to come back under the Communist rule, to visit Poland or to have contacts with anything connected with the Communist system. Connections with an ideal, "genuine" Poland gave them strength to refuse to come back to an actual, "falsified" Poland.

Conclusion

The contents of the Polish press in Australia were well adjusted to maintaining ties with Poland on many levels: family, regional (*ojczyzna prywatna*—private homeland) but, above all, with the whole nation and even state (*ojczyzna ideologiczna*—ideological homeland). Naturally, a majority of the newspapers refused to accept the country's Communist character and its dependence upon the U.S.S.R. As the space devoted to Poland shows, the interest of the Polish press

---

[43]*Wiadomości Polskie*, February 26, 1955.
[44]*Wiadomości Polskie*, March 12, 1955.

in Australia in regards to the situation in the homeland did not decrease. On the contrary, it was subject to rises at the end of the period under discussion.

The newspapers provided a channel for the Polish emigrants. They received domestic news and even familiarized themselves with problems, hopes and everyday cares of life in Poland.

The majority of the newspapers not only informed the public of events in Poland and of its international standing but also attempted to shape opinions of the Poles in Australia in the spirit of political emigrés ideology. This approach predominated in organized circles of the Polish community in Australia, with whom disposers of the most important newspapers were connected. The political function of the analyzed press was most evident in the relationship between Polish emigrants in Australia and Poland, more than in the case of their relationship with Australian society or within their own ethnic group.

The opposition to the Communist system in Poland promoted by the majority of the publications integrated Poles in Australia around definite objectives. Although it encompassed only a part of the Polish community, it was supported by the overwhelming majority of organized Polish emigrant groups. Among these objectives assistance for movements fighting for freedom in the homeland came to the forefront in the second half of the 1970s. This trend not only appeared in the major newspapers. Numerous bulletins also collected money for opposition organizations and for those repressed by the Communist authorities in Poland. They also propagated demands of the Polish anti-Communist opposition in Australian society. Such examples dating back to 1956 included political campaigns for the benefit of Poland, manifestations and meetings with Australian politicians. All of this served the purpose of mobilizing the Polish emigrants in Australia and uniting them around a commitment to Poland's affairs. As events progressed from 1976 this commitment grew stronger. Pre-war political divisions, although relatively permanent in exile, slowly gave way to new divisions according to a criterion of one's attitude towards the situation in Poland. Within the framework of opposition to the Communist system a common attitude of supporting the resistance in Poland developed. Editors of the major Polish newspapers made attempts not to get involved with only one opposition group in Poland. Rather, they made efforts to support the whole opposition movement.

Although attitudes toward the Polish People's Republic and its representatives in Australia divided the Polish community, the political ideas of the fight for Poland's freedom provided its *raison d'etre* and united a considerable part of the whole group.[45] These were the most active circles which had publications at their disposal. It is worth mentioning, that attitudes towards Poland, which were expressed in the columns of the periodicals, brought about or intensified the di-

---

[45]Grzegosz Babiński, *Więź etniczna a procesy asymilacji. Przemiany organizacji etnicznych. Zagadnienia teoretyczne i metodologiczne "Prace Polonijne,"* z. 10, p. 44.

visions within the emigrant community. Frequent polemics discouraged readers from committing themselves to any organizational activities. However, it was the reference to the country of origin that was, apart from the Polish language, tradition and culture, a principal plane of meeting for diversified circles and for individuals coming from different periods of emigration from Poland. This tendency grew more evident as the demographic structure of the Polish group in Australia developed with increasing complexity. The duration of emigrants' stay in Australia became more differentiated, while the ties based upon the older generation's common experience (World War II and simultaneous settlement in Australia) could no longer remain the reason for the integration of all Polish emigrants. It should be made clear, however, that the Polish-language press in Australia, throughout the entire period under scrutiny, never ceased to be an emigrant press. Nor was it taken over by the Australians of Polish decent, who infrequently (if ever) could read or write in Polish.[46] This explains why the Polish press did not have any immediate influence upon their ties with their parents' homeland, nor upon their attitudes towards the political situation in Poland.

---

[46]R. Harris and J. Smolicz, *Australijczycy polskiego pochodzenia* (Wrocław, 1984), pp. 100, 106-107.

Mr. Dybek's Neighborhood:
Toward a New Paradigm
for Ethnic Literature

by

Thomas Gladsky[1]

The difficulty of defining, describing, or even locating the ethnic writer appears to grow increasingly more troublesome. Even a casual glance at the introduction to *Ethnic Perspectives in American Literature*[2] reveals the problem. Turf wars, biological insiderism, and questions of definition haunt the essays offered in this 1985 collection of ethnic literary histories. The issue of authenticity, raised most recently in connection with Forrest Carter's *The Education of Little Tree*,[3] continues to complicate matters. In addition, current thinking about ethnic literature continues to be influenced by theoretical models that do not apply evenly to all ethnic groups and historical periods. Daniel Aaron's influential essay "The Hyphenate Writer and American Letters"[4] exemplifies this situation. Reflecting an opinion that had almost become axiomatic by the 1960s, Aaron confidently divides ethnic literature into three stages or phases. He

[1]Thomas Gladsky is Dean of Graduate Studies at Central Missouri State University in Warrensburg, Missouri.
[2]Edward Ifkovic and Robert J. DiPietro, eds., *Ethnic Perspectives in American Literature* (New York, 1985).
[3]Forrest Carter, *The Education of Little Tree.*
[4]Daniel Aaron, "The Hyphenate Writer and American Letters," *Smith Alumnae Quarterly* (July 1964), pp. 213-217.

describes the earliest ethnic writer as a "kind of local colorist," aiming to humanize stereotypes and win sympathy. In stage two, ethnic writers "lash out at the restrictions" and incur the risk of "double criticism.;" In the third stage, according to Aaron, the ethnic writer passes "from the periphery to the center" while continuing to possess a "double vision."[5] As Thomas Ferraro points out, Aaron's paradigm is rooted in the aesthetics of universality and modernism and in a commitment to the notion of literary evolution.[6] Moreover, his model fits only those groups which have a literary history that spans generations and that includes a substantial body of immigrant literature. In the case of cultural groups relatively new to the United States—Caribbean peoples, Southeast Asians, immigrants from the Indian subcontinent, or Euro-ethnics who have not developed a literary voice—this kind of paradigm presents difficulties. So too does the more recent effort of Werner Sollors to discuss literary ethnicity through consent and descent models.[7]

American writers of Polish descent are a case in point. Since the 1830s when Poles began to arrive in measurable numbers, the Polish experience has been chronicled almost exclusively by host-culture writers from Samuel Knapp, Willie Triton, Edith Minitier and Nelson Algren to such recent, influential works as James Michener's *Poland* and William Styron's *Sophie's Choice*.[8] Only since the 1960s have significant numbers of writers of Polish descent turned to their own ethnicity for material; and only recently have writers such as W. S. Kuniczak, Anthony Bukoski, Gary Gildner, Darryl Poniscan, Anne Pellowski, Richard Bankowsky, and Stuart Dybek begun to receive deserved recognition as the literary voice of an American cultural group.[9]

Unfortunately, Sollors' call to move beyond ethnicity—to interpret literary ethnicity through non-inclusive models—tends to diffuse this literary phenomenon. As the first generation ready to record its own ethnic experience, contemporary writers of Polish descent must first make literary history before they can move beyond it. Without a recognizable literary tradition of their own and

---

[5]Carter, p. 214.

[6]Thomas J. Ferraro, "Avante-Garde Ethnics," in William Boelhower, ed., *The Future of American Modernism: Ethnic Writing Between the Wars* (Amsterdam, 1990), p. 18. In this article, Ferraro tries to reconcile modernism and ethnicity by examining Henry Roth and Henry Miller. In the process, he warns that Aaron assumes that modernism and universality are synonymous.

[7]See Werner Sollors, *Beyond Ethnicity* (New York, 1986), p. 198.

[8]Samuel L. Knapp, *The Polish Chiefs* (New York, 1832); Willie Triton, *The Fisher Boy* (Boston, 1857); Edith Minitier, *Our Natupski Neighbors* (New York, 1916); Nelson Algren, *Never Come Morning* (New York, 1942); James Michener, *Poland* (New York, 1983); William Styron, *Sophie's Choice* (New York, 1979).

[9]This is not to say that writers of Polish descent did not exist prior to the 1960s; but the publications of contemporary writers I have named and those included in anthologies such as *Of My Blood* (1980) and John Minczeski, ed., *Concert at Chopin's House* (St. Paul, 1987) indicate that a literary movement may be blossoming.

separated by considerable time and distance from their cultural roots, they must establish ethnic identity even while distancing themselves from it. They must bridge the chasm between modernity and the eccentricities of ethnicity, and they must balance between typicality and atypicality. They must, in addition, characterize both old and new ethnicities and transform the ethnic past, ethnic memories so to speak, into representations of the post-modern self in a trans-ethnic landscape. The literary ethnicity that results in such cases may be disappointing to readers who would look for an ethnic self frozen in images of first-generation transplant or in literary forms associated with the immigrant generation. Readers and scholars alike might also wonder what kind of ethnicity they are encountering, especially one which appears to renounce self-consciousness, cultural ethnocentrism, and traditional ethnic markers.

Although one might "read" a number of current ethnic writers this way, the work of Stuart Dybek represents both the limitations of traditional paradigms of ethnic literature and the special circumstances of the contemporary Euro-ethnic writer who resists such categories. Unlike many of his colleagues, Dybek is rather difficult to classify. Some readers associate him with region; some with issues of social class. A goodly number of the stories in *Childhood and Other Neighborhoods* and *The Coast of Chicago*,[10] his two collections of fiction, have no visible ethnic dimension. Others do. In some ethnicity hovers only along the edges, either in the form of urban trans-ethnicity or in the specific but shadowy outlines of Polishness and Polonia. His reviewers appear reluctant, however, to refer to Dybek's ethnic dimension despite the fact that he has from time to time connected his artistry to his Polish descent[11]; and despite the fact that most of his stories are set in ethnic Chicago neighborhoods where many of the characters have a Polish heritage of some degree or another.

Even so, Dybek's stories can hardly be described as "classic" examples of ethnic fiction. For one thing, the period of immigration has long ago ended for the people in his neighborhood. Consequently, he does not offer examples of assimilation and acculturation or generational conflict; nor are his protagonists defending their Old World heritage, or preserving ethnic rites of passage. For another, Dybek's protagonists—young, urban, outsiders—know little, if anything, about Poland or the cultural nuances of the immigrant generation from which they are descended. Moreover, Dybek ignores traditional cultural markets such as language, foods, religious feasts, folk music, dance, and allusions to Old World history and legend—all of which mark both host-culture literature about

---

[10]Stuart Dybek, *Childhood and Other Neighborhoods* (New York, 1986); Stuart Dybek, *The Coast of Chicago* (New York, 1991).

[11]Interestingly enough, Dybek's reviewers have concentrated on style, noting the grotesque, the bizarre, the fantastical, and the dark in his two collections of short stories, *Childhood and Other Neighborhoods* and *The Coast of Chicago*. Dybek has also been linked to regionalism—a Chicago writer in the style of Nelson Algran, as Howard Kaplan describes him. Dybek admits, in addition, to having more than a passing "interest in class."

Polish Americans as well as the work of earlier descent writers such as Monica Krawczyk, Helen Bristol and Victoria Janda. In what sense then, one might ask, does Dybek draw upon his ethnic roots and how does he represent the ethnicity of Americans far removed from their native grounds? What kind of ethnic literature is Dybek writing, if in fact we may even call it ethnic?

To begin to answer these questions, we must first recognize that as a contemporary writer of Polish descent, Dybek does not fit into the particular stages described by Aaron as appropriate to, let us say, Jewish American writers. On the contrary, Dybek operates on all three stages simultaneously. In other words, he must, of necessity, function as a local colorist, as a critic of both the ethnic experience and the mainstream culture, and as a writer who manages to stand one foot within the mainstream, the other on its edge.

To be sure, in Dybek's fiction ethnicity is a distinct and recognizable presence, in part because he supplies enough cultural details to establish particularity. On one level, he is a local colorist-information giver. For example, his characters have names like Swantek, Marzek, Vukovich, Kozak, and Gowumpe. Even those with Anglo names have a Polish frame of reference: grandmothers named Busha, churches names St. Stanislaus. Relatives call soup *zupa*; the neighbors listen to the *Frankie Yankovitch Polka Hour*; passers-by stammer in foreign-sounding English. In a few stories, Dybek "introduces" the Polish experience in ways similar to host-culture writers like Edna Ferber, Karl Harriman, and Russell Janney.[12] For example, in "Chopin in Winter," Dzia Dzia tells his young grandson about the music and life of Chopin and his own trek from Kraków to Gdańsk to avoid being drafted into the Tsarist army, and in "Blood Soup," Dybek builds his story around peasant cuisine, mysticism, and old country temperament.[13] In virtually all his stories, Dybek artfully introduces some aspects of Polish culture even in those ostensibly about non-ethnic concerns. Here and there we run into *mazurkas*, Polish diminutives, Paderewski, Our Lady of Częstochowa, *babushkas*, and DPs, the standard reference for Old World Poles. Yet neither his characters nor narrators refer to themselves as Polish or Polish American. Polishness is understood and assumed; ethnicity, to paraphrase Carlos Bulosan, is in the heart,[14] as Dybek implies that the post-modern ethnic self needs few labels and little or not introduction.

If anything, Dybek shows a generation resisting its ethnic impulses even as it rushes toward them. In one sense his young protagonists are not ethnic at all but modernists who, like Stephen Daedalus or Prufrock, wander city streets con-

---

[12]See, for example, Edna Ferber, *American Beauty* (New York, 1931); Karl Harriman, *The Homebuilders* (New York?, 1903); Russell Janney, *The Miracle of the Bells* (New York, 1946). All of these rely heavily on peasant folklore, stereotypical cultural characteristics, and the icons of Polish legend and history.

[13]See Dybek, "Chopin in Winter" and "Blood Soup."

[14]See Carlos Bulosan's autobiography, *America is in the Heart* (Seattle, 1943). Bulosan talks about America in metaphysical terms as a state of mind to immigrants and even the icons of Polish legend and history.

tent with their own alienation and superior to the urban bight and social chaos that surround them. They are loners, eccentrics, budding intellectuals. They have no conscious sense of themselves as Polish American or as ethnic. They are consumed instead with adolescence, environment, friends, with life in deteriorating and charging southside Chicago. They prefer Kerouac, the White Sox, Edward Hopper and rock music to Sigismund, Silesia, and *szczowiowa*. Dybek best captures their state of mind in their rejection of Polish mysticism and parochial education. Frequently, he gives us post-adolescents turning their backs on the religion of their ancestors. The narrator in "The Woman Who Fainted" complains that "Perhaps I had already attended too many masses ... and had come to resent the suffering, death, and, even more, the fear underlying religion."[15] In "Visions of Budhardin," the protagonist, in a rage of pent-up resentment, ravages the church which so callously ignored his childhood needs. But Marzek, in "Sauerkraut Soup," speaks for all Dybek's disillusioned Polish Catholics when he says: "I had already developed my basic principle of Catholic education—the Double Reverse: *(1) suspect what they teach you; (2) study what they condemn.*"[16] Marzek's statement serves not only as an indicator of protest and revolt, but also as a sign of the distance between the ethnicity of his generation and that of his immigrant ancestors who, "dressed in black coats and babushkas ... sustained the intensity of their grief."[17] In this fashion Dybek functions as a critic of the perceived provinciality of his ethnic Chicago neighborhood.

Dybek's young ethnics are not happy. They thrive on melancholy, feast on loneliness, inhabit the "hourless times of night."[18] They are refugees from Edward Hooper's *Nighthawks.*[19] At the same time, they are acutely aware that they ache for something they cannot name "but knew was missing," as the narrator of "The River" phrases it; and that "things are gone they couldn't remember, but missed; and things were gone they weren't sure ever were there."[20] In part theirs is a remembrance of youthful things past. Dybek also implies, however, that this loss also involves the cultural past. For one thing, a reverential relationship between Old World Poles and their ethnic grandchildren occurs frequently in the stories. In "Blood Soup," "Chopin in Winter," and "The Apprentice," youngsters listen to, observe, attend to and assimilate cultural mores. As the title of "The Apprentice" implies, Stefan is initiated into grandfather's sense of history, displacement, fatalism, and the strangeness that defines the Polish temperament in Dybek's fiction. For another, Dybek continually laments the disappearance of the Polish southside. As the narrator of "Blight" phrases it, "I was back in my neighborhood, but lost."[21]

[15]Dybek, *Chicago*, p. 120.
[16]Dybek, *Childhood*, p. 127.
[17]Dybek, *Chicago*, pp. 154-155.
[18]*Ibid.*, p. 84.
[19]Edward Hopper, *Nighthawks.*
[20]Dybek, *Chicago*, p. 25.
[21]*Ibid.*, p. 71.

Ethnicity is complex, pervasive, and dynamic in these stories. The neighborhood defies traditional national boundaries. In "The River," a Ukrainian kid fiddles a nocturne. The girl in "Laughter" is Greek. The upstairs neighbors in "Chopin in Winter" speak Czech. The eccentric teacher in "Farwell" comes from Odessa. Chicanos are almost as prevalent as Poles. The multi-cultural society that surfaces is, in fact, trans-ethnicity in the making. Dybek's protagonists are not Poles; they are not even Polish American by traditional definition. To paraphrase Michael Fischer, they have, paradoxically reinvented and reinterpreted themselves.[22] Theirs is a new identity—in part a fusion of consent and descent perfectly captures in a conversation between Dzia Dzia and his grandson in "Chopin in Winter." Grandfather is teaching the boy about the music of Chopin and mentions that Paderewski dearly loved Chopin. The boy, however, does not know Paderewski, a sign of his distance from his cultural heritage. Instinctively, Grandfather connects their dual heritages by asking, "Do you know who's George Washington, who's Joe Dimaggio, who's Walt Disney? ... Paderewski was like them, except he played Chopin.... See, deep down inside, Lefty, you know more than you think."[23]

Lefty and all of Dybek's protagonists do indeed know more than they think. They know that ethnicity in America never stands still; that Polishness differs from generation to generation, and that when all is said and done "what they are" does not really matter in terms of the past. On a number of occasions Dybek looks at the new urban ethnic who accepts ethnicity while rejecting nationality. In "Hot Ice," for example, Eddie Kapusta arrives at this insight: "Most everything from that world had changed or disappeared, but the old women had endured—Polish, Bohemian, Spanish, he knew it didn't matter; they were the same ... a common pain of loss seemed to burn at the core of their lives."[24] And in the same story, Eddie further discounts the significance of national origins when he admits to himself, "Manny could be talking Spanish; I could be talking Polish.... It didn't matter. What meant something was sitting at the table together."[25]

In Dybek's fiction Chicanos and Americans of Polish descent often "sit at the table together": Ray Cruz and the narrator in "The Palatski Man," Eddie Kapusta, Manny, and Pancho in "Hot Ice," Ziggy, Pepper Rosado and the narrator in "Blight." The commingling of Latino and Slav is economic and sociological more than cultural—a product of shifting urban people and resulting neighborhood changes, the result of shared environment and social class. From this a new sense of ethnicity—an emblem of contemporary America—arises. On the surface, the new ethnicity appears to be nothing more than the camaraderie of friends thrown together by demographics. In reality, the union of Pole and Chicano represents the changing face of America and of Polish Americanness.

---

[22]See Werner Sollors, *The Invention of Ethnicity* (New York, 1989), p. xi.
[23]Dybek, *Chicago*, pp. 20-21.
[24]*Ibid.*, p. 154.
[25]*Ibid.*, p. 151.

Stanley Rosado is Pepper to some and Stashu to others, reflecting his Mexican father and Polish mother. When David, the descendant of Poles, goes to a bar with a friend, he drinks a Coco-Nana rather than vodka or *piwo* [beer]. The Mexican music on the jukebox sounds "suspiciously like polkas." David now listens to *"CuCuRuCuCu Palona"* on the radio, and Eddie Kapusta sings in Spanish. Tellingly, Eddie identifies more with Spanish than he does with the Polish language. He is stuck with the word *juilota* pigeon. It seems the perfect word because in it "he could hear both their cooing and the whistling rush of their wings." Equally telling, Eddie cannot remember "any words like that in Polish, which his grandma had spoken to him when he was little."[26] Eddie's relatives may likely turn out to be Hispanic in the sense that Richard Rodriguez, in *Hunger and Memory*, believes that he may become Asian.[27]

The Polish ethnic self, also addressed recently by Gary Gildner in *The Warsaw Sparks*,[28] assumes what some may regard as a strange identity. And Dybek emerges as a writer who eludes and absorbs traditional paradigms while suggesting a new one. To be sure, he does write about an identifiable ethnic group, supplying the preciousness of local color among the way. He is, at the same time, eager to resist the parochialism of ethnicity. His characterization of his young protagonists as romantic rebels, updated versions of Keats, Proust, Dosteyevsky and others whom they read, also leads him away from ethnic realism even though his fiction is rooted in region and in the cultural neighborhoods of southside Chicago. Without consciously trying, Dybek encompasses all three of Aaron's stages, functioning as a spokesperson for all generations of Americans of Polish descent and producing a multi-layered and multi-dimensional ethnic self. This self reflects the image of a trans-ethnic transcends national origins but remains vital and where the ethnic and the modern self are not only compatible as Ferraro would argue, but are the essence of post-modernism and "a way of being American," as Andrew Greeley puts it.[29]

---

[26]*Ibid.*, p. 136.

[27]Richard Rodriguez, *Hunger of Memory* (Boston, 1982). Rodriguez speculates at one point about the course of American demographics and applies the changing cultural face of the nation to his own situation. He wonders if his presence is an Asian community might not naturally and inevitably lead to Asian descendants.

[28]Gary Gildner, *The Warsaw Sparks* (Iowa City, 1990).

[29]Andrew Greeley, "Is Ethnicity Unamerican?" *New Catholic World,* Vol. 219 (June 1976), pp. 106-112. Greeley disposes of the notion that ethnicity is "unamerican," arguing instead that ethnicity as Americanness is a "critically important phenomenon" (p. 111).

Johann Stanislaus Kubary:
A Polish Ethnographer's Adventures and Contributions in the 19th Century Pacific

by

Dirk Anthony Ballendorf[1]

The traditional native monetary system for Palau is unique in Micronesia. Except for Yap, where large aragonite stone discs, as well as shells and other kinds of valuables, are used for money, Palau's is the most highly developed and complex monetary system. The money itself consists of polychrome and clear glass beads, crescentic and prismatic bar gorgets, and beads of pottery. All these are generically called *udoud*. The ceramic and glass prismatic pieces are called *ba'al*, and the bead-like pieces are called *bleob*. Ceramic *udoud* are found in yellow, red or orange varieties; the glass beads come in a wide variety of colors and degrees of transparency. All *udoud* feature a hole through which a string or cord can be passed. All are of foreign origin. Palauan money today remains a very important part of the society. It continues to be used for traditional social purposes and increasingly is worn for status purposes by contemporary Palauan women. But the origins of the money, and how its usage evolved, is largely forgotten or unknown by most Palauans, especially younger people whose family might not possess any. It is important then to shed light on the money, and

---

[1]Dirk Anthony Ballendorf is Professor of History and Micronesian Studies at the University of Guam's Micronesian Area Research Center. Palauan words and names have been Anglicized for convenience.

its "culture-history place" in Palau.

The German-Polish ethnographer and naturalist Johann Stanislaus Kubary was the first European to seriously investigate the origins and usage of the Paluan money and report on it in the late nineteenth century. While most monographs on this period in Micronesia assign this competent and dedicated scholar some mention in their bibliographies, reading much of his reportage leaves one with the feeling that some contemporary researchers have little more than a secondary knowledge of Kubary's contributions. Of course, for English-speaking scholars, it must be remembered that he wrote in German and Polish, and many of his contributions and brief biographies are found in obscure publications tucked away in the archives of German museums. Kubary, however, was not dull. He was a dedicated scholar, an adventurer, and finally a tragic figure.

Johann Stanislaus Kubary was born in Warsaw in 1846 of a German mother and a Hungarian father. His father died early, his mother remarried, and so he was reared in the home of his Polish stepfather. Following a troubled childhood, Kubary began to study medicine at the age of seventeen. However, his youthful enthusiasm got him involved in agitation for Polish independence, and after several bouts with the authorities, he fled from Poland to Hamburg where he soon became stranded without support and had to seek work by his wits. Through the good offices of one J. D. S. Schmeltz, a man important in museum circles, he was introduced to Johann Godeffroy, one of the most prominent and wealthy shippers of his day, and whose company was the parent of today's great *Hamburg Sued Line*.

Herr Godeffroy, whose Pacific offices were in Samoa, had a passion for ethnography and artifact collecting. The young, scientifically-inclined Kubary was eager to work for Godeffroy, and so it came to pass that at age twenty-two he found himself bound for the south seas where he was to serve as a collector for the Godeffroy Museum and an amasser of information for the *Journal des Museum Godeffroy*. From 1870 to 1874 Kubary did extensive field work throughout Micronesia; however, he is not remembered commensurate with his contributions. In his book, *The Caroline Islands* the Englishman F. W. Christian paid Kubary, who was his friend, hard-earned tribute:

> Those who would do work in Micronesian waters might well take exam-
> ple from the unobtrusive, painstaking work of this true man of science
> ... pushed aside into unknown oblivion.[2]

But posterity has not seen fit thus far to enlarge upon Christian's succinct eulogy. William Lessa provides a neat capsule of Kubary's work in an extensive survey he made of fragmentary accounts of pre-Kubary Micronesia, while John Fischer's well-known work, *The Eastern Carolines*, does not even include Kubary in the bibliography.[3]

---

[2]F. W. Christian, *The Caroline Islands* (London, 1899).
[3]John L. Fischer, *The Eastern Carolines* (New Haven, CT, 1957).

Palauans, and those who study Palau, will be more appreciative of Kubary as time passes, for his lucid and careful descriptions of the origin and usage of the Palauan *udoud*. Kubary discusses Paulauan money at length in two separate articles. The first is "Die Palau-Inseln in der Suedsee" [The Palau Islands in the South Seas] in the *Journal der Museum Godeffroy* (Hamburg, 1873), where Palauan money is discussed under the heading "The Palauan Money."[4] Later, in a collection of five articles published in Leiden between 1889-95, the first article, entitled: "Concerning the Indigenous Money of the Island of Yap and the Palau Islands," Kubary treats Palauan money at greater length.[5]

Palauan Legends

Kubary presents four legends of how Palauans traditionally accounted for the origins of their money. These legends are interesting and short enough to be considered here in some detail.

The legends claim the money was brought into Palau at four different places: Ngkeklau village (in Ngaraard) on the northeast coast of Babelthuap; Ngcheangel (Kayangel) Atoll; Ngeaur (Angaur) Island, and the peninsula of Ngerechelong at the northern end of Babelthuap. The longest legend concerns Ngear and is given first.

A starling came from Neursar hamlet in Airai to Keklau and drank water from the knothole of a bars tree. It became pregnant and bore a small fish that remained in a water pouch in the bark of the tree until the people found it. Someone took it home in a shell, where it grew so quickly that, as a result it had to be placed in even larger shells until it occupied a large tridacna shell; it finally had to be put out to sea as a young sea bass. The dukel, (a large trigger fish) was its spouse, and the large sea bass that bore an entire country, Norot, on its back, from which it took its name, went to Angaur, where it bore a young girl. The child was named Ardirgun, and she went ashore and played with the children of the island, where she was invited into the residence of Werbelau. During the day the strange child played ashore, but went to the beach in the evening to go out to sea with her mother. But, since the people had grown to love her, they wanted to keep her. With her mother's permission, Ardirgun remained in the family or Werbelau until she became a woman. She grew so quickly and became so large, just as her mother had earlier in Keklau, that soon people were disgusted by her, so they built a separate house for her and threw food to her.

[4]Johann Stanislaus Kubary, "Die Palau-Inseln in der Suedsee," *Journal der Museum Godeffroy* (Hamburg, 1873).

[5]Johann Stanislaus Kubary, "Uber des Einheimische Geld auf der Insel Yap und auf den Palau Inseln," *Ethnographische Beitraege zur Kenntnis des Karolinen Archipels* (Leiden, Holland, 1880). Translation by M.L. Berg.

This treatment grieved the woman, and she complained to mother of her sorrow, who advised her to leave Angaur. Ardirgun took her leave from her stepparents saying, "I am pregnant. If you cared about me until my time, all my insides would be money and this would have been your property. Since it has turned out differently, you shall have only this much." At this she scratched her thick fingers and genuine Palauan money fell onto the ground. Afterwards, the woman left and disappeared into the ocean with her mother.[6]

This was how the family of Werbelau, the Matelkou, had become the richest in Palau at an early period.

The second legend concerns Keklau, and is regarded as the most authoritative and the earliest of the four:

The fish mentioned, as said above, carried on its back the land of Nrot, whose shore was covered with genuine Palauan money. In the same place lived the daughter and many redshank birds who were her children. One of these, known by the name of Adalrok, visited Palau and came to Keklau, the home of its grandmother. Here it began to break a piece of *udoud* with its beak. The woman of the house, Narueleu, saw it, and when her son just returning from shark fishing addressed Adalrok, it announced its death and bid him look into its beak in which money would be found. In all, Keklau obtained seventy pieces, all yellow money, and the family of Narueleu was the second wealthiest in Palau. Later the family grew poor, and the money went over to the family Karman in the same region.[7]

In the 1873 article, Kubary mentions that the family of Karman still had the largest *barak*, called *adaltal a barak* (which means "mother of barak") which was of an indeterminately great value" in the 1880s.[8] The third legend concerns Kayangel and its chief, Deor:

Deor, chief of Kayangel, went fishing with his son, and reaching the Kossol reef, fastened his canoe to a coral block, that was really a quill of the dorsal fin of the dukel fish, the spouse of the atomagay fish. While the father slept, the dukel carried the canoe to the land of Nrot where the son awoke, disturbed by the rustling of the canoe on the beach. He went ashore, gathered a basket full of the brightly colored stones on the beach and threw them at the numerous redshanks, so that only a few remained in the basket. When the father awoke they found themselves again at the former place, and the father took the rest of the stones, which proved to be *udoud*.[9]

---

[6]*Ibid.*
[7]*Ibid.*
[8]Kubary, "Die Palau-Inseln."
[9]Kubary, "Uber des Einheimische Geld."

The last and shortest legend deals with a woman from Araka long:

> [Another story has it that] Arakalong also obtained its money from
> an unknown country. The wife of the Iratey (Uong era Etei, the chief of
> Mengellang village) was put on the reef because of her quarrelsomeness;
> here she was saved by a sea snake and taken by it to a country from
> which she returned with *udoud*.[10]

Palau and Yap

All these legends acknowledge that the origin of Palauan money was outside
of Palau. While Palauans in the 1870s and 1880s still believed in an island
swimming about freely in the ocean dispensing money, Kubary tried to connect
the source of the money with other islands in the region and with southeastern
Asia. People in Yap said Palauan money was used and known before the large
aragonite discs came into fashion; many pieces of it are found in Yap even today,
some with holes drilled for threads, some not. Kubary knew first hand that the
Yapese took such pieces to Palau to exchange for Palauan articles. Another circumstance connecting Palau and Yap was that Keklau was founded by the Yapese
and was the home of Palauan money inside Palau.

But it is Kubary's contention that, although the Yapese played an important
role in Palau at an early time (including the founding of the *Idid* clan of Koror,
from which the *Ibedul* is chosen), the societies had grown so different by the late
nineteenth century that they had little in common besides names of people and
places.

It was more probable, Kubary thought, that the people who had introduced
the money to Yap and Palau came from someplace else, and settled in both
places and elsewhere. The Yapese claimed they had come from the north. Judging by the materials used to make the pieces of money—clay, glass, imitation
pearls, and porcelain—Kubary surmised the origin of the materials could not be
the Carolines, but only a place with well-developed porcelain and glass industries; those were only found in Asia. In concluding his article on Yapese and
Palauan money, he stated his belief that the materials had been brought by proto-
Malayan peoples to the Western Carolines:

> However, the principals of Palauan political, district and economic
> life bear the ur-Malayan [*sic*] character, as described in the writings on
> the old Menangkabau on Sumatra, and many savage Malayan tribes of the
> Malay Archipelago. The *udoud*, on emanation from the Malayan culture,
> came from the west with the bearers of this culture; that the *udoud* could
> have been brought from Malaya can be grasped if one considers that the
> people paid their fines to the chieftains in the form of large Chinese

---

[10]*Ibid.*

plates; that on Celebes, a few tribes most carefully treasure ageless vessels as sacred legacies from their ancestors; and finally, that most of the islands traded with the Chinese, from whom they learned about quite early, and exchanged for porcelain goods.[11]

This reference of Kubary's is partially, or circumstantially validated by the fact that the German naturalist Karl Semper had noticed the reverence Palauans paid to such legacies when he was in Palau in 1862 and 1863.

Organization of Palauan Money

Subsequently, Kubary discourses on the economy, distribution and usage of the money:

> The amount of money is restricted; there can be no more than the gods gave during their time. There are pieces of similar worth, but there are none exactly identical. The worth of the smaller pieces is fixed by custom; for the larger pieces, the worth is essentially arbitrary and depends on the assessment of the possessor.[12]

Kubary divides Palauan money into three groups: (1) those made of porcelain-like materials or fired clay (subgroups are yellow money: *barak* and red money: *bunau*; (2) those made of artificial pearls (subgroups are *kalebukeb*, *kluk* and *adolobok* and, (3) those made of glass (subgroups are transparent *kaldoyok* opaque and those inlaid with enamel.

The unit of value for the smaller money pieces was ten baskets of *taro*, "approximately sixty small roots or thirty to forty large ones." The unit was known as *mor a kaymo* [literally, "go to ten"]. The next unit of value was the *honiakel* or *matal adolobok* worth twice the first; *adolobok* followed and was the sum of the first two, then came *matal a kluk* worth the first and third together. The last four units were: *kluk*, or the sum of *matal a kluk* and *adolobok*; *eket a kelkul*, worth from one to two *kluk*; *kalebukeb*, up to five *kluk*; and *eket a kalbakabil*, more than a *kalebukub*.

The lowest two units were used to buy *taro*, coconut oil, coconut syrup, and tobacco. The third class was used for buying sails. In many cases, however, the money paid or given was determined by the rank of the buyer or giver. The upper three classes were too valuable to exchange and were guarded.

Frequently, people would have to borrow money on which they would have to pay interest. There are several examples of the interest to be paid. To borrow an *adolobok*, a *matal a adolobok* or *honiakel* of almost identical worth given as interest. To borrow a *kluk*, a *matal a kluk* had to be given as security and an

---

[11]*Ibid.*
[12]*Ibid.*

adolobok in interest; for a *kalebukeb an eket* a *kelkul* had to be given as security and a *kluk* paid as interest.

In addition to these recognized features bearing on the interest charged, pieces often had to be exchanged for other pieces required on several occasions or for various exchanges. Such money changing transactions became quite complicated since money would have to be paid for each of several different considerations involved in the deal. Kubary lists four considerations to be paid for in the exchange of a *kluk*: (1) "propitiation for the feeling" of the money; (2) the body of the money; (3) the money received in exchange; and (4) the transfer fee. As the value and class of money increased, so did the number of considerations to be paid. Kubary himself once exchanged a *barak* with the chief of Melekeok, the *Reklai*, for which the chief gave him six lesser pieces. According to Kubary, he only received half of what value he had coming, but he realized that:

> since I am a stranger and a friend of the chief as well, it was proper. Yes the chief could be said to be liberal. It is easy to realize that business carried out with this money is quite difficult, and since all relationships in life are regulated by this means and it is only in the hands of the important people, it is easy to reach a conclusion about a later investigation of the Palauan objects.[13]

Kubary used a comparison of life in the western Carolines with life in the eastern Carolines to point up the pervasive influence of Palauan money.

> Considering the economic institution of Palauans, one clearly sees that its complete, rounded development has to thank the presence of the *udoud*; one cannot even imagine this development without the *udoud*. This is best shown by the economic condition of the eastern peoples of the Carolines, who, although they have close kinship descent ties with the Palauans, and found their social institutions on entirely similar basic concepts, but lack the *udoud*, have formed an entirely different and unprofitable one.[14]

In the article "Das Palau-Geld," Kubary runs through a miscellaneous list of uses for this money. They are payments for the help of a deity in battle; fines for crimes; repealing a death sentence; the support of village chieftains if you had too wait too long for a title and wanted to kill your brother (these chieftains say *kabom!*—"go to it!"—many chiefs and chieftains got titles this way); restoring friendship with a friend; or marital sex ("a man has to pay his wife for each hug").[15]

---

[13]*Ibid.*

[14]*Ibid.*

[15]Johann Stanislaus Kubary, "Das Palau Geld," *Journal des Museum Godeffroy* (Hamburg, 1873). Translation by M.L. Berg.

On an earlier page in the same article, Kubary gives an accurate summary statement of the dominance of Palauan money:

> *Udoud* means everything here; there is no other wealth to compare with it. Even our goods, which universally play the major role among uncivilized peoples, are here not regarded as highly. The wealth of an islander is a state is solely determined by the possession of this money. The money of a family consists of money that the head of the family personally possesses. There is a privilege of the heads throughout the country. There is also a state treasury used for military defeats and politics. Personal wealth is the collective possession of a whole family, never of a single person.[16]

Palauan culture, of course, is quite complicated, and with many anomalies woven through its fabric. The precision with which Kubary recorded the values and protocols of *udoud*, might be more reflective of his European penchant for structure and exactness, than it was for the ambiguities of Palauan culture, society and personality. However, this should not minimize his contributions and recordings, but merely be a factor in their interpretations. The work of Johann Stanislaus Kubary is very important to Palauans and all who are interested in the history of the Carolines. He provided great insights into the Palauan society and culture of his time and as he saw it.

His own life and adventures, after his discourses on the Palauan *udoud*, are intrinsically interesting. As is the case today, it was always a narrowly-interested few who paid charmed and enthused attention to the Caroline Islands. Once, in 1874, aboard a homeward-bound Godeffroy ship with reportedly one hundred barrels of carefully-packed specimens—which undoubtedly included a number of valued specimens of Palauan *udoud*—Kubary was shipwrecked near Jaluit in the Marshalls and arrived finally in Hamburg with only a small portion of his irreplaceable collection intact. Herr Godeffroy, however, was quite enthusiastic over the remnants; and since Kubary was still *persona non grata* in Poland, the merchant hastily sent him back to the Pacific with his guarantee of unlimited support. This small amount of *udoud* Kubary brought back to Germany is today in the collections of the *Museum fuer Volkerkunde* in Leipzig, Germany.

Later Life

In 1875 Kubary went to the eastern Carolines and established himself at Pohnpei where he purchased land and established some botanical gardens which were also one of his loves. There he met and married a beautiful Pohnpeian woman who bore him a son and a daughter, and who was to be his faithful com-

---

[16]*Ibid.*

panion in his worldwide wanderings. With Godeffroy's mandate of support in mind, Kubary went off to investigate Nukuoro, Satawan, and Truk—where he lived for over a year—when he received an abrupt notice that Godeffroy had gone bankrupt, and hence his services would no longer be needed. The Franco-Prussian War had intervened in Europe, and was the ruin of the Godeffroy Company; both Kubary and the Museum were casualties. In the months which followed his abandonment by Godeffroy, he mortgaged his holdings on Pohnpei and went to Japan where he made an ill-fated attempt to start a museum in Tokyo. From there he returned to Palau where he sought to start a collection under the auspices of a private museum in Leiden, but this also fell through. Then, for a brief time, he undertook artifact collecting for the *Museum fuer Volkerkunde* in Berlin which sponsored him to Yap, Sonsorol and Merir islands. After that support ended he was again without backing.

Kubary's Death

Discouraged and depressed, Kubary withdrew from his scientific work and took employment as an interpreter on a German warship cruising the Pacific. At New Guinea he and his family disembarked and he got a job as a shopkeeper for a German trading company. Finally, in 1895, Kubary returned to Pohnpei with his family. But, again there was dejection and tragedy. His only son died of a fever and was buried in his beloved botanical gardens. These were subsequently destroyed by fire which resulted from a naval bombardment by the Spanish against some Pohnpeian rebels. Not long afterwards Kubary took his own life.

Kubary's land on Pohnpei eventually passed into the hands of the Etscheit family who still holds some of it today. Kubary's European peers, shortly after his death, erected a small monument to him at Pohnpei which also still stands, slightly dissolute, in the ruins of the old Spanish fort at Kolonia.

Conclusion

In all, Kubary spent twenty-six years in the Pacific, most of them in Micronesia. In addition to his vast collections and manuscripts, he authored several basic ethnographic reports, all of which have found their way into various other reportive and interpretive publications in more than a dozen languages and spanning almost a century. His writings on the Palauan *udoud* and on many other ethnographic and historical matters remain a basis for our knowledge of late nineteenth century Micronesia. Nothing can replace or deprecate Kubary's painstaking efforts at collecting and participating and finally by following through and recording much of what he had seen experienced. F. W. Christian's eulogy is fitting:

Such men as Kubary during their lives receive scant thanks, but their praise should be a grateful duty duty to all who admire pluck and enterprise.[17]

---

[17]Christian, *Caroline Islands.*

Part II

Essays on the Effects of
Government Policy on
Polish Immigrants
in the United States

The Effects of U.S. Government Policy on Polish Americans, 1900-1925

by

James S. Pula[1]

The years between 1900 and 1920 are usually referred to as the Progressive Era, a time when a coalition of political reform groups advocated a variety of changes they thought would make America a better place to live. For Polonia, however, the Progressive Era brought a growing nativist movement that resulted in the United States government sanctioning the development of an ugly and degrading ethnic stereotype and the closing of America's shores to further immigration, moves that still cast their shadow on Polish Americans in the 1990s.

Prior to the American Civil War, Poland and the Poles in the United States generally enjoyed a positive status in the minds of most Americans. The images of Kościuszko and Pułaski fighting for American independence were well-known and Americans generally sympathized with and supported the Poles during the November Uprising in 1830-31. Polish music was in vogue in society, and Polish themes often appeared on the stage or in publications such as Jane Porter's *Thaddeus of Warsaw*.

[1]James S. Pula is Editor of *Polish American Studies*, the journal of the Polish American Historical Association, and a member of the Boards of Directors of that organization and the Polish Institute of Arts and Sciences of America.

Between 1880 and 1910, rapid population increases in American cities led t growing popular fears of rising crime rates, the evils of city bossism, increase congestion, and decreasing standards of living. Coming as they did during a perio of steadily increasing immigration, Americans began to view the influx of "foreigners" as one cause for their rising fears and to question whether the natio could continue to welcome all who wished to enter.

Designed to at once increase and influence public awareness, articles began t appear in the popular press arguing for an end to unrestricted immigration. By th turn of the century the "Progressives" were joined by the American Federation of Labor and various Nativist groups in demanding a literacy test for immigrants as means of limiting both their number and type. By 1906, continued lobbying et forts by the Immigration Restriction League and the American Federation of Labc brought the issue of immigration to the fore in Congress once again, resulting i the establishment of a government commission to study the entire immigratio question. Thus was born the United States Immigration Commission, which em ployed a staff of more that 300 people for over three years, spent in excess of million dollars, and accumulated a mass of data and conclusions that it publishe in forty-two volumes. The Commission's findings supported the prevailing preju dices of the proponents of restriction, officially declaring for the first time tha there was a fundamental qualitative difference between immigrants from Souther and Eastern Europe and those groups from Northern and Western Europe. Restric tion of the former, it concluded, was "demanded by economic, moral, and socia conditions."[2]

The United States Immigration Commission was organized in April, 1907. included three Senators, three Representatives and three special experts. The fir: six positions were quickly filled by the appointment of members of the Senate an House Committees on Immigration, selections which left little doubt that ther would be a distinctly restrictionist bias among the Congressional members of th Commission. From the House of Representatives came Benjamin F. Howel John L. Burnett, and William S. Bennet. Of the three, both Howell and Burne were on record as favoring the restriction of immigration. Bennet, while not vocal anti-restrictionist, could be considered as sympathetic to the problems an concerns of immigrants and thus could be viewed as a friend by the anti-restrictio ists.

The Senate's contribution to the Commission was even more weighted i favor of restrictionism than that of the House. Asbury C. Latimer was an avowe opponent of immigration. Among the first actions which he took as a Commi: sion member was the appointment of James H. Patten, an activist in the Immigra tion Restriction League.[3] Joining Latimer, and serving as chair of the Commi: sion, was William P. Dillingham of Vermont whom historian John Higham cha

---

[2]Robert A. Divine, *American Immigration Policy 1924-1952* (New Haven, CT: 1957), p. 14.

[3]Barbara Miller Solomon, Ancestors and Immigrants (Cambridge, MA: 1956), p. 197.

acterized as a "moderate restrictionist." The Commission chairman was already on record as favoring the restriction of European immigration through the use of the literacy test and a quota system. It was Dillingham, in fact, who proposed establishing a maximum annual immigration quota, and supplementing this with separate nationality quotas.[4]

The real power and direction behind the Commission lay with its remaining Senate appointee, Henry Cabot Lodge. As a freshman Congressman in 1888, he was already concerned about the rising tide of European immigration. A founding member of the Immigration Restriction League, he sponsored a literacy bill in the Senate in 1895 and defended his action in an impassioned speech in the following year.[5] At a time when Progressivism stirred the minds of political reformers, Lodge voted against the direct election of United States Senators and opposed women's suffrage and other political reforms. As an author, his writings were as tainted by his political and social philosophies as were his activities in favor of immigration restriction and his subsequent actions on the Immigration Commission.[6]

To complete the Commission, the three "special experts" were appointed by President Theodore Roosevelt as representatives of the executive branch of government. Roosevelt, who had already proclaimed himself to be a strong advocate of immigration restriction, spoke in his correspondence and his messages to Congress of his uneasiness at the influx of "foreigners" into the country.[7] This same attitude was apparent in Roosevelt's selection of the "special experts."[8] He appointed William R. Wheeler, Charles P. Neill, and Jeremiah W. Jenks. Wheeler, an Assistant Secretary of Commerce and Labor, had been active in the anti-Japanese movement in San Francisco.[9] Neill, the Commissioner of Labor, subscribed to the general anti-immigration beliefs of organized labor.[10] Jeremiah Jenks was a professor at Cornell University where he argued for immigration restriction based on the belief that there were innate racial differences which permanently separated national groups.[11]

When viewed together, the nine members of the Commission charged with investigating the impact of immigration on the United States included eight avowed restrictionists and only one person who might be considered moderately anti-restrictionist. This bias quickly became evident in the Commission's selection

---

[4]John Higham, *Strangers in the Land: Patterns of American Nativism, 1860-1925* (New York: 1970), p. 310; *Dictionary of American Biography*, p. 310.

[5]Solomon, p. 118; Higham, p. 96.

[6]*Dictionary of American Biography*, pp. 347-348.

[7]Prescott Hall, "The Recent History of Immigration and Immigration Restriction," *Journal of Political Economy*, Vol. XXI (1913), p. 737.

[8]Oscar Handlin, *Race and Nationality in American Life* (Boston: 1957), p. 101.

[9]*Ibid.*, p. 105.

[10]Hall, p. 736.

[11]Handlin, pp. 101, 108.

of key staff members and in the methodology it employed in its investigations
When, for example, it examined the impact of immigration on labor, a subjec
dear to the collective heart of the American Federation of Labor, the preconceive
stereotype was that immigrants from Southern and Eastern Europe would hav
lower industrial skills than those from Northern and Western Europe. When th
raw data suggested that this was in fact not true, the Commission purposely in
cluded among the data for Southern and Eastern Europeans in a category marke
"no occupation," all people listed as "accompanying women and children." Whe
viewed in statistical terms, this raised the percentage of unemployed people in thi
group and gave the false impression that these people were unskilled and unem
ployed. This resulted in an increase of almost 22% in the number of Poles classi
fied as unskilled and unemployed.

In another examination of the labor question, the Commission concluded tha
Southern and Eastern European immigrants were responsible for lowering wag
scales. In calculating this the Commission used aggregate numbers for people c
varying nativity, without regard to occupation, length of service, or other var
ables. The fact that wages might be affected by mechanization, seniority, or racia
prejudice was not considered.

Finally, in its study of the relationship of immigrants to the union movemer
the Commission, rather than conduct its own study of the issue, asked leaders c
the AFL about their impressions of the situation. Long an opponent of unre
stricted immigration, the AFL was at that point in history a craft union that di
not appeal to unskilled workers in general and refused, except in certain isolate
cases, to enroll unskilled immigrant workers in particular. It was in the AFL's in
terest to show that immigration had a deleterious effect on labor, so that is what
told the Commission. Since this information fit into the Commissioners' ow
preconceptions, they accepted it at face value.[12]

In similar fashion, the Commission conducted "investigations" of criminality
housing, education, and other issues of the day. In each case, as with the investiga
tion of the condition of labor, in order to prove its own preconceptions in the fac
of often contradictory evidence, the Commission knowingly accepted faulty evi
dence and consciously manipulated data to "prove" its case. The result, publishe
for the benefit of the entire world by the United States government, professed t
indicate that the various "races" of European immigrants each had its own particu
lar characteristics. Italians, for example, were prone to violent crime, while Pole
were considered physically strong but mentally weak and docile.

Although based upon faulty research, reasoning, and reporting, the conclu
sions reached by the U.S. Immigration Commission extended federal sanction t
the stereotyping of millions of Americans and provided an aura of "legitimization
to calls for immigration restriction. These pronouncements had an immediate e

---

[12]Paul H. Douglas, "Is the New Immigration More Unskilled than the Old?"
Quarterly Publications of the American Statistical Association, Vol. 16, No. 126
(June 1919), pp. 394, 396-397; *U.S. Immigration Commission Reports*, Vol. I,
pp. 367, 376.

ect on the image of Poles and other Southern and Eastern Europeans. Before the final conclusions were even published, such reputable figures as education leader Ellwood Cubberly publicly characterized these groups as "Illiterate, docile, lacking in self-reliance and initiative and not possessing the Anglo-Teutonic conceptions of law, order, and government." For these reasons, he concluded "their coming has served to dilute tremendously our national stock, and to corrupt our civic life...."[13] Similarly, Robert Hunter, a leading social reformer at the turn of the century, argued in a passage from *Poverty*, published in 1912, that "In the United States the peasantry from other countries, degraded by foreign oppression, are supplanting the descendants of the original stock of this country."[14]

This new rationale became a favorite of popular writers such as Madison Grant whose *The Passing of the Great Race*, published in 1916, argued that the pure, superior American racial stock was being diluted by the influx of "new" immigrants from the Mediterranean, the Balkans, and the Polish ghettos. Thinly cast in the guise of scientific theory, Grant's racist diatribe gained wide popularity among the American public and greatly influenced federal immigration legislation.[15]

The results of the U.S. government's sanctioning of ethnic stereotyping can be seen in T. J. Woofter's survey of popular literature between 1900 and 1930. Woofter found that concurrent with the dissemination of the findings of the U.S. Immigration Commission, "there occurred a marked change in public sentiment toward immigration" in which the old restrictionist arguments based upon economics yielded to a rationale based upon "the undesirability of certain racial elements."[16]

The Immigration Commission's reports also led to further discriminatory actions by the federal government. In March 1919 Senator Albert Johnson introduced a bill designed to restrict total immigration by assigning quotas based upon national origin.[17] The new bill cleared both Houses of Congress and on May 19, 1921, President Warren G. Harding signed into law the first legal act in American history designed specifically to restrict European immigration. The First Quota Act of 1921 imposed a maximum of 357,803 as the number of immigrants that could enter the country from outside the Western Hemisphere in any single year. The number was considerably less than the average of 625,629 who entered annually between 1901 and 1920. Each nationality group was given a separate quota based upon the number of people from that group residing in the United States in 1910. This provision discriminated directly against Southern and Eastern Euro-

---

[13]Anthony J. Kuzniewski, "Boot Straps," pp. 21-22.

[14]Victor Greene, "Polish American Worker," p. 68.

[15]James S. Pula, "Dillingham Commission," *Polish American Studies*, Vol. XXXVII, No. 1 (1980), pp. 7-8.

[16]T. J. Woofter, *Races and Ethnic Groups in American Life* (New York: 1933), p. 31.

[17]Handlin, pp. 97-98.

peans.[18]

Although the 1920 census had just been completed and its results would ha
been available soon, the law specifically required use of the earlier 1910 cens
because, as its proponents argued, "the number of the older and better immigran
coming has been relatively much smaller during the last ten years, and the numb
from southern Europe, Italy and Russia much greater, which will be reflected
the 1920 census. The making of the 1910 census as the basis will give us more
the better and less of the less desirable immigrants than if it were based on t
census of 1920."[19] Clearly, this was a conscious attempt to discriminate again
Southern and Eastern Europeans.

The quota reversed a trend in pre-war years that saw Southern and Eastern E
ropeans outnumbering Northern and Western Europeans by four to one. It is cle
that the law was designed specifically to limit, in a discriminatory fashion, imm
gration from Southern and Eastern Europe. Under its provisions, Poland was a
signed an initial quota of 25,827.[20] The National Origins Act of 1924 reduced t
total number of immigrants per year from 357,803 to 164,667. Further, to insu
the predominance of immigrants from Northern and Western Europe, the quo
percentage of each nationality was reduced while the base year was moved ba
from 1910 to 1890. This was yet another clear attempt to decrease the number
immigrants from Southern and Eastern Europe who entered in large numbers aft
1890. For Poland, this resulted in a new annual quota of only 5,982, a loss
more than 80% from its previous level.[21] The net effect of these nationality quot
imposed by Congress in 1921 and 1924 was to sharply reduce the influx of near
100,000 Poles per year to a fraction of that number.

The official U.S. government actions promulgated first in the specio
machinations of the U.S. Immigration Commission and then in the equally di
criminatory actions of the First Quota Act and the National Origins Act, had tw
very serious consequences for Polonia. First, by extending official governme
sanction to the actions and conclusions of the U.S. Immigration Commission t
government appeared to "legitimize" a derogatory ethnic stereotype that continu
to haunt Polish Americans to this day. Although the Progressive Era is known
a period of great political, economic and social reform, for Polish Americans t
era resulted in the U.S. government officially labeling them as people of limit
mental capacity fit only for strong physical work; people at once submissive a
docile, yet dangerously undisciplined and prone to alcoholism and criminali
people who aspired to nothing more than the poor, overcrowded, unsanitary conc
tions of the urban slums.[22] In time, this image, reinforced in literature and fil
gradually developed into the stereotypes found in the vicious and degrading "Poli

[18]Pula, pp. 8-10.
[19]Handlin, p. 96.
[20]Pula, pp. 11-12.
[21]*Ibid.*, pp. 12-13.
[22]Bicha, "Hunkies," pp. 22-23.

jokes" of recent decades.[23] It was the U.S. Immigration Commission that gave this stereotype the "blessing" of the federal government, and it has been the federal court system, reluctant to prosecute discrimination based on national origin, that continues to look the other way at stereotypical slurs and socio-economic discrimination against Polish Americans that would not be condoned were they directed against other groups in society.

The second major effect that U.S. government actions of the Progressive Era had upon Polish Americans was to deprive Polonia's communities of the continuing influx of immigrants from Poland that was necessary to their vitality, their cultural survival, and their psychological well-being. The drastic reduction in Polish immigration served not only to cut off the external source of immigrants necessary to the vitality of life in the urban ethnic communities, but also cut off direct access to cultural renewal from Poland. After the passage of the quota acts the river of Polish immigrants was diverted to France and Belgium. The result was that fewer Poles came to the United States during the period between 1921 and 1940 than came in any single year between 1900 and 1914.[24] The exact number, of course, depended upon how you defined a "Pole." In one study, Helena Lopata compared the arrivals and departures listed by the U.S. Bureau of Immigration by "race or people" and found that between 1920 and 1932 there was a net *exodus* of 33,618 Poles from the United States.[25]

Finally, for Polish Americans the interwar period was a time of complex socioeconomic change that saw the second generation grow to maturity and begin to not only strengthen the established Polonia and contend for its leadership, but move more into the mainstream of American society. Within this context, the desire to adapt enough to participate fully in the American socioeconomic milieu, while at the same time preserving their Polish cultural heritage, was greatly hampered by the lack of ongoing contacts and cultural renewal provided by a continuing flow of immigrants.[26]

While the first generation of Polish Americans, the immigrants themselves, generally developed a sense of psychological security within the confines of their ethnic communities, a security that provided psychological support for them in the face of a sometimes hostile and foreign environment outside their enclaves, the second generation found itself in an awkward transitional phase between loyalty to the heritage of their parents and the desire to take advantage of opportunities in a society beyond the confines of the ethnic culture that tended all too often to ridicule and discriminate against those who manifested outward signs of Polishness. Conflict between the first and second generations of Polish Americans arose as traditions and perspectives of parents pulled in one way, while americanization pulled the other. As Thaddeus Radzilowski eloquently explained, for the second generation "The dilemma of their lives involved, as we all know, the problem of

---

[23]*Ibid.*, p. 26.
[24]Zyblikiewicz, "Foreign Policy," p. 75.
[25]Helena Z. Lopata, "Problems of Estimation," p. 95.
[26]Kuzniewski, review of Brozek, p. 70.

negotiating between identities, with all of the attendant pain and alienation tha
brought. Because they were Americans, because their identities were less secure
than those of their parents, because they could not avoid intimate contact with
American society as successfully as their parents could and because they were
drawn to American culture, they felt more acutely and painfully the insults of
nativism and prejudice and the sting of exclusion. Their struggles, negotiation
and compromises, as a result, are much more responsible for the shaping of th
modern Polish-American identity than are the experiences of the immigrants. The
created the context within which succeeding generations discovered what it mean
to be a Polish American."[27]

   "To repudiate one's parent's culture in favor of the culture of Protestant Amer
ica," Daniel Buczek argued, "leads to a generational war between parents and chil
dren.... It leads to the condition of *anomie*, which may be defined as loss of per
spective, rootlessness, aimlessness, cultural deprivation."[28] As a result of these
conflicts, members of the second generation were more prone to exhibit character
istics of the "marginal man" complex. Some adopted a negative view of their her
itage which led them to shun it. Those who developed this form of "marginality"
were lost to Polonia forever. Others, rejected by the dominant society because of
their Polishness, often developed the self-doubting or self-deprecating actions of
those who feel guilty about leaving their parents' culture and heritage. Thus, th
U.S. government policy of discriminating against would-be Polish immigrants
by impairing the healthy transmission of ethnic culture which could have bee
used as psychological support for communities undergoing transition and ameri
canization, further placed upon Polish Americans an insidious stereotypical por
trait that inhibited their ability to compete equally in America's socioeconomi
sphere and at the same time caused them to reject or feel guilty about their ow
heritage.

   Similarly, as Edward Kolodziej has shown, Poles who migrated to America
during the interwar period constituted a much closer reflection of Polish societ
than did the earlier migration and would, if allowed to continue without artificia
government restriction, have led to both a cultural and economic renewal withi
the Polish American communities.[29] The lack of this important cross-section of
Polish society further served to stereotype Polish Americans as undereducatec
unskilled peasant laborers.

   Deprived of the continuous cultural contact with their Old World heritage tha
would have been possible without immigration restriction, Polish American cul
ture became static--a culture anchored on the fading memories of the peasant fol
culture of the original immigrants and the often fragmentary or faulty knowledg
of their offspring who preserved some customs from "tradition" without a clea
understanding of their importance.

---

[27]Radzilowski, "Second Generation," pp. 8-9.
[28]Buczek, "Polish-American Parish," p. 160.
[29]Kolodziej, "Emigration From," p. 179.

Rather than a vibrant, living culture that shaped and supported the lives of those it touched, the Polish communities increasingly remembered their heritage only as isolated curiosities of the past. Lacking the vitality created by ongoing contacts with Poland, Polonia became to a certain extent "frozen in time" so that when Polish Americans did have an opportunity to visit the Old Country they felt strangely out of place and when Poles arrived in America they could not relate to a Polonia whose speech was riddled with unfamiliar Americanisms, whose knowledge of contemporary Poland was based upon general and fragmentary newspaper reports, and and whose culture resembled an imperfect version from half-a-century past. A vital, thriving culture that could have stood as a psychological support against the vicious ethnic slanders both permitted and fostered by U.S. government policy could have lent valuable psychological support to Polish Americans, providing them with a positive self image. That this did not happen is due to the lack of further immigration, which resulted from the overt discriminatory actions of the United States government.

The Effects of Civil Rights Legislation on Americans of European Ancestry

by

Shelly Lescott-Leszczynski[1]

Until 1954 it was legal in the United States to maintain separate schools for black and white children. The *Brown v. Board of Education* decision, reversing the 1896 *Plessy vs. Ferguson* ruling upholding "separate but equal" facilities for blacks and whites, declared such a system "inherently unequal" and discriminatory. The Court based its views on the due process and equal protection clauses of the Fourteenth Amendment. Southern states resisted desegregation, even after the 1955 implementation decree. Only two years later, in 1957, a new Civil Rights Act guaranteed black Americans the right to vote.

Those of us who came of age during these years remember the bitter and violent times, as well as the bright hopes of black Americans led by the charismatic and impassioned Dr. Martin Luther King. One result of the period was that by 1964 a comprehensive Civil Rights Act was passed. In succeeding years, the policies built upon this Act, particularly the policy called "affirmative action," became catalysts for enormous social change in our country.

Before going into specific ways in which these policies affected Polish Americans and other Americans of European ancestry, I shall briefly review the ways in which they evolved.

---

[1]Shelly Lescott-Leszczynski, Ph.D., owns a publishers' service bureau in Reno, Nevada.

Overview of Affirmative Action

The concept of "equal opportunity" was espoused throughout the 1964 Civil Rights Act which guaranteed assurances of non-discrimination in all spheres and activities of American daily life for all Americans, regardless of race, color, religion, sex, or national origin. In order to ensure compliance with the non-discrimination mandates of the Act, such as the desegregation of public facilities, data had to be collected from government agencies as well as from institutions that received federal funds or contracts. "Black," "White," and "Other" were the categories used in data collection prior to 1964. But now, because the federal government was concerned with identifying groups in American society who suffered past and present discrimination, and whose socioeconomic disadvantages were attributed to such discrimination, additional categories were created. Since the 1970s, the expanded categories have been:[2]

White, not of Hispanic Origin: Persons having origins in any of the original peoples of Europe, North Africa, or the Middle East.

Black, not of Hispanic Origin: Persons having origins in any of the Black racial groups of Africa.

Hispanic: Persons of Mexican, Puerto Rican, Cuban, Central or South American or other Spanish culture or origin, regardless of race.

American Indian or Alaskan Native: Persons having origins in any of the original peoples of North America, and who maintain cultural identification through tribal affiliation or community recognition.

Asian Origin: Persons having origins in any of the original peoples of the Far East, Southeast Asia, the Indian Subcontinent, or the Pacific Islands. This area includes, for example, China, Japan, Korea, the Philippine Islands, and Samoa.

Data collection for any white ethnic group other than Hispanics has never been mandated—or even suggested—by the federal government. In a sense, then, European ethnics have become "hidden factors" of the "White" data collection category.

While non-discrimination guarantees apply to each individual, equal opportunity guarantees evolved into a policy of preferential treatment and special protections for members of ethnic and racial groups of every data collection category

---

[2]The foregoing categories were detailed in Directive No. 15: Race and Ethnic Standards for Federal Statistics and Administrative Reporting, *Federal Register*, April 4, 1977.

except "White." All non-whites and Hispanics were designated as "minorities," a term that has had connotations of "victimization" since 1945, when sociologist Louis Wirth defined a minority as "a group of people who are singled out from the others in the society in which they live for differential and unequal treatment and who therefore regard themselves as objects of collective discrimination."[3]

This program of preferential treatment for designated minorities is called *affirmative action*. More recently, women from all racial and ethnic groups have been identified as a minority and therefore eligible for many affirmative action programs.

Affirmative action programs are many and varied. Their history dates back to executive orders issued by Presidents John F. Kennedy and Lyndon B. Johnson. Kennedy's Executive Order No. 10925 (1961) guaranteed equality of opportunity in federal employment and authorized the review of practices by federal agencies and contractors to enforce their compliance with the equal opportunity aspects of earlier Civil Rights Acts. Johnson's Executive Order No. 11246 (1965), calling for "affirmative steps" to be taken to ensure equal opportunity, directed federal agencies to issue guidelines to all institutions and corporations which had contracts with the federal government.

Affirmative action was intended to help the disadvantaged minority groups achieve upward mobility. Affirmative "steps" would provide individuals with expanded job and training opportunities. In addition, there would be an active recruitment program within federal agencies and, on a voluntary basis, in private industry and educational institutions as well.

Neither quotas nor deadlines for achieving affirmative action goals were suggested originally. However, toward the end of the 1960s, and certainly by the beginning of the 1970s, a "goals and timetables" approach to achieve proportionate representation of minorities on a broad, national scale had become the official interpretation of affirmative action policy.[4]

Challenges to Affirmative Action Practices[5]

Affirmative action programs faced legal challenges almost as soon as public institutions and private companies began implementing them. With attention focused on creating benefits exclusively for the designated racial and ethnic minorities, legal questions of "reverse discrimination" and "adverse impact" were raised. European ethnics, the "majority's minority," had also faced discrimination. Many had assimilated only at the painful cost of their cultural identities.

---

[3]Louis Wirth, "The Problem of Minority Groups," cited in *The Chronicle of Higher Education*, October 16, 1991.

[4]Adapted from John Lescott-Leszczynski, *The History of U. S. Ethnic Policy and Its Impact on European Ethnics* (Boulder, CO: Westview Press, 1984).

[5]This analysis is adapted from Lescott-Leszczynski, pp. 53-54. Mikulski's comments are quoted on p. 54.

Socio-economically speaking, their positions in the middle class had been relatively recently won. For the most part, they were hardworking, blue-collar taxpayers, often stereotyped and joked about in the media.

Because of their color they were not victims; because they went to work every day (often husband and wife) and earned money to support their families, however modestly, they were not "disadvantaged," and because they were "White," even their ethnic distinctiveness was officially blurred. The traditional neighborhoods they had carved out in the urban landscape—a source of pride and pleasure for all city dwellers—were also changing, as new groups (the disadvantaged minorities) began encroaching on their boundaries. Congresswoman Barbara Mikulski summed up the resentment that many European ethnics were feeling in 1970: "America is not a melting pot," she said, "It is a sizzling cauldron for the ethnic American who feels that he has been politically extorted by both government and private enterprise.... He is overtaxed and underserved at every level of government."

Many affirmative action programs are focused in the areas of education, employment, and business development. Recently, there has been an effort to reevaluate the principles upon which they are based. Echoes of the reverse discrimination challenges of twenty years ago are heard today, by a more receptive public—minority *and* non-minority.

Education

In the field of education, affirmative action policies have led most colleges today to routinely reserve places for minority candidates. Sometimes this takes the form of a quota based upon a targeted percentage of minority students to the general student population of the college or university. "Diversification" of the student body is one current justification for this practice. Admissions officials have maintained that racial and ethnic criteria have never been intended to *replace* academic criteria. Rather, membership in a disadvantaged minority group lends additional weight to otherwise qualified minority applicants.

There are many non-quantifiable, non-academic factors which are normally taken into consideration in the selection process, for example: residence, political or alumni contacts, veteran status, and physical handicaps. *Membership in a minority group is an automatic presumption of disadvantage* and, as such, becomes a positive factor in the application process.

A famous challenge to admissions quotas was raised by Alan Bakke in 1976. Bakke, who was white, accused the University of California's medical school at Davis of discriminating against him in favor of minority candidates, for whom the school had set aside 16 places. The quota, contended Bakke, was a form of "reverse discrimination" and violated his constitutional rights.

The medical school created the "set-asides" as part of its affirmative recruitment goal of "remedying" past discrimination. However, the school was unable to prove that the quota actually redressed prior discrimination *at the school*—rather, it was an attempt to redress general societal discrimination.

The Supreme Court decided that Bakke's civil rights had indeed been violated under Title VI of the Civil Rights Act (exclusion from participating in any federally funded program on the basis of race not being permissible). But it also decided that race-conscious remedies for past discrimination were justified by the same Title VI as well as the Fourteenth Amendment. Bakke won his case; but at the same time, racial and ethnic diversity in the student body was recognized as a desirable goal in admissions policies, and affirmative admissions programs were upheld.

The Civil Rights Commission made the following comment: "Academic achievement is measured not only by how high the applicant stands, but also by how far he has had to climb from where he began."[6]

That diversity is desirable has never been challenged by any European ethnic. However, many of the same non-academic factors that have handicapped the designated minorities may well have impeded upward mobility of European ethnics, too. Second and third generation Americans of European ancestry also enrich and diversify our predominantly Anglo-Saxon, Protestant society.

Quotas for minority group members are once again being challenged. *The Chronicle of Higher Education* reported in January 1992 that the Middle States Association of Colleges and Schools has adopted a policy stating that diversity standards "would not be used as a condition for accrediting institutions and that colleges could define for themselves how the standards would be applied."[7] This is an important issue because students can receive federal aid only if they attend colleges that are accredited by agencies which are recognized by the Department of Education.

Another way in which schools increase their minority enrollments is to offer "race-based" scholarships and grants to students from racial and ethnic minorities. This policy has been effective in nurturing gifted and deserving minority students, particularly blacks and Hispanics. However, it has effectively shut out many middle class and blue-collar white ethnics, whose (often combined) family earnings make them ineligible for income-based scholarships.

The Education Department is now proposing "race-neutral" guidelines. During the Bush administration, Secretary of Education Lamar Alexander published proposed new regulations in December 1989 that called into question the legality of race-based scholarships. Secretary Alexander declared that this type of set-aside deprived non-minorities of an "equal opportunity" to receive such assistance.[8]

---

[6]The summary of the Bakke challenge and the quote from the Civil Rights Commission are adapted and quoted from Lescott-Leszczynski, pp. 95-96.

[7]*The Chronicle of Higher Education*, January 8, 1992, p. 24.

[8]*The New York Times*, December 7, 1991, p. A9 and February 6, 1992, p. A7.

The new guidelines aroused heated debate and turmoil, as they appeared to negate decades-old practices founded upon the philosophy of special protections for Hispanics and non-whites. March 1992 was the deadline for comments on the matter; however, at the time of this writing in June, 1990, the Education Department has not made the new guidelines final.

In issuing its proposals, the Education Department suggested that private donors of scholarships are not covered by Title VI of the Civil Rights Act. It would seem from this that private donors should be able to offer scholarships specifically intended for needy white students—to European ethnics, for example. This may be a matter for the courts to interpret. *The Chronicle of Higher Education* reported a situation at a Colorado community college concerning a fund which was set up three years ago to award $1200 annually to a female business student. Although the donor had originally suggested that the award go to a white student, the college made the award race-neutral. This year the donor insisted that the recipient be white, and when the college refused—after a Hispanic student charged that the race-based stipulation was discriminatory—the donor requested her money back.[9]

A recent case involving a race-based scholarship for black students at the University of Maryland illustrates the contradictions that often arise between implementing judicial mandates and determining their constitutionality. This case had a slightly different twist in that Daniel Podbersky, the twenty-year-old sophomore who brought the suit, described himself as "Hispanic" when applying for a scholarship that was open to all students. When he failed to qualify, he applied—and was turned down—for a scholarship exclusively set aside for blacks. *This preferential scholarship is financed both by private and public monies.* The university barred Podbersky, the son of a Hispanic mother and Polish-ancestry father, from applying. A Baltimore federal district court upheld the university in the subsequent suit, a decision which Podbersky appealed.[10]

Employment and Business Development Practices

Toward the end of the 1960s, the Civil Service Commission was following a policy of "non-discrimination" in federal personnel actions. In line with Executive Order 11246 it was also utilizing "affirmative steps" in the form of positive actions to enhance the competitive ability of disadvantaged minority employees and potential job applicants. As in the past, the criteria for hiring and promotion within the federal government were based on individual merit—all examinations were scored the same way, and, in theory, advancement eligibility was nondiscriminatory. But the emphasis on *individual* merit and achievement did not produce broad or immediate results for disadvantaged *groups.*

---

[9]*The Chronicle of Higher Education,* June 3, 1992.
[10]*The New York Times,* February 6, 1992, p. A7.

The Equal Employment Opportunities Commission, the Civil Rights Commission, and various civil rights and minority group activists pressured the federal government to move faster. They wanted *proportionate representation* of the designated minorities, and they insisted on *deadlines* for achieving this. Within a few years, the traditional merit system of civil service was supplanted by a representationist approach.

The Office of Federal Contract Compliance (OFCC) had already implemented a representationist approach in the form of quotas, or "set-asides," for employment of minorities, as well as for utilization of minority subcontractors by companies that bid on contracts for federal or federally funded projects. Goals for achieving the quotas were based on local or national statistics. An *affirmative action plan* had to be submitted along with each bid. This practice grew out of an OFCC bid directive for projects issued in Philadelphia. The "Philadelphia Plan" had immediate and long-lasting impact upon federal, state, local, and also private employment practices.

Numerical goals and deadlines were justified on the basis of past and/or currently identified discrimination as evidenced by a scarcity of minority group members in a company or government agency in proportion to their numbers. To this extent affirmative action, as it began to be practiced, became a public policy that was both *remedial* and *compensatory*. Broadly speaking, the federal government was now attempting to correct the socioeconomic disadvantages of certain groups of people by "injecting" them into what was hoped would be an upward mobility path among mainstream Americans. The philosophy was breathtakingly creative, idealistic, and optimistic. The underlying assumption was that the minority individual's socioeconomic disadvantage was attributable to discrimination suffered by the group.

Another example of the effects of business policies can be seen in the Equal Employment Opportunities Act which legitimized numerical goals and timetables. Directives such as the "May Memo" policy statement for public personnel systems issued by the Civil Service Commission in 1971, instructed federal agencies to establish goals and timetables "in those organizations and localities and in those occupations and grade levels where minority employment is not what should reasonably be expected in view of the potential supply of qualified members of minority groups in the work force and in the recruiting area...."[11]

In 1972, Congress passed the Equal Employment Opportunity Act and legitimized goals and timetables. EEOC was given enforcement powers to sue respondents—in public and private sectors—for non-compliance. The Act formally brought federal, state, and local governments under the authority of Title VII of the Civil Rights Act, however, it is interesting to note that since the 1970s the EEOC's own work force has been *unrepresentative* of national statis-

---

[11]Robert Hampton, Chairman of the CSC, "Memorandum for Heads of Departments and Agencies," May 11, 1971.

tics: its composition in the early 1970s was 48.6% black, 12% Spanish-sur-named, and only 35.6% non-minority.[12]

Preferential treatment for minorities in hiring and promotion practices, often referred to as "reverse discrimination," caused many whites to feel that they had been excluded from training programs, promotion opportunities, and jobs. "Reverse discrimination" suits filed throughout the 1970s were often portrayed in the media and by civil rights activists as the result of a white "backlash." In view of the centuries-old discrimination against black Americans that the 1964 Civil Rights Act was intended to redress, many white liberals considered such challenges contemptible, and the Supreme Court continued to support affirmative action for designated minorities.

The most significant of the reverse discrimination suits filed at the time was *United Steelworkers of America v. Weber*. Weber, a white male who felt he had been rejected from a training program at Kaiser Aluminum because of an affirmative action program worked out between Kaiser and the Steelworkers Union, sued on the basis of reverse discrimination. Although the lower court found for Weber, the Supreme Court overturned the decision, maintaining that it is constitutional for a company to implement affirmative action programs *even when there has been no finding of prior discrimination*. As with *Bakke*, the Supreme Court considered the redress of past discrimination by society in general sufficient justification for affirmative action programs within a private company.

The EEOC Guidelines published in 1977 suggest that evidence of prior discrimination can be found by comparing an employer's work force with an appropriate segment of the labor force. If this is true, one should expect to find, for example, that in cities where there is a high density of a particular ethnic group, a representative percentage of the group should be found in various strata of the work force—at least in those businesses that are in compliance with Title VII of the Civil Rights Act. Since there had been no federal data collection for European ethnics, the National Center for Urban Ethnic Affairs commissioned a study to show "the extent to which members of the Polish, Italian, Latin, and Black communities have penetrated the centers of power and influence in Chicago-based corporations."[13]

Dr. Russell Barta surveyed Chicago corporations in 1973—over 100 major companies were involved. The 1970 Census reported that nearly 34% of Chicago's population of seven million were either Polish, Italian, Latin, or Black. Yet Poles (as well as Latins and Blacks) were not part of the upper echelons of management in these corporations. Indeed, 97 of the 106 companies surveyed had no officers who were Polish, and only 4 of them had directors who were Polish. These companies were among the largest in the nation in industry retail, utilities, transportation, and banking. Dr. Barta's findings suggest that if

---

[12]U. S. Civil Service Commission, *Minority Group Employment in the Federal Government* (Washington, DC: U. S. Government Printing Office, 1972), p. 126.

[13]Reported in Lescott-Leszczynski, p. 139.

equal opportunity is measured by comparing the number of *ethnics* employed with those of the same group living in a locality, Chicago's Polish population, for example, was dramatically under-represented in corporate realms of power. Were they victims of discrimination?

Recent Re-evaluations of Affirmative Action Policies

The premises for affirmative action and the concept of merit versus representation are being questioned by many Americans, including many young and upwardly mobile beneficiaries of these policies, the so-called "affirmative action babies."[14]

One practice of federal and local governments has been to "adjust" the scores of black and Hispanic job applicants who take the General Aptitude Test Battery, a test which may affect the recommendations made for job placement by state and local agencies. This adjustment, dubbed "race-norming," is widely applied to the scores of black and Hispanic job applicants who take this and other federally sanctioned aptitude tests. It works this way:

*Individual scores are ranked within three groups—Black, White, and Hispanic.

*Individual scores are *not* compared to all other test scores. (Asian scores are ranked in the White category because they are so high.)

The impact on candidates is clearly in favor of blacks and Hispanics because, on the average, black Americans score 16%-20% lower than white and Asian Americans on the test, and Hispanics score 5%-10% lower. The same *raw* score would therefore result in a higher ranking for individual black and Hispanic test-takers, since their scores would be compared only to other black or Hispanic test-takers. Without the race-norming adjustment, the test is said to "favor" whites.

The 1991 Civil Rights Act makes this practice illegal, according to a spokesperson at the Labor Department. The Labor Department has indicated that it plans to spend some $6 million over the next two years to study ways of improving the test.[15]

The Supreme Court has also begun to place some limit on affirmative action "set asides." According to George R. LaNoue, "The affirmative action practice

---

[14]Notable among recent publications is Yale Law School professor Stephen L. Carter's book *Reflections of an Affirmative Action Baby* (Basic Books, 1991). Stanford economist Thomas Sowell, a well-known black conservative, has questioned affirmative action for minorities for years. And, perhaps, the most notable and most visible "(anti) affirmative-action baby" is Supreme Court Justice Clarence Thomas.

[15]*The New York Times*, December 14, 1991, p. 1.

of setting aside a percentage of contract awards in bid decisions for federal and federally-funded projects is currently being subjected to new, stringent guidelines referred to as the "strict scrutiny" test.[16] This can be seen in a 1989 Supreme Court decision that struck down a 30% set-aside for minority contracting in the city of Richmond. The Court ruled in favor of the Croson company in a suit in which the company had been denied a contract because it could not sub-contract the set-aside required by city regulations.

While not nullifying the right of local entities to develop affirmative action plans, the Court has issued specific guidelines for the use of racial classifications. The application of "strict scrutiny" recommended by the Court involves the following criteria:

*that the racial classification is a necessary *remedy* for continuing effects of discrimination identified in a specific activity;

*that the remedy is tailored to cover only those industries where minority groups were found to have been discriminated against and that it was used only for the time period necessary to compensate for the previous bias;

*that race-neutral means were not sufficient to remedy the discrimination.

Considerations

The trend in U. S. ethnic policy is clearly away from the traditional, liberal interpretation of affirmative action, in which the concept of *group harms and group remedies*, including *proportionate representation* in every sector and activity of society, often takes precedence over individual rights, individual merit, and individual responsibility for one's situation and destiny. What is happening, and why?

Affirmative action over the past twenty or so years has been an extraordinary experiment in *social engineering*. In addition to being responsible for many positive achievements, it has had some unpleasant side effects. For many years it exacerbated urban tensions between European ethnics and the designated minority groups. White ethnics who challenged situations which they deemed unfair to them quickly earned the designation of "racist" or "white backlash." Americans of European ancestry have been put in the position of having to protest public policy, which creates a negative impression of their character. From the start-up of affirmative action policy they have had to bring suit as *individuals* (their ethnic group membership entitling them to no special guarantees) in an effort to

---

[16]Adapted from an analysis by George R. LaNoue, "Race-based Policies: a Court's Guidelines," in *The Chronicle of Higher Education*, April 8, 1992, p. A52.

protect themselves from a new kind of discrimination—discrimination in "reverse." At the same time, minority *individuals*, many of them recent immigrants themselves, are able to benefit from special preferences by virtue of their group membership and an automatic assumption of disadvantage resulting from discrimination.

Affirmative action has been one of our most controversial policies: generous in the eyes of some, unfair and preferential in the eyes of others, long overdue and fully deserved in the eyes of its beneficiaries. While the policy has not singled out European ethnics—or any whites—for discriminatory treatment, it has blurred their ethnic distinctiveness in the eyes of the law. It has attached an aura of "guilt by association" to the European ethnic. Americans of European ancestry have also been the object of certain types of discrimination, from cultural stereotyping to subtle but pernicious "class" discrimination. On a practical level, a minority preference system makes it possible to check the upward mobility of non-minority groups by creating sets of benefits from which they are excluded. If non-discrimination, equal opportunity policy was intended to protect racial and ethnic minorities from further exclusionary treatment, how ethically tenable is affirmative action policy, which continues as an exclusionary policy by practice and intent?

Immigrants from Europe came to this country with a willingness to adapt and a determination to succeed. Those groups who were here first and were conquered, and those who were coerced and enslaved, understandably may not take the same view. As historian Thomas Higham and economist Thomas Sowell have pointed out, there are deep, underlying differences among us. "Our" disadvantages are perceived to have been the result less of discrimination than of language and culture. "Their" disadvantages are attributed solely—and officially—to discrimination, past and continuing.

Over the past quarter of a century minority and non-minority Americans have interacted—in the work place, in schools, in neighborhoods, and in the ubiquitous media—with the assumptions of the 1960s defining their roles and obligations toward each other. Immigration continuously replenishes the first-generation strand of the great and diverse web of our society, ensuring new "blends" for generations to come. It is time to examine some of the old assumptions, for they are too draining on our social relationships and on our ever more finite resources.

At the same time, we need to consider *other possible factors* in the continuing disadvantage and alienation of *sub-groups within minority classifications*, such as urban blacks and Hispanics, whose coexistence with other urban groups—minority and white—is so uneasy that emotions often erupt violently and irrationally, out of proportion to real or imagined offenses. We need to explore new ways to treat their problems and we need to test new assumptions. The old ones cannot be effective or true indefinitely.

America's rapidly changing demographics, such as the influx of immigrants from currently "protected" groups, necessitate that we re-evaluate or reinterpret affirmative action policy. In the next century today's minorities will be the majority in some areas of the country. There will be more interaction and more inter-marriage between minority and non-minority individuals. Shall we continue to consider the resulting offspring as victims?

The deeply felt principles that gave rise to affirmative action are under philosophical scrutiny. The key issues on the agenda for the future are:

1. merit versus representation,
2. individual rights versus group harms and remedies, and
3. are special preferences or special helps still needed, and if so, for which types of people, on what basis, at what cost, in what forms, and for how long?

Expanding the Legal Definition of Discrete and Insular Minorities: From *Carolene Products* Through *Al-Khazraji/Shaare Tefila* and Beyond

Raymond J. Dziedzic[1]

Contemporary legal understandings of race discrimination in the United States begin with the now-famous footnote 4 of *Carolene Products*, wherein Mr. Justice Stone remarked that a constitutional issue may be subjected to heightened scrutiny when it appears that "prejudice against discrete and insular minorities may be a special condition which tends seriously to curtail the operation of those political processes ordinarily relied upon to protect minorities and which may call for a correspondingly more searching judicial inquiry."[2] Thus it was within the seemingly innocuous context of a substantive due process issue (dealing with marketing filled milk) that the Court laid a foundation for later development of civil rights litigation. Since the time of *Carolene Products*, the Supreme Court's

---

[1]Raymond J. Dziedzic, Esq., an Attorney and Counsellor at Law with offices in Buffalo, New York, comes from a prominent Polish American family widely recognized for their efforts on Polonia's behalf. He recently completed a twenty-year teaching career to devote his time to practice law.

[2]*United States v. Carolene Products*, 304 U.S. 144, 58 S.Ct. 778, 82 L.Ed. 1234 (1938).

reference to "prejudice against discrete and insular minorities"[3] has come under extensive analysis with periodic expansion so as to eventually extend constitutional protections to previously excluded groups. The intent of this article is to provide a limited review of where the legal definition of racial discrimination has been in the immediate past, to look at recent developments regarding the expansion of constitutional protections to groups not previously covered, and to suggest how the understanding may be still farther extended within a context the Court seems willing to accept.

When speaking about the modern era of civil rights anti-discrimination legal decision making, the most common starting point selected is the holding of *Brown v. Board of Education*.[4] That holding (dealing with consolidated issues from Kansas, South Carolina, Virginia, and Delaware) announced that the "separate but equal" doctrine allowed under *Plessey v. Ferguson*[5] was no longer acceptable.[6] What escapes attention of the general public is that *Brown* was preceded by a series of pre-and post-World War II Supreme Court decisions that attempted to correct social conditions in the United States in response to abject forms of racism as practiced in Nazi Germany.[7] Assistance was provided through the advocacy of the National Association for the Advancement of Colored People which undertook a campaign against segregation beginning around 1935.[8] Temporarily delayed by the overriding exigency of World War II, the NAACP renewed its desegregation drive in the immediate postwar years. Test cases were taken to the Supreme Court and met with measurable success. *Missouri ex rel. Gaines v. Canada*[9] was reaffirmed by a unanimous court in 1948 with the holding in *Sipuel v. University of Oklahoma Board of Regents*.[10] Each case emphasized that blacks were entitled to in-state school seats at previously segregated law schools. Hastily established schools for black law students would not be acceptable;[11] nor was it acceptable that blacks be required to sit in segregated areas of classrooms, libraries, or cafeterias.[12] Upon these bases, the Court undertook the matter of racially segregated schools when it agreed to hear *Brown*.

---

[3]*Id.*

[4]347 U.S. 483, 74 S.Ct. 686, 98 L.Ed. 873 (1954).

[5]163 U.S. 537, 16 S.Ct. 1138, 41 L.Ed. 256 (1896).

[6]*Brown, id.*, at 495.

[7]Alfred Kelly, "The School Desegregation Case," *Quarrels That Have Shaped the Constitution* (1964) at 243.

[8]*Id.*

[9]305 U.S. 337, 59 S.Ct. 232, 83 L.Ed. 208 (1938).

[10]332 U.S. 631, 68 S.Ct. 299, 92 L.Ed. 247 (1948).

[11]*Sweatt v. Painter*, 339 U.S. 629, 70 S.Ct. 848, 94 L.Ed. 1114 (1950).

[12]*McLaurin v. Oklahoma State Regents*, 339 U.S. 637, 70 S.Ct. 851, 94 L.Ed. 1149 (1950).

By applying the analyses of *Gaines, Sipuel, Sweatt,* and *McLaurin,* the *Brown* Court was able to conclude that "separate but equal ... [is] inherently unequal" and has a detrimental effect by connoting inferiority[13] and called for desegregation with all deliberate speed.

One of the more significant offshoots of the post-World War II civil rights movement was the legal scholarly debate that arose concerning the original understanding of the Fourteenth Amendment, Section 1 of which specifically states:

> No State shall make or enforce any law which shall abridge the privileges or immunities of citizens of the United States. Nor shall any State deprive any person of life, liberty, property without due process of law; nor deny to any person within its jurisdiction the equal protection of the laws.[14]

Section 5 authorizes Congress to enforce the entire Amendment by enacting appropriate laws.[15] An early commentator remarked:

> [S]ection 1 of the fourteenth amendment, on its face, deals not only with racial discrimination, but also with discrimination whether or not based on color. This cannot have been accidental since the alternative considered by the Joint Committee, the Civil Rights formula, did apply only to racial discrimination ... the fact that the proposed constitutional amendment was couched in more general terms could not have escaped those who voted for it.[16]

The difficulty with this perspective is that it appears to attack the anti-discrimination principle. A school of thought developed at the time of the Brown ruling arguing that the ills of the past would only be overcome by extending specific benefits to specifically identified "suspect groups"[17] who were the victims of invidious forms of discrimination. This school maintains that "[t]he antidiscrimination principle fills a special need" to overcome misdirected notions of the "differential worth of racial groups or on the related phenomenon of racially selective sympathy and indifference."[18] Here, the concern turns towards the factor of stigmatic harm resulting from psychic injury arising from racial

---

[13]*Brown, id.,* at 495 (accepting the argument that plaintiffs were denied equal protection under the law as provided by the Fourteenth Amendment).

[14]U.S.C. Constitutional Amendment 14, §1.

[15]*Id.,* §5.

[16]Alexander Bickel, "The Original Understanding and the Segregation Decision," *Harvard Law Review* , Vol. 69 (1955), pp. 1, 59-63.

[17]See, for example, *Korematsu v. United States,* 233 U.S. 214, 65 S.Ct. 193, 89 L.Ed. 194 (1944), where the Court announced the suspect class standard.

[18]Paul Brest, "Forward: In Defense of the Antidiscrimination Principle," *Harvard Law Review,* Vol. 90 (1976), pp. 6-11.

generalizations.[19] Within this school of thought, it is common to see references to a white versus black dichotomy. In that respect, the antidiscrimination proponents use the term "white" to include all Caucasian people leaving the distinct impression that Caucasian physical features are sufficient to prevent one from suffering the effects of racially motivated discrimination.[20]

Superficially, these two positions seem diametrically opposed. Yet a deeper understanding of racial discrimination in the United States leads to the conclusion that the positions might become reconciled. Proponents of the antidiscrimination school of thought employ the word "white" with expansive application. "[W]e are talking ... about the rights of individuals or groups against the larger community, and against the majority...."[21] Thus, whiteness came to be perceived as automatic entrance into the mainstream of society. A more enlightened view moves from pure numeric majoritarianism and towards the dominant-minority relationship. "There is a growing literature that argues that in fact there is no consensus to be discovered (and to the extent that one may seem to exist that is likely to reflect only the domination of some groups by others).... '[D]isputes concerning the legitimate role of race in governmental decision making, whether for purpose of segregation or affirmative action, ... present differences of the greatest magnitude regarding conceptions of justice.'"[22] Upon accepting the theory of dominant-minority relations, a fuller understanding of the intent of the framers of the Fourteenth Amendment will come into focus, one that will enhance the anti-discrimination principle and not detract therefrom. That a non-majority might control a given society is all too clearly illustrated by the practice of apartheid as found in the Union of South Africa.

The Court on several occasions gave cognizance to dominant-minority relations in the United States. *Castaneda v. Portida*[23] recognized a prima facie instance of intentional discrimination against Mexican Americans where, despite constituting a "governing majority" in the county involved, they were virtually excluded from selection to grand juries. Mr. Justice Marshall's concurrence honed in on the matter when he remarked that "[minorities] frequently respond to discrimination ... to the point of adopting the majority's negative attitude towards

---

[19]*Id.*

[20]Cf. James Jacob, "Race Relations and the Prison Subculture," *Crime and Justice: An Annual Review of Research*, Vol. 1 (1979); Paul Brest and Sanford Levison, *Processes of Constitutional Decision-Making: Cases and Materials* (1983) at 511. But, see Alan Freeman, "Legitimizing Racial Discrimination Through Antidiscrimination Law: A Critical Review of Supreme Court Doctrine," *Minnesota Law Review*, Vol. 62 (1978), pp. 1049, 1052-1055, wherein he presents the position of an "innocent" class of whites who were not responsible for discrimination against non-whites.

[21]Laurence Tribe, *American Constitutional Law* (1978), note 7 at 896.

[22]John Ely, *Democracy and Distrust* (1980) at 63-64 (quoting Sanford Levison).

[23]430 U.S. 482, 97 S.Ct. 1272, 51 L.Ed. 2d 498 (1977).

the minorities...."[24] Similar findings were reached in *Reed v. Reed*[25] (females entitled to Fourteenth Amendment equal protection where they are equally qualified with men but deprived by some artificial statutory limitation) and *Frontiero v. Richardson*[26] (female service personnel entitled to a presumption of propriety when claiming their spouses despite statutory language to the contrary). From this perspective it appears that the Court accepted the dominant-minority relationship as lying within the original meaning of the Fourteenth Amendment and was willing to extend antidiscrimination protections to victims of racially motivated forms of discrimination even though they were not black Americans. The promise of fuller coverage was looked towards as a beacon as additional groups of self-perceived American minorities raised the issue in the courts. Yet it seems that this was the point beyond which the Courts were not willing to go.

An indication of this line of judicial resistance against furthering coverage of antidiscrimination protections appeared in the decision of *McDonald v. Santa Fe Trail Transportation Company*.[27] There, white employees were dismissed after committing felonious acts against the employer while a black employee who was also involved was not discharged from employment. Although the Court used Fourteenth Amendment language to find for the petitioners, it did so in very limited fashion so as to keep the anti-discrimination principle from coming to be applied to white males in general.[28] Within a year's time, the Court undertook the matter of *University of California v. Bakke*.[29] There, a white male sought protection under Title VII of the Civil Rights Act of 1964[30] when he was denied a seat in medical school. The Court's analysis cut a specific exception for the respondent as an individual who demonstrated that the preferential treatment extended by the minority admissions program "touch[ed] upon [his] individual race or ethnic background [and] he is entitled to a judicial determination that the burden he is asked to bear on that basis is precisely tailored to serve a compelling governmental interest...."[31] In this way the Court was able to reconcile what it considered to be a personal wrong without distorting the antidiscrimination principle nor bringing white males within the span of discreteness and insularity that sits as the keystone of minority rights theory. The general theory of reverse discrimination was laid to rest when the Court ruled in 1970 that private contracts seeking to voluntarily correct the effects of past discrimination through

---

[24]*Id.*, at 503.

[25]404 U.S. 71, 92 S.Ct. 251, 30 L.Ed. 2d 225 (1971).

[26]411 U.S. 677, 93 S.Ct. 1764, 36 L.Ed. 2d 583 (1973).

[27]427 U.S. 273, 96 S.Ct. 2574, 49 L.Ed. 2d 493 (1975).

[28]*Id.*, at 296, where the Court expressed the thought that as "Unlikely as it might have appeared in 1866 that white citizens would encounter substantial racial discrimi-nation" the Fourteenth Amendment nonetheless covers whites who can establish a prima facie case of race discrimination.

[29]438 U.S. 265, 98 S.Ct. 2733, 57 L.Ed. 2d 750 (1978).

[30]42 U.S.C. §2000 et seq. 78 Stat. 252.

[31]*Bakke, ibid.*, at 299.

bona fide affirmative action plans were constitutionally acceptable provided they were designed to parallel the 1964 Civil Rights Act.[32]

While it may be reasonably accepted that the Court deemed it necessary to protect the antidiscrimination principle from the broadsides of reverse discrimination attacks, a degree of bewilderment arises at the Court's hesitancy to accord constitutional protection to identifiable minority groups under Title VII of the Civil Rights Act of 1964. The language of the statute specifically states:

> No person in the United States shall on the grounds of race, color, or *national origins*, be excluded from participation in, be denied the benefits of, to be subjected to discrimination....[33] (emphasis added)

It appears, however, in spite of this clear reference to national origins (i.e., ethnic nationality minorities) the Court was not prepared to accept ethnic ancestry as a sufficient basis for sustaining a cause of action under the Civil Rights Act of 1964. *United Jewish Organizations of Williamsburg, Inc. v. Carey*[34] involved an attempt on the part of Hasidic Jews to preserve the structure of their New York State assemblymanic and senatorial election districts from being redesigned. The Court's holding was rooted in a view that Hasidic Jews—and by implication all Jews—are members of the white majority so that Jews lacked a "constitutional right ... to separate community recognition...."[35]

A major obstacle encountered by the plaintiffs in *United Jewish Organizations v. Carey* was a device not of their own making. The New York State Legislature's 1974 election district redistricting plan came under exacting review by the United States Attorney General because a literacy test was used in Kings, New York and Bronx Counties as late as 1968.[36] Furthermore, the Director of the Census determined that less than 50% of the residents within those three counties who were eligible to vote actually voted in the 1968 Presidential election.[37] Notwithstanding the New York State Legislature's averment that the complained-of literacy test had not been used for nearly ten years,[38] the U. S. Attorney General concluded that presence of the literacy test and the low rate of voter participation in these three counties was sufficient cause for remediation to

---

[32]See also *United Steelworkers of America v Weber*, 433 U.S. 193, 99 S.Ct. 2721, 61 L.Ed. 2d 480 (1978).

[33]42 U.S.C. §2000d, 78 Stat. 252 (emphasis added).

[34]430 U.S. 144, 97 S.Ct. 996, 51 L.Ed. 2d 229 (1977).

[35]*Id.*, at 153. But see *Fullibone v. Klutznick*, 448 U.S. 448, 100 S.Ct. 2758, 65 L.Ed. 2d 902 (1980), Justice Stevens, in dissenting, noted that "If the national government is to make a serious effort to define racial classes by criteria that can be administered, it must study precedents such as the First Regulation to the Reich's Citizenship Law of November 14, 1935: 1. A Jew is...."

[36]*Id.*, 430 U.S. at 149.

[37]*Id.*

[38]*Id.*

overcome an apparent form of discriminatory affect on minority group voting rights.[39]

In attempting to challenge the perceived detrimental impact that the U. S. Attorney General's finding would have upon the homogeneity of their community, the Hasidic Jews merely argued that the proposed redistricting would dilute the value of their franchise and that such a dilution to overcome past forms of discrimination suffered by protected minority groups abridged the Constitutional rights of the Hasidic community.[40] Nowhere in this argument did the Hasidim contend that Jews should be considered as a separate racial classification entitled to antidiscrimination protections. To the contrary, petitioners in this case said that "[We do not] contend that there is any right ... for permanent recognition of a *community* in legislative apportionment."[41] Thus the Court was able to hand down a ruling rooted in the view that Hasidic Jews—and by implication all Jews—are members of the white majority so that Jews lacked a "constitutional right ... to separate community recognition...."[42]

Following the ruling of *United Jewish Organizations*, the lower federal courts consistently disallowed antidiscrimination cause of action where plaintiffs relied upon national origins theories. *Kurylas v. U. S. Department of Agriculture*[43] concerned a Polish American who sought §1981 antidiscrimination protection pursuant to an Equal Employment Opportunity dispute that arose between this veterinarian and his immediate supervisors. In granting summary judgment for the employer, the U. S. District Court for the District of Columbia Circuit, held that EEO determination suits must not only be brought in a timely fashion[44] but that any §1981 claim must assert that the alleged discriminatory act is racially motivated. In finding that plaintiff in *Kurylas* failed to state a cause of action when using the national origins argument, this court clearly stated that "only nonwhites have standing to bring an action under §1981."[45]

Budinsky v. Corning Glass Works[46] dealt with an alleged improper dismissal of an employee with fourteen years service. Amongst the nine assertions contained in the complaint, plaintiff averred that he was the object of derogatory name-calling by his superiors. In seeking relief, this plaintiff, because of his Slavic heritage, sought antidiscrimination protection under §2000e, et. seq. in addition to §1981. The District Court granted the employer's motion to dismiss and stated:

---

[39]*Id.*, at 156-157.
[40]*Id.*, at 153.
[41]*Id.*, at 154, fn. 14.
[42]*Id.*
[43]373 F.Supp. 1072 (D.D.C. 1973).
[44]*Id.*, at 1074.
[45]*Id.*, at 1075.
[46]425 F.Supp. 786 (W.D. Pa., 1974).

> *Discrimination* grounded on national origin—or, indeed *on anything but "race" ...* —is *not now cognizable* under §1981, and plaintiff has advanced no compelling reason why, ... this Court should expand the ambit of the Statute to cover alleged employment discrimination entirely on non-racial factors.[47] (emphasis added)

Thus, a third instance of federal court hesitancy to accept nation origins claims for antidiscrimination protection was recorded.

A similar ruling was rendered in *Petrone v. City of Reading*.[48] There plaintiff presented a claim that he was denied equitable treatment in a matter concerning zoning code enforcement for his proposed pizza franchise business. Amongst the complained-of acts allegedly committed by the municipality in this case were allegedly defamatory remarks pertaining to plaintiff's Italian ancestry while plaintiff made no allegation that he was looked upon as being non-white.[49] The federal circuit court for the Eastern District of Pennsylvania found for the defendant and dismissed the changes holding that plaintiff failed to state a maintainable cause of action under the Civil Rights Act of 1964. Here the Court held that the 1964 Civil Rights Act speaks directly to race and does not concern disparity in treatment on the basis of religion, sex, or national origin[50] and that "[s]ince plaintiff has asserted discrimination based only upon his heritage and that there is no allegation that plaintiff is generally perceived as a non-white...."[51]

It appears, therefore, that the federal courts grounded their opinion that ethnic Americans lacked standing to maintain race discrimination claims when claims of that sort did not raise a substantial issue of racism. Perhaps these lower courts relied upon the dictum of *Jones v. Alfred H. Mayer Co.*,[52] where it was stated that racial discrimination claims are to be distinguished from religious or national origins discrimination. What is apparent is that by the close of the 1970s the Court maintained the position that antidiscrimination protections were to be extended to blacks, Hispanics, females, American Indians, Eskimos and Asian Americans. Groups outside the "suspect classifications" listed directly above would be dealt with only on the most restrictive individualized bases where one of their members demonstrated an individual *prima facie* case of racially motivated discrimination.

Beyond the race-sex-nationality-religion line of cases seeking anti-discrimination protections, theories of fundamental rights were raised testing the extent

---

[47]*Ibid.*, at 787.

[48]541 F.Supp. 735 (E.D. Pa. 1982). But see *Manzanares v. Safeway Stores*, 593 F.2d 968, 971 (10th Cir. 1979) allowing a claim by a Hispanic Caucasian Mexican American.

[49]*Id.*, at 738.

[50]*Id.*, citing *Boddorff v. Publicker Industries, Inc.*, 488 F.Supp. 1107, 1109 (E.D. Pa. 1980). Contra, *Harris v. Norfolk and Western Rg. Co.*, 616 F.2d 377, 378 (8thCir. 1980; dictum).

[51]*Id.*, 541 F.Supp. at 738-739.

[52]392 U.S. 409, 413, 88 S.Ct. 2186, 20 L.Ed. 2d 1189 (1968).

of constitutional coverage for claims that could not be directly identified from within the Constitution. The Court dealt with these peripheral notions, especially as regards sex-related status,[53] by deploying the theory of penumbra coverage. "[The] specific guarantees in the Bill of Rights have penumbras, formed by emanations from those guarantees that help give them life and substance."[54] Primary amongst these penumbra rights accepted by the Court is the right to privacy.[55] This avenue of sexual self-determination protected by the penumbra of the Constitution was followed by the gay community in its attempt to earn similar due process coverage.

Relying upon its perceived plain language understanding of the terms sex, sexual preference, and privacy in association, homosexuals brought the matter to court in *Doe v. Commonwealth's Attorney for Richmond*.[56] This three-man District Court denounced the theory in rather summary terms and attempted to convert sexual privacy into the limited context of marital privacy.[57] Although the Supreme Court affirmed the finding of the District Court,[58] it is maintained that the matter has not been given final judicial determination. In anticipation of a future constitutional argument, one commentator has suggested that the time may be ripe for the Court to reconsider the foundation for antidiscrimination protections by substituting "anonymous and diffuse minority" terminology in lieu of the "discrete and insular minority" language relied upon by the Court.[59]

Thus the matter stood. The Court maintained adherence to the element of racism as the capstone for antidiscrimination protection from the 1938 *Carolene Products* enunciation through the 1985 commentary suggesting a rephrasing of the standard. It seems as if an impregnable citadel had been erected. At that particular juncture, however, a further theory was developed—within the framework of the *Carolene Products* model—that was able to pierce the apparently impregnable.

To earn judicial cognition, a cause of action filed by nominally Caucasian plaintiffs had to argue that civil rights protection and anti-discrimination coverage should go beyond consideration of mere physiological manifestation. Rather than focusing upon "race," a more correct standard would be to measure whether

---

[53]For example, *Griswold v. Connecticut*, 381 U.S. 479, 85 S.Ct. 1678, 14 L.Ed. 2d 510 (1965); *Roe v. Wade*, 410 U.S. 113, 93 S.Ct. 705, 35 L.Ed. 2d 147 (1975).

[54]*Griswold, id.*, at 484.

[55]*Id.*, at 483; *Roe v. Wade, ibid.*, at 153-154.

[56]403 F.Supp. 1199 (E.D. Va. 1975).

[57]*Id.*, at 1203-1205.

[58]Aff'd, 425 U.S. 901 (1976).

[59]Bruce Ackerman, "Beyond Carolene Products," *Harvard Law Review*, Vol. 98 (1985), p. 713.

alleged discriminatory acts are "racial" in character.[60] Simply restated, proper analysis could be applied by reviewing whether acts directed against a particular group are invidiously discriminatory if the victims of such acts are looked upon by the discriminators as belonging to a group that shares certain inborn (i.e., racial) characteristics. This approach is quite unlike the "anonymous and diffuse," reverse discrimination, religious identity, or national origins theories previously rejected by the Court. At the same time, by demonstrating that an individual/group suffered from an act of racially motivated discrimination, the victims of such discrimination would demonstrate that they fall within the "discrete and insular" minority standard. Such a matter came to the Supreme Court in the consolidated cases of *Saint Francis College v. Majid Ghaidan Al-Khazraji*[61] and *Shaare Tefila Congregation v. Cobb.*[62] In those cases, the main issue raised was:

> [W]hether ... minority group members who do not belong to distinct "non-white races," but who are the victims of racially-motivated discrimination, are entitled to seek relief under section 1 of the Civil Rights Act of 1866, U.S.C. §§ 1981 & 1982.[63]

To arrive at an affirmative conclusion, the Court was required to undertake an extensive review of the original intent of the framers of the 1866 Civil Rights Act and whether the proffered construction was constitutionally acceptable. The Court found that it could answer affirmatively.

The Court has consistently maintained that the Civil Rights Act of 1866 should be broadly construed and emphasized that "'ingenious analytical instrument'... [may not be used] to carve ... expectation[s]" from that statute.[64] 42 U.S.C. §1981 guarantees that

> [a]ll persons within the jurisdiction of the United States shall have the same rights in every state and Territory to make and enforce contracts, to sue, to be parties, give evidence, and to the full and equal benefit of all laws and proceedings for the security of persons and property as is enjoyed by white citizens, and shall be subject to like punishments, pains,

---

[60]See, e.g., "Beyond a Black and White Reading of Sections 1981 and 1982: Shifting the Focus from Racial Status to Racial Acts," *University of Miami Law Review*, Vol. 41 (1987), pp. 823-857.

[61]481 U.S. 604, 107 S.Ct. 2022, 94 L.Ed. 2d 582 (1987).

[62]481 U.S. 615, 107 S.Ct. 2019, 94 L.Ed. 2d 594 (1987).

[63]Anti Defamation League of B'nai B'rith et al., Amicus Brief supporting *Majid Al-Khazraji* and *Shaare Tefila Congregation* (Docket Nos. 85-2169 and 85-2156, filed November 20, 1986).

[64]*Jones v. Alfred H. Mayer Co.*, 392 U.S. 409, 437; 88 S.Ct. 2186, 20 L.Ed. 2d 1189 (1968) (quoting *United States v. Price*, 383 U.S. 787, 801; 86 S.Ct. 1152, 16 L. Ed. 2d 267 (1966)).

penalties, taxes, licenses, and exactions of every kind, and to no other.[65]

As is seen from the holdings of *Kurylas*,[66] *Budinsky*,[67] *Petrone*,[68] and *United Jewish Organizations*,[69] the federal courts have consistently held that antidiscrimination suits have to be grounded in language that substantially addresses the question of whether the complainant has suffered from racially motivated discrimination. Neither national origins claims nor those founded upon community cohesiveness/religion have been deemed sufficient to carry the burden necessary to sustain a Civil Rights Act of 1964 cause of action. From the precedents rendered, it is highly improbable that the national origins, religion, community identity theories would be able to prevail. For a plaintiff to succeed under the 1964 Civil Rights Act, a claim should assert, and be able to substantiate, that a claimant was wronged because of race animus. To that end, the term race takes on an ambiguous character that may be resolved only by analyzing the clear meaning of the word race and its intended use at the time the statute was enacted.

Analysis of the concept "racial character" requires broad construction to determine the extent of protection Congress intended under sections 1981 and 1982.[70] The legislative history of the statutes clearly demonstrates that the 39th Congress intended that far more than just "non-whites" be protected and that the 39th Congress understood and used the term "race" differently from today's generic usage.

It is well settled that statutes are to be interpreted by using the clear meaning of plain language employed by the framers. Words are to be looked at not as a precise scientific formulae but with a degree of feeling for the ordinary intelligence of common usage present amongst the general public at the time of enactment.[71] Deliberate care when interpreting statutes dating back more than a century is most appropriate. This care must recognize that words are not static but undergo etymologic changes with the passage of time. "Race" is in that category of words that have changed—substantially—since the framing and enactment of the Civil Rights Act of 1866. The *Al-Khazraji/Shaare Tefila* Court reiterated this standard of statutory construction.

---

[65]42 U.S.C. §1981, 16 Stat. 144.

[66]*Supra*, at 9.

[67]*Supra*, at 11.   But see J. Merhige dissenting at 1205.

[68]*Supra*, at 11.

[69]*Supra*, at 12.

[70]See *City of Memphis v. Green*, 451 U.S. 100, 120; 101 S.Ct. 1629, 67 L.Ed. 2d 769 (1981), (statute to be "broadly construed"); *Sullivan v. Little Hunting Park, Inc.*, 396 U.S. 229, 237; 101 S.Ct. 1584, 67 L.Ed. 2d 769 (1969), ("...narrow construction ... inconsistent with protection afforded").

[71]*Maillard v. Lawrence*, 57 U.S. (16 How.) 251, 261; 14 L.Ed. 925 (1853).

In *Al-Khazraji*, the Court examined the "full and equal benefits of all laws ... as is enjoyed by white citizens, ..." clause as it appears in §1981[72] to determine whether this Caucasian plaintiff had standing to bring a race discrimination action under this statute. In noting that §1981 does not specifically use "race" within its structure, the Court cited *Runyon v. McCrory*[73] to reiterate that the section nonetheless forbids all racial discrimination in making private and public contracts.[74] The Court's reliance upon *Runyon v. McCrory* is significant because that holding allowed the Court to incorporate by reference a thorough examination of §1981's legislative history wherein it was clearly demonstrated that §1981 was rooted in both the Civil Rights Act of 1866[75] and the Voting Rights Act of 1870.[76] On this point, the Court declared:

> The debates [of the 1866 Civil Rights Act] are replete with references to "Scandinavian races," *Cong. Globe*, 39th Cong., 1st Sess., 499 (1866) (remarks of Sen. Cowan), as well as the Chinese, *id.*, at 523 (remarks of Sen. Davis), Latin, *id.*, at 238 (remarks of Rep. Kasson), Spanish, *id.*, at 257 ([remarks of Sen. Davis related to District of Columbia suffrage]) and Anglo-Saxon races, *id.*, at 722 (remarks of Rep. Dawson). Jews, *ibid.*, Mexicans, *ibid.* (remarks of Rep. Dawson), blacks, *passim*, and Mongolians, *id.*, at 498 (remarks of Sen. Cowan), were noted as racially distinct. Gypsies, *ibid.*, (remarks of Sen. Cowan) and Germans, *id.*, at 1294 (remarks of Sen. Shellabarger) were identified as separate races.[77]

The history of the 1870 Voting Rights Act, as reviewed in *Runyon v. McCrory*, revealed a similar intent to protect immigrant group civil rights from racially motivated discrimination. Rep. Bingham referred to §16 of that Act (partial authority for §1981) when he said that, "'the States shall not hereafter discriminate against the immigrants from China and in favor of the immigrants from Prussia, nor against the immigrants from France and in favor of the immigrant from Ireland.' (remarks of Rep. Bingham, Cong. Globe, 41st Cong. 2d Sess. at 3871)."[78] Parallel views were expressed in the Senate. *Id.*, at 1536, 3658, 3808 (1870).[79]

Upon this analysis, the *Al-Khazraji* Court concluded that Congress intended to protect identifiable classes of people from international discrimination that was based on ancestry or ethnic characteristics whether or not such identifiable groups would be classified as distinct races under contemporary scientific theory.

---

[72]42 U.S.C. 1981, 16 Stat. 144.
[73]427 U.S. 160, 168, 174-175; 96 S.Ct. 2586, 49 L.Ed. 415 (1976).
[74]*Al-Khazraji, supra,* 481 U.S. at 609.
[75]14 Stat. 27.
[76]16 Stat. 40, 144.
[77]*Id.*, 481 U.S. at 612.
[78]*Id.*, at 613.
[79]*Id.*

"The Court of Appeals was ... right in holding that §1981 ... reaches discrimination against an individual ... of an ethnically and physiognomically distinctive subgrouping of *homo sapien*. It is clear ... that a distinctive physiognomy is not essential to qualify for §1981 protection."[80] Thus, Majid Ghaidan Al-Khazraji, although a Caucasian, was found to have standing in bringing a §1981 civil rights action by unanimous vote of the Court.

Plaintiffs in *Shaare Tefila Congregation v. Cobb*[81] sought relief and punitive damages under §1982.[82] The operative language provided there guarantees all citizens of the United States "the same right ... as is enjoyed by white citizens...."[83] The difficulty rose over the construction of the statute's reference to "white citizens." A series of earlier decisions indicated that Caucasian status was enough to deny physiognomically Caucasian people standing to sustain a §1982 civil rights cause of action.[84] The *Shaare Tefila* Court expressed similar resistance when it said:

> ...a charge of racial discrimination within the meaning of §1982 cannot be made out by alleging only that the defendants were motivated by racial animus; it is necessary as well to allege that defendants' animus was directed towards the kind of group that Congress intended to protect when it passed the statute.[85]

Following the line of reasoning expounded upon in *Al-Khazraji*, the *Shaare Tefila* Court raised the analytical question of "whether Jews [i.e., an ethnic minority group] are considered to be a separate race ... at the time §1982 was adopted, [and whether] Jews [i.e., an ethnic minority group] constituted a group of people that Congress intended to protect."[86] Alluding to the ruling held in the consolidated case of *Al-Khazraji*, Mr. Justice White wrote a unanimously agreed upon opinion stating that it is reasonable for the Court to conclude "that the section was 'intended to protect from discrimination identifiable classes of persons who are subjected to *intentional* discrimination solely because of their ancestry or ethnic characteristics.'"[87] Referring back to the etymological study employed in *Al-Khazraji*, Mr. Justice White concluded that "definitions of race when §1982 was passed are not the same as they are today...."[88] Building upon

---

[80]*Id.*

[81]*Supra*, see fn. 61.

[82]42 U.S.C. §1982, 14 Stat. 27..

[83]*Id.*

[84]See, e.g., *Budinsky v. Corning Glass Works*, 425 F.Supp. 786 (W.D. Pa. 1974) re Slavic Americans; *Kurylas v. Department of Agriculture*, 373 F.Supp. 1072 (D.D.C. 1973) re Polish Americans; *Petrone v. City of Reading*, 541 F.Supp. 735 (E.D. Pa. 1982) re Italian Americans.

[85]*Sharre Tefila, supra*, 481 U.S. at 617.

[86]*Id.*

[87]*Id.*

[88]*Id.*

that understanding, it then became possible for the *Shaare Tefila* Court to find that "Jews [i.e., an ethnic minority group] were among the peoples then considered to be distinct races and hence within the protection of the statute."[89] Therefore "Jews are not foreclosed from stating a cause of action against other members of what today is considered to be part of the Caucasian race."[90]

An interim recapitulation is appropriate here. By turning to an etymological study of the term "race," the Court was able to accept race discrimination arguments from amongst Caucasian groups who had formerly been denied standing for want of belonging to a "non-white" class. That is, where national origins civil rights actions failed for lack of standing, ethnic nationality minorities now seem to be able to sustain a civil right cause if they are able to establish that they were the victims of racially motivated discrimination falling within the scope of congressional intent dating from the time the civil rights laws were originally written.

That today's understanding of "race" is quite different from that used when the 1866 Civil Rights Act was written is apparent from a review of dictionary listings dating back to 1830.[91] Noah Webster, in *An American Dictionary of the English Language,* listed race as a "continued series of descendants from a parent who is called a *stock.*"[92] Noah Webster, in *A Dictionary of the English Language,* wrote of race as "[t]he lineage of a family."[93] J. Donald, in *Chamber's Etymological Dictionary of the English Language,* spoke of "descendants of a common ancestor."[94] The 1887 edition of Noah Webster's *Dictionary of the English Language* stated that race represented "[t]he descendants of a common ancestor; a family, tribe, people or nation, believed or presumed to belong to the same stock."

Similarly, nineteenth century encyclopedias described race in ethnic ancestry terms. The 1858 edition of *Encyclopedia Americana* referred to such races as Finns, Gypsies, Basques, and Hebrews.[95] In 1863 the *New American Cyclopaedia* spoke of a number of subsidiary Arab races, the Hebrews as the Semitic race, and other races such as the Swedes, Norwegians, Germans, Greeks, Finns, Italians, Spanish, Mongolian, and Russians, among other racial groups. The ninth edition of the *Encyclopedia Britannica* (1878) categorized Arabs, Jews, Germans, Hungarians, and Greeks as racial groups.[96]

---

[89]*Id.,* 481 U.S. at 617-618

[90]*Id.,* at 618.

[91]*Al-Khazraji, supra,* 481 U.S. at 610-612, provides a synopsis of these listings.

[92]666 New York 1830, emphasis in the original.

[93]441 New Haven 1841.

[94]415 London 1871.

[95]*Id.,* 481 U.S. at 611 contains specific citations.

[96]*Id.*

Taking the above under consideration makes it possible to more clearly understand the remarks of Senator Trumbull of Illinois as he introduced the 1866 Civil Rights Act as a "bill ... to protect *all* persons in the United States in their civil rights" with application to "every race and color."[97] That Congress intended to protect all races is clear from the debates over the proposal. Sen. Howard, a supporter, spoke of the bill as giving "to persons who are of different races or colors the same civil rights...."[98] The opposition attacks even conceded that "the white as well as the black is included,...." (remarks of Sen. Johnson);[99] and "[the bill] provides, in the first place, that the Civil Rights of all men, without regard to color, shall be equal" (remarks of Sen. Hendricks).[100] Thus it has been said that:

> The statutory structure and legislative history persuade us that the 39th Congress was intent upon establishing in the federal law a broader principle than would have been necessary simply to meet the particular and immediate plight of the newly freed Negro slaves. And while the statutory language has been somewhat streamlined in re-enactment and codification, there is no indication that §1981 is intended to provide any less than the Congress enacted in 1866 regarding racial discrimination against white persons.[101]

With the findings of *Al-Khazraji* and *Shaare Tefila* establishing the propriety of ethnic ancestry civil rights causes of action a further logical step would be to project towards a next ethnic minority group that might seek to institute similar litigation. Such a group may be found in the Polish Americans.

Within the Polish American community it is widely maintained that "the heritage of Polish Americans and their history in America is inextricably involved in the fight against discrimination...."[102] An example frequently employed by Polish Americans to underscore this position relates to the treatment of the Jamestown Polonians. Brought to the young Virginia Colony as skilled craftsmen in 1608, these artisans were quite responsible for the eventual economic success of this colonial endeavor. In 1619, when the colony was granted the privilege of self-government, the Polanders found themselves excluded from the House of Burgesses. These Poles responded with a work stoppage to demand a part in the political process. The historic record reports the outcome:

---

[97]*Congressional Globe*, 39th Congress, 1st Session (1866), at 211.

[98]*Id.*, at 504.

[99]*Id.*, at 505.

[100]*Id.*, at 601.

[101]*McDonald v. Santa Fe Trail Transportation Co.*, 427 U.S. 273, 296; 96 S.Ct. 2574, 49 L.Ed. 2d 493 (1976).

[102]Polish American Congress et al., Amicus Brief in both *Bakke, supra,* and *United Steelworkers v. Weber, supra,* at 2.

Upon some dispute of the Polonians resident in Virginia, it was now agreed (notwithstanding any former order to the contrary) that they shal be enfranchised and made as free as any inhabitant there whatsoever: and because their skill in making pitch and tarre and sope-ashes shall not dye with them, it is agreed that some young men shalbe put unto them to learne their skill and knowledge therein for the benifitt of the Country hereafter.[103]

Despite the promise of this early effort, the Polish community in America was relegated to a position of secondary importance as, first, the colonial and then the Old Immigration populated the new nation with people predominantly from Northern and Western Europe. The North-West Europeans came to form the core of dominant, white American society. People unlike this dominant group would often feel pains of discrimination incident to their ethnic ancestry. Notwithstanding the influx of the New Immigration, the dominance of the self-perceived nativists found expression in the form of growing resistance towards Southern and Eastern Europeans culminating in the passage of America's first blanket anti-immigration laws.[104] One analysis of the advent of restrictive immigration by a Polish-American author is critical of the Dillingham Commission's Report as being racist.[105]

The general rule for attempting to measure the effects of invidious forms of discrimination is to seek data on the rate at which a particular suspect group may have gained entrance into the mainstreams of society. The studies that have focused upon the Polish American community generated some incisive information. Professor Obidinski's work on Buffalo's Polonia is notable for the identification of a trend wherein second and third generation Polish Americans expressed dismay in being made to feel different from the "downtown" society.[106] Another study of Polish, Italian, Latin, and Black representation in the upper echelons of large Chicago corporations presented a rather dismal finding, reporting that out of 1,355 possible director/officer positions, merely 52 (i.e., 3.8%) were held by the groups under consideration. In particular, Poles held but 0.7% of the total

---

[103]Cf. Frank Renkiewicz, ed., *The Poles in America 1608-1972* (Dobbs Ferry, NY: Oceana Press, 1973), p. 42.

[104]E.g., *Annual Reports* (1899) of the Bureau of Immigration and Naturalization wherein race classifications were established that remained in regular use until the 1930s (see especially p. 6 for Polish); see also "Race Classification," *Report of the Commissioner General of Immigration 1904*, at 10a; and the 1911 Commission Report urging literacy tests for eastern and southern Europeans as relied upon by the House in 1916. H.R. No. 95, 64th Congress, 1st Session, at 4-5 (1916).

[105]James S. Pula, "American Immigration Policy and the Dillingham Commission," *Polish American Studies*, Vol. 37 (1980), at 5-31.

[106]Eugene Obidinski, *Ethnic to Status Group: Polish Americans in Buffalo* (1980), with special focus on chapter 1.

positions (i.e., 10 out of 1355).[107] It is suspected that the numbers have not significantly changed since Dr. Barta's study was completed.

Paul Wrobel's study[108] of attitudes amongst Detroit's Polish Americans goes to reinforce the findings of Obidinski and Barta. Together, these three sociological studies demonstrate the pervasive degree to which the effects of perceived indigenous discrimination has been felt across the width and breadth of the Polish American community.

Attendant to the rise of this internal apprehension was the widespread appearance of the "Pollock" jokes. Recognized as a form of racially motivated discrimination, the main theme of this reverse variety of ethnic humor was the characterization of Poles as stolid, dull and quasi-human—i.e., a less-than-desirable life form.[109] It may be that there was some carryover from Nazi racist programs of World War II, where severe forms of anti-Semitic and anti-Slavic ethnocentrism resulted in the merciless deaths of millions of Jews and Poles.[110] The Poles, like the Jews, were defined in racial terms by the Nazis.[111]

The startling paradox of understanding the above is that Poles in America, when seeking antidiscrimination protection under national origins theories, were held to lack standing because of their Caucasian traits.[112] It appears, rather, that the courts of the 1970s were more intent on establishing limited parameters of antidiscrimination protections than in grasping the invidious discrimination perspective that lay at the heart of civil rights actions brought by Polish Americans. When learning of rejections from antidiscrimination protection, Polish Americans complained that they were not being accorded equal protection.

> We raise these questions and issues not to be difficult or resentful for we believe that the groups now being favored deserve attention to their plight. We raise these questions and issues to point out there are others who have similar problems and also deserve attention and similar effort.[113]

---

[107]Russell Barta, Minority Report, *The Representation of Poles, Italians, Latins and Blacks in the Executive Suites of Chicago's Largest Corporations* (Washington, DC: The National Center for Urban Ethnic Affairs, 1973).

[108]Paul Wrobel, *Our Way: Family, Parish and Neighborhood in a Polish-American Community* (1979).

[109]Michael Novak, "The Sting of Pollock Jokes," *Newsweek*, April 12, 1976, at 13.

[110]See, e.g., Document No. 1880, Prosecution Exhibit 1314, Nuremberg Trial Documents; Document 1919 PS International Military Tribunal, Nuremberg, Germany.

[111]Document No. 862.4016/2184 PS/FF, in the National Archives, Washington, DC. See also Justice Stevens, dissenting in *Fullibone* as cited in note 35, *supra*.

[112]*Kurylas, supra,* at 1076.

[113]Polish American Congress et al., Amicus Brief, *United Steelworkers v. Weber, supra,* at 7.

Furthermore, the Polish American Congress maintained that "an uneven approach ... [with] an indifference to solving the problems of *all* who have been discriminated against"[114] can only result in unequal protection of groups that deserve antidiscrimination coverage. The language of the Fourteenth Amendment specifically states: "No State shall ... deny to any person within its jurisdiction the equal protection of the laws."[115]

It would seem that equal protections would be extended in an equal fashion. Yet that has not always been the case. Joseph Tussman and Jacobus tenBroek wrote a commentary in which they attempted to demonstrate that most laws are either underinclusive, overinclusive, or both.[116] Tussman and tenBroek's work provides an analogous basis for analyzing the relative position of Polish Americans regarding both mainstream society and how Polish Americans have been affected by antidiscrimination laws.

Drawing from *Hirabayashi v. United States*,[117] wherein Tussman and tenBroek demonstrate that the World War II sequestering of Japanese Americans may have been an overly generalized reaction that ran afoul of the Fourteenth Amendment's equal protection guarantee, it may logically be argued that classification of Polish Americans within the ranks of America's dominant class was similarly based upon an unwarranted overgeneralization. Blacks, Hispanics, American Indians, Asiatics, females, and most recently Jews and Arabs have been identified as amongst discreet and insular minorities on the basis of the physiological and historic incidents each group bears and that these perceived differences serve as the basis for past and current acts of racially motivated discrimination. Polish Americans, as earlier legislatures and courts have maintained, have not been permitted suspect group status but rather, based largely on their Caucasoid appearance, are claimed to have been readily accepted into mainstream white dominant society. Yet, as demonstrated above,[118] a closer analysis of the circumstances would show that Polish Americans have not been favored with ready social acceptance. Instead, they have faced invidious forms of discrimination similar to those experienced by the identified minority groups.

An important predicate in attempting to define the suspect class seems to rest with an understanding of nineteenth century pseudo-scientific theories concerning the nature of man and supposed near-man (i.e., sub-humans). Through a process of dehumanization, the dominant group could not only express satisfaction with their dominance but also justify the need for continued control over those to be dominated. Medieval notions that came to justify eighteenth and nineteenth century slavery eventually became formalized in the work of the pseudo-scientists. Employing Darwinian theory, late nineteenth/early twentieth

---

[114]Polish American Congress, Amicus Brief, *Bakke, supra*, at 4.

[115]U.S.C. Const. Amend. 14, §1.

[116]Joseph Tussman and Jacobus tenBroek, "The Equal Protection of the Laws," *California Law Review*, Vol. 37 (1949), at 341.

[117]320 U.S. 81, 63 S.Ct. 1375, 87 L.Ed. 1774 (1943).

[118]*Supra*, at 23 and 24.

century writers attempted to standardize race theory in a manner that would support Aryan/Nordic domination. Primary amongst these attempts was *The Inequality of Human Races*.[119] In this widely accepted book, Arthur De Gobineau proclaimed the "superiority of the white type," particularly the "Aryan family."[120] De Gobineau denigrated non-white people by characterizing them as being of lesser intelligence and asserting that non-whites ranked lower on the evolutionary ladder.[121] Upon publication, these race theories gave form to a hitherto abstract belief.

It is important to note that De Gobineau's work was preceded by another expression of pseudo-scientific racist thought. In "The Expansion of the Slavs,"[122] T. Peisker wrote that Slavic people are the product of the Pripet Marshes where, among other factors, the miasmatic gases and pestering gnats spread fevers that brought a degenerating effect upon this stock of humanity, thereby relegating it to a lesser developed station relative to the Gothic (i.e., Nordic) race.[123] To understand Peisker properly, two factors must be taken into consideration: First, the Pripet Marshes are located in the eastern portion of those lands that traditionally have belonged to the Polish nation. Therefore, the implication that the Poles were amongst those most detrimentally affected by the degenerating influence is to be clearly inferred from Peisker's theory. Secondly, this work appeared at the time when Poland was under partition by Austria, Prussia, and Russia and where each of these partitioning powers attempted to destroy Polish culture in favor of their own. Thus, it may be reasonably recounted that Peisker attempted to rationalize continued partition based on the notion that Poles were subhumans incapable of governing themselves. For the purpose of this discussion, however, Peisker's work was published coincidental with the last stages of the New Immigration. The era of free access to America closed with the passage of the Emergency Quota Act (1921)[124] closely followed by the National Origins Act (1924)[125] as a reinforcement of the nativist discrimination against Poles as less-than-desirable Eastern Europeans.[126]

The parallels between De Gobineau and Peisker are clear. It is reasonable to presume that De Gobineau's work had an effect upon the twentieth century institutionalization of racially motivated discrimination directed against blacks. It should be just as reasonable to presume that Peisker's work had a similar impact with regard to the rise of racially-motivated discrimination against Poles in

---

[119]Arthur de Gobineau, *The Inequality of Human Races* (New York: G. P. Putnam's Sons, 1915).

[120]*Id.*, chapter 16.

[121]*Id.*

[122]T. Peisker, "The Expansion of the Slavs," *Cambridge Medieval History* (New York: 1913), Vol. II, chapter XIV, at 418-479.

[123]*Id.*, at 420, 425-426, and 428.

[124]42 Stat. 5.

[125]8 U.S.C. §145 et seq., 43 Stat. 153.

[126]*Id.*

America. Both works were published in America at the beginning of the twentieth century. This element, by itself, should serve as sufficient basis for presuming that those decision makers who would enact racist legislation or develop sociological theories had access to both De Gobineau and Peisker. To deny such access would be equivalent to denying the very existence of either writing. Yet, while it is widely accepted that De Gobineau's work is significant to understanding the application of Fourteenth Amendment equal protection in the effort to eradicate the racism lying at the heart of the invidious forms of discrimination cast against the identified minorities, Peisker's work has been virtually ignored in formulating an understanding of Poles as victims of invidious discrimination and therefore eligible for anti-discrimination protection.

Conclusion

With the findings of *Al-Khazraji* and *Shaare Tefila*, compelling authority now exists to allow for strict scrutiny of properly framed antidiscrimination claims that might be raised by victimized Polish Americans. In seeking remedy for a complaint of an act of racially motivated discrimination, redress should be sought under 42 U.S.C. §§1981, 1982, 1985(3) and 2000(d),[127] with additional charges, whenever appropriate, grounded in the Common Law theories of nuisance, trespass, and/or the intentional infliction of emotional distress.

---

[127]42 U.S.C. §§1981, 1982, 1985(B) and 2000(d). 16 Stat. 144, 14 Stat. 27, 17 Stat. 13, and 78 Stat. 252.

A Bottle of Milk for Poland:
Nelson Algren and I

by

Anthony Bukoski[1]

I.

In a November 1989 letter to me, Professor Thomas Gladsky, author of
Princes, Peasants, and Other Polish Selves: Ethnicity in American Literature,
recalled how that month he had attended an Institute entitled "Cultural Diversity
and Liberal Education: Negotiating Difference in the Academy." Presented by
the University of Chicago's Office of Continuing Education, the Institute pur-
ported to explore "ways in which the academy might responsibly embrace cultural diversity within a liberal arts agenda." The Institute hoped, furthermore,
"to provide opportunities to listen carefully to voices which have previously
been muted within the academy."

In his letter Gladsky commented on how restrictive the term "diversity" has
become:

> I never heard a word [at the conference] mentioned about Euro-ethnic
> groups or most of the world's cultures for that matter. Diversity is the
> exclusive terrain of women and African Americans, with a nod toward

[1]Anthony Bukoski is Associate Professor of English at the University of
Wisconsin-Superior.

Asians and Native Americans. After a talk about "our wonderful ethnic studies" program by a Bowling Green University academic, I asked in which courses [at Bowling Green] one might study East-European cultures. He looked over the course selection and unashamedly pointed to Ethnicity and Aging, a sociology course. He did not laugh when I asked him if he were serious! That's the way it is. ... we [Polish Americans] are out before we're in.[2]

Gladsky's experience parallels mine that fall when I telephoned the University of Wisconsin-Madison to inquire about reading a paper at a conference on "Design for Diversity," the University of Wisconsin System's then-new initiative for increasing multi-cultural awareness and education. At "The Challenge of Diversity: Curriculum Development for the Twenty-First Century" conference co-sponsored by the Office of the Special Assistant to the President for Minority Affairs and the Undergraduate Teaching Improvement Council, I wished to offer a plan for incorporating into the University liberal arts curriculum a course of Polish-American history and culture. Having proposed the topic, I was politely told that it did not fall within the purview of the conference, which, it turns out, was open only to African-, Asian-, Native-, Hispanic-American and women's issues. The letter announcing the conference from the University of Wisconsin System's former Vice President for Academic Affairs, however, listed no such restrictions and, in fact, noted that some panels would "discuss individual and institutional approaches to ... meeting the ethnic studies requirements."[3]

Stanislaus Blejwas, past president of the Polish American Historical Association, has suggested reasons why American culture, and I think by extension today's "multi-cultural" and "cultural diversity" issues on campus, too often exclude Polonia; or perhaps why or how Polonia has excluded herself. At least partly the reason has to do with Polish Americans' lacking a strong cultural and political voice. In his Presidential Address at the December 1987 Polish American Historical Association meeting, an address later published as "Voiceless Immigrants" in *Polish American Studies*, Blejwas recounts attending a National Endowment for the Humanities seminar whose twelve participants represented different racial and ethnic backgrounds. Together the participants "explored the rich body of immigrant and ethnic literature—rich, that is, except for the Polish American experience," writes Blejwas.

Remarkable as it might seem, there does not exist a Polish American literature; that is, a literature penned by Polish immigrants and Polish ethnics about their experience in America, and readily available to the American reading public. While my seminar colleagues overwhelmed us with pages of ethnic literary bibliography (novels, poetry, plays, essays, biographies, and literary criticism), it was, and still is, impossible

---

[2]Thomas Gladsky, Letter to the author, November 27, 1989.
[3]Eugene Trani, Letter to the University of Wisconsin System Vice Chancellors, September 22, 1989, p. 1

to locate more than a dozen Polish American novelists and short story writers, while there is not a major Polish American poet or dramatist.[4]

Blejwas posits several *possible* causes for the dearth of Polish-American writing as recently as 1987.[5] Among possible causes for the lack of a Polish-American literature, Blejwas suggests that the oral tradition Polish peasants brought with them to America did "not fare well in a (an) urban, industrial society," that these immigrants wanted their children's education to be "economically productive ... the idea of graduate study in history, English, sociology, or anthropology ... not seem[ing] to offer a profitable economic return," that strict adherence to "the inerrancy of [church] dogma and structure, may have effectively stifled intellectual curiosity about the world in which man lives and struggles," and that the rapidity with which many second generation American Polonia denied their ancestors' peasant roots "manifested a sense of cultural and psychological inferiority" toward the past.[6]

Suggesting why each of the above may or may not be true, Professor Blejwas also offers what he calls "serious" external causes for Polonia's lacking a voice—American publishers' perceptions that Polish topics do not sell or that Polish Americans as a group do not read, the lack of national Polish-American literary prizes, a national Polish-American literary journal, or a residency for its writers.[7]

Gladsky's, my own, and no doubt other Polish Americans' experience of being left out of the diversity issue is, I think, partly related to our lacking the literary voice of which Blejwas speaks. As an ethnic group, Polish Americans have much in their history and culture that may go untold, perhaps more so today when "ethno-" and "Eurocentrism" are commonly viewed as culturally restrictive and so the thinking goes, necessarily bad. In a special number of *Mid-American Review* devoted to "Works by Latino Writers," Luis J. Rodriguez discussing "Multicultural Diversity in the Arts" recently opined that "to be white is to engage in dominance behavior.... The so-called Eurocentrist view of the world [is] the historical view of the power elite."[8] On one hand, as Polish Americans

---

[4]Stanislaus A. Blejwas, "Voiceless Immigrants," *Polish American Studies*, Vol. 45 (1988), pp. 5-11.

[5]Out of 133 novels and short stories cited in Joseph Zurawski's 1972 *Polish American History and Culture: A Classified Bibliography*, for example, Blejwas finds only 15 by "individuals of Polish origin." See Stanislaus A. Blejwas, "Voiceless Immigrants," p. 5.

[6]Blejwas, "Voiceless Immigrants," pp. 7-8.

[7]Blejwas, "Voiceless Immigrants," p. 9.

[8]Luis J. Rodriguez, "Living on the Hyphen: Multicultural Diversity in the Arts," *Mid-American Review*, Vol. 12 (1992), pp. 3-7, quote from p. 6. Rodriguez, speaking of how people of color are marginalized in American society, notes that only when whites see themselves as "Italian or Irish or Swedish or Jewish"—in terms of their ethnicity, in other words—can they avoid the "dominance behavior" that comes from being white. He quotes the poet Jack

then we are associated with white Europe, "the power elite" Eurocentrists. On the other, as white ethnics we are insufficiently attractive to what Michael Novak calls "the highly educated members of superculture [in America who] have been diligently taught that ethnicity is the source of evil"[9] to warrant real consideration of our story in the academy. When, for example, has a journal or magazine devoted a special issue to Polonia's creative writers? (A major theme, by the way, of the University of Chicago's Cultural Diversity Institute was "De-Centering the West.") As Gladsky wrote, we Polish-Americans "are out before we're in." What happened to the ethnic revival foreseen for the 1970s? Are Poles, Italians, Greeks, and Slavs (Monsignor Geno Beroni uses the acronym PIGS to describe these ethnic groups)[10] any more at the forefront of American consciousness and the way this consciousness is formed by the print and electronic media or by serious inquiry in the academy than twenty years ago?

Stanislaus Blejwas in his address notes that Polish Americans "are an ethnic group, but not an ethnic presence on the American cultural scene."[11] The danger is that we may be relegated to "cultural oblivion"[12] or continue to be stereotyped by those who understand neither us nor our experience. Objections to its "worshipful and unscholarly" sample entries notwithstanding, one wonders whether such stereotyping played a part when a 1991 application to the National

---

Foley: "The only way for the 'majority' to conceive of itself as a majority is to conceive of itself as white; without whiteness there are only 'minorities.' To speak of multiculturalism, therefore, is to speak of a way of seeing the world without whiteness—though one has to admit that whiteness (power, dominance) is much in evidence." Rodriguez then writes: "Although, in effect, we are still 'multicultural,' in the interplay of dominance-signifying terms, to be multicultural is to be other than white. And this in turn becomes other than 'mainstream'.... [T]here is a liberating potential in multi-cultural diversity. It can challenge the lie of a 'superior' culture by the affirmation of 'other' cultures. And ... it can also help do away with the dominance-creating power that is really at stake: Class rule in America."

At the same time as it encourages "whites" to see themselves ethnically, such "multicultural" thinking assumes that the PIGS—Poles, Italians, Greeks, Slavs—in America, since they are white, have themselves not been marginalized. Michael Novak comments on the fallacy of equating Polish Americans with the "dominant" white American culture: "One day on a platform, an American Indian was telling a group of Polish nuns and me what our ancestors did to *his* ancestors. I tried gently to remind him that *my* grandparents (and theirs) never *saw* an Indian. They came to this country after that. Nor were they responsible for enslaving the blacks (or anyone else). They themselves escaped serfdom barely four generations ago—almost as recently as blacks escaped slavery." See Michael Novak, *The Rise of the Unmeltable Ethnics: Politics and Culture in the Seventies* (New York: 1973).

[9]Novak, p. xvii.
[10]Novak, p. xxxiv.
[11]Blejwas, "Voiceless Immigrants," p. 6.
[12]Blejwas, "Voiceless Immigrants," p. 9.

Endowment for the Humanities for support of a Polish-American dictionary was denied. Though "attracted to the idea of ethnic dictionaries," stated a summary of the panelists' comments, and though while understanding that Poles comprise "the second largest migrant group to the United States in the twentieth century" yet still have no standard reference work about them, nonetheless the panel found it "difficult to be enthusiastic about a Polish dictionary."[13]

As harmful can be presumed familiarity with Polonia. When I submitted a collection of short stories to the University of Illinois Press Short Fiction Competition in 1988, one of their readers responded thus to three of the six Polish-American stories:

> I have a real problem with these [stories], and it's subjective. I spent my formative years in a household where English was not the native tongue; I hung around with the Polish for a while and then moved to a town where Italians formed half the population. So when I read these [Bukoski's] stories I say, Sure, that's right; but everybody knows that [about Polish Americans]. I guess the question is, Does everybody REALLY know that?[14]

Had this university press reader dwelt at some later time among "the Greeks" and "the Slavs" (the "G" and "S" in "PIGS"), he or she would have come full circle through America's unpopular ethnics, the PIGS whose experience is unequal—in the minds of some—to the suffering and exploitation of those whom so-called "diversity" conferences, multicultural programs, and special journal issues are designed to celebrate. "[P]rejudices against ethnic Americans have seldom been challenged on the Left, as prejudices against blacks have been,"[15] Michael Novak writes. Partly this is so because ethnic Americans' history and culture—as African-Americans' was until the 1960s and Native-, Hispanic-, and Asian-Americans' until more recently—white ethnic Americans' history still is, I think, irrelevant to many American educators.

Professor Blejwas' assessment of our forebears "voicelessness" notwithstanding; having done so little to tell our story, to *force* our story told as Werner Sollors says African Americans have,[16] I wonder how Polish Americans can now expect to be included in discussions of multiculturalism and diversity? How can we expect if not equal, then at least some, *any!* representation in anthologies, special journal issues, and multi-cultural readers? Left to the non-Polonian text editor or diversity-conference coordinator to include materials about Polish-American life in their projects, we may very well end up with the kind of "cultural

---

[13]NEH Division of Research Program's Panel Comment Sheet Number RT-21280.

[14]Ann Lowry Weir, Letter to the author, October 6, 1988, p. 1.

[15]Novak, p. 8.

[16]Werner Sollors, *Beyond Ethnicity: Consent and Descent in American Culture* (London: 1986), p. 36.

amnesia" our immigrant great-grandparents and grandparents sometimes developed to forget the old country, the voyage across, and their struggles and humiliation here.[17] Our own amnesia will be forced on us from outside by an indifferent academy and by a seemingly hostile media. In his history of the Polish-Americans, John J. Bukowczyk has chronicled how "the purveyors of American mass culture ... [have] treated Polish-Americans with disdain. Postwar mass culture absorbed none of the positive elements of Polish-American culture as it had adopted and accepted Jewish, Yiddish, and Black forms."[18] How few valuable, positive images we saw of Polish America outside our communities in the 1950s and 1960s. I am not sure much has changed.[19] This lack of a positive image is the focus of the second, the more personal part of my essay, and where Algren comes in.

II.

Aside from noting with mild curiosity that a movie had been made of *The Man with the Golden Arm* (1949)—a 1951 Pocket Books edition describes the movie and novel as "the powerful, tender story of a dope addict and gambler who never dealt a hand so bad as the one life dealt him"—I was not interested in Algren in 1956, the year of the movie's release. My father having followed the Catholic Legion of Decency ratings where *The Man* had been condemned, nor was I permitted to see the movie.

By sixth or seventh grade, I had heard of Pułaski and Kościuszko, but Poland's language, art, and history had no regular place in the *Szkoła Wojciecha* curriculum—this being perhaps less typical of larger cities where "first- and second-generation immigrants and their children who attended Polish-American parochial or after hours Polish language schools were taught about Adam Mickiewicz ... Henryk Sienkiewicz and Władysław Reymont...."[20] I learned from my mother about the Black Madonna and other religious and national heroes, and my father had read *Quo Vadis?* and some of Joseph Conrad in English. Suffering "cultural amnesia," my grandparents, however, hardly spoke of Poland.

I neither knew nor cared about an ethnic identity. In Catholic high school we read Conrad's "The Lagoon" and heard Madame Curie's name, but in no Pol-

---

[17]Novak, pp. xx-xxi.

[18]John J. Bukowczyk, *And My Children Did Not Know Me: A History of the Polish Americans* (Bloomington, IN: 1987), p. 112.

[19]John Bukowczyk discusses American mass culture's negative portrayal of Polish America, one which continues seemingly unabated. In fact, as recently as March 24, 1992, the NBC sitcom "Empty Nest" presented through an "entire program ... a sloppy, stupid character named Mrs. Polsky. The story was made from some of the Polish jokes we hear." See Virginia C. Lada, letter to the editor, *Polish American Journal*, June 1992, p. 3.

[20]Stanislaus Blejwas, Letter to the editor, *The New York Times Book Review*, November 22, 1987, p. 47.

ish context. I doubt whether I heard the words "Polish" or "Polish American" in four years of high school. Except for a few sports figure, for me no well-known Polish Americans existed after whom I could psychologically, intellectually, or emotionally model myself, or in whose lives I could see mine reflected. For all I knew, American Polonia never existed in the culture outside Superior, Wisconsin. Possibly I would have cared about Polish-American identity earlier in life had American culture provided occasional glimpses of—and thus validated—who we, the Polish Americans, are. As John J. Bukowczyk notes, in the post-war years, "[a]bsent in the media were both positive depictions of Polish-American characters and characters to whom blue-collar ethnic viewers and their children could relate. Instead, they regularly encountered anti-Polish bias and stereotypes that undercut group identity."[21] Now in the decade of "diversity" and "multiculturalism" we are being denied ourselves again, this time by the diversity planners.

Not until I was an eighteen-year-old university student did I see for the first time a view of Polish-American life imaged in fiction. In one of my world literature reading assignments, Algren's "A Bottle of Milk for Mother," Bruno "Lefty" Bicek, a Chicago street tough having robbed an old man, is being interrogated by the police, a *Dziennik Chicagoski* reporter looking on. Uncertain of the value and values of his ethnic background, and consequently unsure of his own worth, the posturing, bragging Lefty soon confesses:

> You wouldn't think a old boobatch like that'd have so much stren'th left in him, boozin' down Division night after night, year after year, like he didn't have no home to go to. He pulled my hand off his mouth 'n started hollerin', *"Młody bandyta! Młody bandyta!"* 'n I could feel him slippin.' He was just too strong fer a kid like me to hold—.[22]

As Lefty "sings," Sergeant Adamovitch thinks how the kid is a "low-class Polak," whereas he, the Sergeant, is a "high-class Polak because his name is Adamovitch and not Adamowski." He speculated that Irish not Polish run Chicago because of people like Lefty, "Polaks [who] stayed on relief and got drunk and never got anywhere and had everybody down on them."[23] Thus my first view of Polonia in American literature. My second was of a "survivor of the stone age" in his undershirt and grease-stained pants who says to his visiting sister-in-law Blanche as the "music of the polka comes up," "I'm afraid I'll strike you as being the unrefined type."[24]

---

[21]Bukowczyk, p. 112.
[22]Nelson Algren, Nelson, "A Bottle of Milk for Mother," *The Neon Wilderness* (New York: 1960), p. 78.
[23]Algren, p. 84.
[24]Tennessee Williams, *A Streetcar Named Desire* (New York: 1947), pp. 72, 31.

Stanislaus Blejwas, Thomas Napierkowski, and others have discussed how "the literary imagination spins unflattering and exaggerated pictures, which most often reinforce the negative stereotypes that Americans possess of their Polish neighbors."[25] To *this* college freshman in 1963, any image, even unfavorable, indicated that Polish Americans were worthy of notice. In Algren's story I saw for the first time names like my neighbors' and mine, even though Algren's Idzikowskis, Nowagrodskis, and Benkowskis were thieves, pimps, and murderers. The pleasure I found in his short story was the desperate pleasure of a young ethnic not wanting to be invisible, the desperation of realizing I had been invisible until reading about people who sometimes spoke my parents' and grandparents' language and who had, as I say, a name like mine. I myself was a kind of voiceless immigrant. Vicious or not in his portrayal, Algren's was a voice for which I was desperate.

Michael Novak has written:

> Those Poles of Buffalo and Milwaukee--so notoriously taciturn, sullen, nearly speechless. Who has ever understood them? It is not that Poles do not feel emotion--what is their history if not dark passion, romanticism, betrayal, courage, blood? But where in America is there anywhere a language for voicing what a Christian Pole in this nation feels...? Of what shall the young man of Lackawanna think on his way to work in the mills, departing his relatively dreary home and street? What roots does he have? What language of the heart is available to him?
> The PIGS are not silent willingly. The silence burns like hidden coals in the chest.[26]

For a long time after reading Algren's story, I did not think about the disadvantages of being an invisible ethnic—thirty-five years to be exact, not until the summer of 1991 when I read *Never Come Morning* (1942),[27] where Algren's story appears in expanded form as the novel's second book. Despite Algren's attempt to justify his portraits (in *The Man With the Golden Arm*, *Never Come Morning*, and assorted stories) of Chicago's Division Street Polonia by claiming he was giving a voice to the voiceless, I agree with Thomas Napierkowski that, given Algren's portrayal:

> even the fair-minded reader receives the impression that Polish American life is as debased, impoverished, and subhuman as the national mythology has claimed; and the privacy and obscurity of that life make it capable of anything in the public's imagination.[28]

---

[25]Blejwas, "Voiceless Immigrants," p. 10.
[26]Novak, pp. 63-64.
[27]Nelson Algren, *Never Came Morning* (New York: 1987).
[28]Thomas Napierkowski, "The Image of Polish Americans in American Literature," *Polish American Studies*, Vol. 40 (1983), p. 14.

I believe too, however, that as Algren's jailed club-fighter Lefty Bicek in the novel composes a letter to a boxing magazine, Algren speaks beautifully for the voiceless, and that this scene alone should in some way mitigate what many have seen as Algren's insult to Polonia.[29] At key places as he writes his letter, Lefty Bicek formulates questions about Poles, about the Polish fighter Stanley Ketchel (Kiecel), for instance. Lefty knows the answers. He simply questions in order to validate himself, as I saw myself validated in Algren's story, as neither a voiceless nor an invisible Pole. The passage in *Never Come Morning* is poignant, I think, because Lefty's is the search of many young men and women for self-validation within the larger culture:

> How do you rate Tiger Pultoric? Does Irish Eddie Boyle represent anything but the Irish? What nationality was Ketchel? Do you spell his name with one L or two? Is it true that Jack Dempsey is part Polish? What was Joe Choynski? A boxer has been knocked down and at the VERY SECOND that the ref is saying TEN the round ends. He is ready to answer the bell for the next round. Did the gong save him from a kayo?[30]

Next Lefty asks the "Question-Box" how best to protect his teeth in the ring.

> Where can I obtain details of the fight between Jack Johnson and Stanley Ketchel? Is it true Kid McCoy came out against Tom Sharkey with plaster in his gloves. Who won...? How do you rate Casey Benkowski?
> He paused, pencil poised and tongue between his teeth, then resumed:
> Who invented the trick of pointing to an opponent's shoelaces and knocking him out when he looked down? Can this still be done?
> He knew the nationalities of Choynski and Ketchel as well as he knew his own; he merely sought printed assurance that they too were Poles and they too were unbeatable....[31]

Too many of us seek this assurance from the larger American culture. How sad that my own initial encounter with Polonia in American literature was of a Polonia "devoid of culture, education, and values."[32] How sad, too, that a person would embrace such an image, no other being available. I doubt whether today's multicultural text editors and diversity specialists know or care about the truly

---

[29]Algren's response to *Zgoda*'s and the Polish Roman Catholic Union of America's protest of *Never Come Morning* is reprinted in the 1987 *Four Walls Eight Windows'* edition.

[30]Algren, *Never Come Morning*, p. 134.

[31]Algren, *Never Come Morning*, pp. 134-135.

[32]Napierkowski, p. 14.

voiceless.

One hears often how "the story must be told" of our Polish immigrant fore-bears. Also important is the story of postwar and contemporary American Polo-nia. With such literary critics as Thomas Gladsky and Thomas Napierkowski encouraging Polonia's authors, perhaps the story is not yet lost. Among those writing fiction and poetry about Polish America are Verlyn Klinkenborg, Stuart Dybek, Gary Gildner, John Guzlowski, John Minczeski, Natalie Kusz, Victor Contoski, Paul Milenski, Jan Kubicky, Anne Pellowski, and myself.

Still, what Polish America needs is one big book, a fiction masterwork to draw America's eyes to us. In a letter to *The New York Times Book Review*, Czesław Miłosz wrote in 1987:

> I have never denied my expression of sympathy for and my recogni-tion of Polish-Americans' achievements in building churches, schools, creating numerous organizations and clubs. I also continue to believe that the story of hardships, deprivations and tragedies which were the lot of the Polish mass immigration to this country makes a vast epic and perhaps one day this epic will be told.[33]

Who will be the writer? Where will he or she come from? "The silence burns like hidden coals in the chest."

---

[33]Czesław Miłosz, Letter to the editor, *The New York Times Book Review*, November 22, 1987, p. 47.

Appendix

In June, 1992, several hundred scholars met in an International Congress at Yale University to celebrate the fiftieth anniversary of the Polish Institute of Arts and Sciences in America. The following is the complete program of that Congress.

Thursday, June 18, 1992

Opening Session
Chair: Thaddeus V. Gromada, Vice President and
Executive Director, Polish Institute of Arts & Sciences
Welcome: Gaddis Smith, Yale University
Welcome: Feliks Gross, President, Polish Institute of Arts & Sciences

Address: Piotr Wandycz, Yale University

Keynote Session
Chair: James S. Pula (SUNY-Empire State College)
Introduction of Speakers: Feliks Gross (Polish Institute of Arts & Sciences)

Remarks: Stanisław Mrozowski,
Former President of the Polish Institute of Arts & Sciences (1965-1974)

Address: His Excellency Kazimierz Dziewanowski,
Ambassador of the Republic of Poland

Concurrent Sessions

1. Democratic Thought in Poland: 1863-1914
Co-sponsored by the Kościuszko Foundation.

Chair: James S. Pula (SUNY-Empire State College)

"The Democratization of the Democratic Ideal: Polish Politics 1864-1900,"
Stanislaus Blejwas (Central Connecticut State University)
"The Rise of Political Parties: 1890-1914," Robert Blobaum (University of
West Virginia)

2. Economic Issues in Contemporary Poland

Chair: Holley Groshek (SECA, Council of Governments)

"Poland's Revolution of 1989: Political, Social or Economic?" Andrzej W. Ty-
mowski (Yale University)
"Polish Privatization Policy," Lucja Swiątkowski Cannon (Washington, DC)
"Political, Social and Moral Dilemmas in Building a Market Economy in
Poland," Halina Niedzielska (New York University)

Comments: Padraic Kenney (University of Michigan)

3. Women in Poland: The Impact of Recent Political, Social and Economic Changes on Women's Lives

Chair: Krystyna Zamorska (Network of East-West Women)

Panelists: Joanna Regulska (Rutgers University), Anna Popowicz (Former
Assistant to the Minister, Office of Women and Family Affairs)

4. Nationality Problems in Post-Communist Eastern Europe

Chair: Paul Best (Southern Connecticut State University)

"Overcoming the Past: Polish-Lithuanian Relations, 1990-1992," Stephen R.
Burant (United States Information Agency)
"Soviet Nationality Problems: Dynamics of Decolonization and Upholding the
Status Quo," Tadeusz Swiętochowski (Association for the Study of Nation-
alities)

Comments: Paul Best

5. Philosophical Influences in Polish History

Chair: Jerzy Krzywicki-Herburt (CUNY-Queens College)

"Wojtyła's Philosophy," Dariusz Sleszyński (Cambridge Center for the Study of Faith and Culture, Boston)
"Tradition and Modernity in the Polish Experience," Ewa M. Thompson (Rice University)
"The Polish Society of Friends of Science (1800-1831) and a Late Spokesman on its Behalf: Wacław Berent (1872-1940)," Joachim T. Baer (University of North Carolina-Greensboro)

6. Democratic Thought and Ideas in Poland: 1600-1800

Chair: Andrzej Kamiński (Georgetown University)

"Polish Constitutional Development in Comparative Perspective," Rett R. Ludwikowski (Catholic University of America)
"Polish Democratic Thought Before May 3, 1791," W. J. Wagner (University of Detroit)
"Religious Freedom in 17th Century Poland: Forgotten Ideas," M. Hillar (Houston, Texas)

7. Computational Models of Cognition and Language Acquisition

Chair: Raymond Sowinski (Rochester Institute of Technology)

"Neural Screen: Towards a Computational Model of Human Cognition," Andrzej Buller (CUNY-Graduate Center)
"Stay Tuned in Polish—Teaching and Learning Polish with a NeXT Computer," Waldemar Martyniuk (Stanford University)

Comments: Michael Mikoś (University of Wisconsin-Milwaukee)

8. The Effects of U.S. Government Policy on Polish Americans
Co-sponsored by the Polish American Historical Association.

Chair: Anthony Kuzniewski, S.J. (College of the Holy Cross)

"The Effects of the Dillingham Commission Reports on Ethnic Communities in the United States," James S. Pula (SUNY-Empire State College)

"The Effects of Federal Civil Rights Legislation on Americans of European Ancestry," Shelly Lescott-Leszczyński (University of Nevada)

"The Effects of Supreme Court Decisions on Polish Americans," Raymond Dziedzic, Esq. (Buffalo, NY)

Comments: John Kromkowski (Catholic University of America)

9. Women's Issues in Polish Literature

Chair: David Goldfarb (CUNY-Graduate Center)

"Restructuring the Woman: Nineteenth Century Polish Women Writers," Maria Makowiecka (CUNY-Graduate Center)

"Maria Dąbrowska," Iwona Misiak (Literary Critic, Kraków)

"A Woman or a Lady: Anna Swierczyńska," Maya Peretz (SUNY-Binghamton)

10. The Polish Air Force in World War II: A Participant Remembers

Chair: Michael Peszke (Perry Point, MD)

A presentation of personal remembrances by Captain Witold Aleksander Herbst, a veteran of 303 and 308 Squadrons in World War II.

Comments: Kazimierz Rasiej (Polonia Technica)

Evening Program

"The Wanderer"
A Performance by the Internationally Renowned Mime Rajmund Klechot

Friday, June 19, 1992

Plenary Session
Theme: The Future of U.S.-Polish Intellectual and Cultural Cooperation

Chair: M. B. Biskupski (St. John Fisher College)

A panel discussion in English and Polish.

Panelists: Andrzej Pelczar (Rector, Jagiellonian University), Kazimierz Kowalski (Polska Akademia Umiejętności), Andrzej K. Wróblewski (Rector, University of Warsaw), Wojciech Wrzesiński (Rector, Wrocław University), Bolesław Wierzbiański (Editor & Publisher, *Nowy Dziennik*), Thaddeus V. Gromada (Vice President for Academic Affairs, Polish Institute of Arts & Sciences)

Concurrent Sessions

11. Polish American Literary Images

Chair: Thomas J. Napierkowski (University of Colorado-Colorado Springs)

"Paradigms of Literary Ethnicity: Stuart Dybek, a Case Study," Thomas Gladsky (Central Missouri State University)
"A Bottle of Milk for Poland: Nelson Algren and I," Anthony Bukoski (University of Wisconsin-Superior)

Comments: Thomas J. Napierkowski

12.   Democratic Thought in Poland: 1914-1939
Co-sponsored by the Kościuszko Foundation.

Chair: M.B. Biskupski (St. John Fisher College)

"The Evolution of Polish Democratic Thought During the Great War," Włodzimierz Suleja (University of Warsaw)
"Polish Democratic Thought and Politics in the Second Republic," Andrzej Ajnenkiel (University of Warsaw)

Comments: M. B. Biskupski

13.   The Holocaust in Contemporary Polish-Jewish Relations

Chair: Irving Levine (Institute on Pluralism & Group Identity, American Jewish Committee)

"Polish Foes of Antisemitism in the 1930s," Ronald Modras (Saint Louis University)
"The Holocaust: Its Implications for Contemporary Church-State Relations in Poland," John T. Pawlikowski (Catholic Theological Union)
"The Polish American-Jewish American Council: A Model for Inter-ethnic Cooperation," Leonard Chrobot (Culver Military Academy)

14. Scholarly and Cultural Organizations on Eastern Europe in America: Their Role at Home and Abroad

Chair: Joseph Gore (The Kościuszko Foundation)

Panelists: Feliks Gross (Polish Institute of Arts and Sciences), Taras Hunczak (Shevchenko Scientific Society), John Iatrides (Modern Greek Studies Association), John Bukowczyk (Polish American Historical Association), Vytaut Kipel (Belorussian Society of Arts & Sciences), Elona Vaisnys (Association for the Advancement of Baltic Studies)

15. Poland in World War II

Chair: John Micgiel (Columbia University)

"Was Poland's Fate Decided in 1942?" Anna Cienciala (University of Kansas)
"Sikorski's Strategy During World War II: 1939-1943," Robert Szymczak (Pennsylvania State University-Beaver)
"American Aid to Poles in the Gouvernement General, 1939-1941," Hal Elliott Wert (Kansas City Art Institute)

Comments: Roman W. Rybicki (Archiwum Wschodnie)

16. Early Modern Polish History

Chair: Paul Knoll (University of Southern California)

"Poland and the Baltic 1558-1721," Robert I. Frost (University of London)
"The Polish Renaissance: Its Originality and Dependence on European Trends," Maria Bogucka (University of Warsaw)
"The War of the Polish Succession and the Reign of Stanisław Leszczyński," Edwin C. Blackburn (Sioux City, Iowa)

Comment: Paul Knoll

17. Environmental Aspects of Polish-European Integration

Chair: Stanisław Gross (New York Medical College)

Panelists: Zbigniew Bochniarz (Humphrey Center, Minneapolis), Wojciech Rosta-fiński (NASA, ret.), Hubert Romanowski (Counselor for Science and Technology, Embassy of the Republic of Poland)

18. Social Organization and Change in American Polonia

Chair: Theodore Zawistowski (PNCC Commission on History and Archives)

"The Great Depression and Mobilization of Second Generation Polish American Women in Detroit, 1930-1937," Thaddeus Radzilowski (Southwest State University)
"Organized Lobbying and Benevolent Actions on Poland's Behalf: The Role of American Polonia in the Twentieth Century," Donald E. Pienkos (University of Wisconsin-Milwaukee)
"The Evolution of Traditional Wedding Customs in the Polish American Community in Central Wisconsin," Dennis Kolinski (Illinois Humanities Council)

Comments: Thaddeus V. Gromada (Polish Institute of Arts & Sciences)

19. Democratic Thought in Poland: The Second World War
Co-sponsored by the Kościuszko Foundation.

Chair: Piotr Wandycz (Yale University)

"Democratic Thought in the Polish Underground in Occupied Poland," Rafał Habielski (University of Warsaw)
"Democratic Thought in Emigré Politics," Andrzej Zakrzewski (University of Warsaw)

Comments: Piotr Wandycz

20. Accounts of Poland in the Work of Two Polish Writers in America

Chair: Anthony Bukoski (University of Wisconsin-Superior)

"Searching for Eden: Poland in Singer's Childrens' Stories," John Guzlowski (Eastern Illinois University)
"The Fiction of Litka De Barcza: Reporter of Post-World War II Poland to America," Thomas J. Napierkowski (University of Colorado-Colorado Springs)

Comments: Anthony Bukoski

21. Polish Military History

Chair: Michael Guzik (SUNY-Buffalo)

"Recruiting Haller's Army," Joseph T. Hapak (Moraine Valley Community College)
"The Militarization of the Polish Legal System at the End of World War II," John Micgiel (Columbia University)
"The Social History of the Virtuti Militari," Zdzisław P. Wesolowski (Florida Memorial College)

22. Teaching Polish Language and Culture

Chair: L. Louise Rozwell (Monroe Community College)

"The Pedagogy of Teaching Polish Language, Literature and Culture," Joanna R. Williams (SUNY-Stony Brook)
"Towards a Video-Based Curriculum," Krystyna Wachowicz (Defense Language Institute)
"The Polish Proficiency Test and Its Applications," Xixian Jiang (Center for Applied Linguistics)

Comments: Krystyna Olszer (CUNY-Hunter College)

23. Issues in Interwar Poland

Chair: Alice-Catherine Carls (University of Tennessee-Martin)

"Averill Harriman's Business Interest in Interwar Poland," Daniel Stone (University of Winnipeg)
"The Roman Catholic Church and Polish Democracy," Neal Pease (University of Wisconsin-Milwaukee)
"American Diplomacy and Polish-Jewish Relations After World War I," Andrzej Kapiszewski (Jagiellonian University)

24. New Research in Biology

Chair: Wanda Wolinska (Sloan Kettering Memorial Cancer Research Institute)

"Fish as a Model in Medical Research: the Vitamin C Example," Konrad Dabrowski (Ohio State University)
"Comparison of Giemsa-Stained Thick Film and Blood Cultivation for Detection of Experimentally Induced *Falciparum* Malaria in Humans," Thaddeus Graczyk (Johns Hopkins University)

25. Thematic Studies in Polish Poetry

Chair: Regina Grol-Prokopczyk (SUNY-Empire State College)

"The Power of the Erotic in Polish Women's Poetry," Maya Peretz (SUNY-Binghamton)

"Judyta and Other Jewish Spirits in the Poetry of Juliusz Słowacki," Joanna R. Clark (Princeton University)

"Time, Impotence, Despair: Polish Poetry in the 1980s," David Malcomb (Olivet College)

Evening Program

"I Lech Wałęsa"
A One-Man Performance Featuring
Jarosław Stremien

Saturday, June 20, 1992

Concurrent Sessions

26. Pope John Paul II

Chair: Zygmunt Malinowski (John Wiley Publishers)

"The Fourth Pilgrimage of Pope John Paul II to Poland," Zygmunt Malinowski. A slide presentation.

"Church Under the Sun," Tadeusz Chabrowski (Temple University)

27. Piłsudski

Chair: Roman Szporluk (Harvard University)

"Piłsudski as a Stateless Military Leader" by David Stefancic (Saint Mary's College)

"Piłsudski's Image in the Solidarity Era" by John Slyce (University of Michigan)

Comments: Tadeusz Swiętochowski (Association for the Study of Nationalities) and M.K. Dziewanowski (University of Wisconsin-Milwaukee, Ret.)

28. Language, Folklore, and the Theater in Polish Culture

Chair: Alexander Schenker (Yale University)

"The Linguistic Heritage of the Old Polish Commonwealth in Contemporary Polish," Zbigniew Gołąb (University of Chicago)

"Teatr Obywatelski: Polish Citizen's Theater," Kazimierz Braun (SUNY-Buffalo)

"Teaching Polish and Slavic Folklore at an American University," Alex Alexander (CUNY-Hunter College)

29. Contribution of Poles to Sociology, Ethnography and Management

Chair: Helena Znaniecka-Lopata (Loyola University, Chicago)

"The Collaboration of William I. Thomas and Florian Znaniecki in the Study of Social Organization Among Polish Americans," Evan R. Thomas (Grand View College)

"Johann Stanislaus Kubary: A Polish Ethnographer's Adventures and Contributions in the 19th Century Pacific," Dirk A. Ballendorf (University of Guam)

"Karol Adamiecki and the Polish Contribution to the Scientific Theory of Management," Zdzisław Wesolowski (Florida Memorial College)

30. Poland's Economy: The International Situation

Chair: Bogdan Mieczkowski (Ithaca College)

"A Measure of the International Cost of the East European Economic Readjustment," Bogdan Mieczkowski (Ithaca College) and Elia Kacapyr (Ithaca College)

"The Polish Stabilization Program," Zbigniew Fallenbuchl (University of Windsor)

"Monetary Stabilization," by Savo Javremovich (Alfred University)

"Recent International Financial Developments in Poland," Robert Bacondi (L.W. International Financial Research, Inc.)

Comments: Andrew Ezergailis (Ithaca College) and Stanisław Wąsowski (Georgetown University)

31. Language and Culture:
Individual and Interpersonal Dimensions
Developed by the PIASA Section on Psychology and Mental Health.

Co-Chairs: Erna Hilfstein (CUNY-Graduate School) and Nonna Slavinska-Holy (Postgraduate Center for Mental Health)

Panelists: Leslie Bachman (CNN), Leslie Curtis (Albert Einstein Hospital), Regina Gelb (American Translator's Association), Mohammed Hamid (LaGuardia College), Simone J. Scheumann (Valhalla Medical University), George Schwab (CUNY-Graduate School)

32. Poland's Economy: The Domestic Situation

Chair: Bogdan Mieczkowski (Ithaca College)

"Macroeconomic Changes in Poland and Their Microeconomic Underpinnings," Stanisław Wąsowski (Georgetown University)
"Recent Impressions from Poland," Aleksander Gella (SUNY-Buffalo)
"Recent Economic Developments in Poland," Krzysztof Badach (L.W. International Financial Research, Inc.)
"Economic Incentives in Poland," Bozena Leven (C.W. Post College)

Comments: Yanek Mieczkowski (Columbia University) and Zenon Wasyliew (Ithaca College)

33. Changing Perspectives in the Arts:
Romanticism, Realism, and Post-Modernism

Chair: Anne Swartz (CUNY-Baruch College)

"The Role of the Szlachta and Peasant in the Development of Regional Village Music Practices," William Noll (Harvard University)
"The Malczewskis Legacy: From 19th Century Kraków to 20th Century Montreal," Jerzy Krzyżanowski (Ohio State University)
"Chopin as Modernist in Nineteenth Century Russia," Anne Swartz (CUNY-Baruch College)

34. The Polish Diaspora in the 19th Century

Chair: Joseph Wieczerzak (CUNY-Bronx Community College, Emeritus)

"Heroes and Aliens: Everyday Life of Polish Refugees in France During the July Monarchy," Kenneth F. Lewalski (Rhode Island College)

"The English Publications of Polish Exiles in the United States, 1808-1888," Zygmunt Wardziński (Montgomery County Community College)

"The Polish Press: A Link Between Australian Polish Immigrants and Their Homeland, 1942-1980," Jan Lencznarowicz (Jagiellonian University)

35. Scholarly Library Resources in Poland and America

Chair: Wojciech Zalewski (Stanford University)

"American Assistance to Polish Research Libraries and Its Impact on Polish Collections in North America," Wojciech Siemaszkiewicz (New York Public Library)

Comments: Alicja Altenberger (Harvard University)

36. Thematic Interpretations in English Literature

Chair: Michael Kiskis (SUNY-Empire State College)

"An Unrecognized Polish Nobleman in Conrad's *Nostromo*," Jean M. Szczypien (SUNY)

"Jane Porter's Kościuszko," Francis E. Zapatka (American University)

"Of Huck and Marlowe: The Compelled Storytelling in Mark Twain and Joseph Conrad," Michael Kiskis

37. Poland's Transition to a Market Economy: A Roundtable

Chair: Bogdan Mieczkowski (Ithaca College)

A panel discussion: Włodzimierz Chodzko (Commercial Counselor, Polish Embassy), Stanisław Wąsowski (Georgetown University), Krzysztof Badach (L.W. International Financial Research, Inc.), Witold Sulimirski (New York), and Piotr Stasiński (*Nowy Dziennik*)

38. East European Influences on Art

Chair: Pamela Kladzyk (Parsons School of Design)

"Polish American Connections in the Art of Arthur Szyk," by Joseph P. Ansell (Otterbein College)

"Placzki: The Motif of Sadness in Polish Sculpture," Pamela Kladzyk (Parsons School of Design)

"Ukrainian Themes in Polish Art in the Second Half of the Nineteenth Century" by Tamara Tarnawski-Ramstad (Radio Liberty, Munich)

Comments: Marek Bartelnik (New York City)

39. Mental Health Perspectives in Eastern Europe: A Renaissance.
Developed by the PIASA Section on Psychology and Mental Health.

Chair: Nonna Slavinska-Holy (Postgraduate Center for Mental Health)

A panel discussion: Gerard Chrzanowski (International Federation of Psychoanalytic Societies), George Kamen, (Washington Square Institute for Psychotherapy and Psychoanalysis), Zvi Lothane (Mount Sinai School of Medicine), Grazyna Marmajewska (New York), Barry H. Smith (The Health Foundation), Eva Wellisz (Council of Psychoanalytic Psychotherapists), Danuta Mostwin (Loyola College, Baltimore)

40. New Perspectives in Polish-Latin American Studies—I

Chair: Edmund S. Urbański (Howard University, emeritus)

"Reflections of a Polish Engineer on Brazil During the Period 1972-1981 and References to Transitional Changes in Contemporary Poland," Krzysztof Z. de Montfort Krakowski (Pittsburgh)

"Recent Polish and Polish-American Participation in Latin American Scholarship," Edmund S. Urbański (Howard University, ret.)

"Reflections on Polish History in Spanish Theater of the Golden Age," Henryk Ziomek (University of Georgia)

41. The 1990 Treaty on Economic Relations Between the United States and Poland

Chair: Susanne Lotarski (U.S. Dept. of Commerce)

"From Association to Accession: An Evaluation of Poland's Aspirations to Full Community Membership," Anne Wagner-Findeisen (Fordham University)

"The 1990 Treaty of Economic Relations Between the United States and Poland," Jan N. Sajkiewicz (Duquesne University)

"Implications of the 1990 Treaty of Economic Relations Between the United States and Poland," Blair C. Kolasa (Duquesne University)

42.   Perspectives on Polish Migration
Co-sponsored by the Polish American Historical Association.

Chair: John Gutowski (St. Xavier College, Chicago)

"Migrants and Polish Territories in the Era of Mass Migrations: The Impact on the Old Country, 1880-1920," Adam Walaszek (Jagiellonian University, Kraków)

"In Search of Myself: From Ethnic Identity to the Concept of the Third Value," Danuta Mostwin (Loyola College, Baltimore)

"Stara Polonia-Nowa Emigracja: Transformations of Social Image," Anna D. Jaroszyńska-Kirchmann (University of Minnesota)

Comments: John Gutowski

43.   New Perspectives in Polish-Latin American Studies—II

Chair: Edmund S. Urbański (Howard University, emeritus)

"Polish Historic Contributions to Latin American Medicine," Stanisław Rola-Szutkiewicz (University of Virginia, ret.)

"The Twentieth Century's Polish Explorers of the Tropical Amazon," Jerzy W. Kozłowski (University of Warsaw)

"Reception of Spanish American Literature in Contemporary Poland," Elżbieta Skłodowska (George Washington University)

44.   Polish Literature and Visual Arts

Chair: Bozena Shallcross (CUNY-Bronx Community College)

"*Tworzenie świata*: Witkacy and Primitivism," David A. Goldfarb (CUNY)

"Sławomir Mrożek as a Writer and a Cartoonist," Regina Gról-Prokopczyk (SUNY-Empire State College)

"Bruno Schulz's Lines and Words: Visualizing a *Sanatorium Under the Sign of the Hour Glass*," Bozena Shallcross (CUNY-Bronx Community College)

45.   Mental Health in Poland
Developed by the PIASA Section on Psychology and Mental Health.

Chair: Nonna Slavinska-Holy (Postgraduate Psychoanalytic Institute)

"Altered Stated of Consciousness: Regression or Evolution?" Andrzej Kokoszka (Copernicus School of Medicine, Kraków)

"Wpływ muzyki na reakcje psychofizjologiczne u pacjentów w stresie przedoperacyjnym," Barbara Miluk-Kolasa (Medical University, Łódź)

Banquet

Chair: Thaddeus V. Gromada, Vice President and Executive Director,
Polish Institute of Arts & Sciences of America
Remarks: Feliks Gross, President, Polish Institute
of Arts & Sciences of America

Principal Address: Hon. Zbigniew Brzeziński
Center for Strategic & International Studies,
and Former National Security Advisor

Index